Frameworks for Blockchain Standards, Tools, Testbeds, and Platforms

Yanamandra Ramakrishna
School of Business, Skyline University College, Sharjah, UAE

Priyameet Kaur Keer
Department of Management Studies, New Horizon College of Engineering, India

IGI Global
PUBLISHER of TIMELY KNOWLEDGE

A volume in the Advances in Systems Analysis, Software Engineering, and High Performance Computing (ASASEHPC) Book Series

Published in the United States of America by
IGI Global
Engineering Science Reference (an imprint of IGI Global)
701 E. Chocolate Avenue
Hershey PA, USA 17033
Tel: 717-533-8845
Fax: 717-533-8661
E-mail: cust@igi-global.com
Web site: http://www.igi-global.com

Library of Congress Cataloging-in-Publication Data

Names: Ramakrishna, Yanamandra, 1966- editor. | Keer, Priyameet, 1985- editor.
Title: Frameworks for blockchain standards, tools, testbeds, and platforms / edited by: Yanamandra Ramakrishna, Priyameet Keer.
Description: Hershey, PA : Engineering Science Reference, [2024] | Includes bibliographical references. | Summary: "This book develops models and frameworks of blockchain and its applications and identifies strategies and best practices for implementation of blockchain"-- Provided by publisher.
Identifiers: LCCN 2023049075 (print) | LCCN 2023049076 (ebook) | ISBN 9798369304051 (hardcover) | ISBN 9798369304068 (ebook)
Subjects: LCSH: Blockchains (Databases)--Industrial applications.
Classification: LCC QA76.9.B56 H347 2024 (print) | LCC QA76.9.B56 (ebook) | DDC 005.75/88--dc23/eng/20240403
LC record available at https://lccn.loc.gov/2023049075
LC ebook record available at https://lccn.loc.gov/2023049076

This book is published in the IGI Global book series Advances in Systems Analysis, Software Engineering, and High Performance Computing (ASASEHPC) (ISSN: 2327-3453; eISSN: 2327-3461)

British Cataloguing in Publication Data
A Cataloguing in Publication record for this book is available from the British Library.

Advances in Systems Analysis, Software Engineering, and High Performance Computing (ASASEHPC) Book Series

ISSN:2327-3453
EISSN:2327-3461

Editor-in-Chief: Vijayan Sugumaran, Oakland University, USA

MISSION

The theory and practice of computing applications and distributed systems has emerged as one of the key areas of research driving innovations in business, engineering, and science. The fields of software engineering, systems analysis, and high performance computing offer a wide range of applications and solutions in solving computational problems for any modern organization.

The **Advances in Systems Analysis, Software Engineering, and High Performance Computing (ASASEHPC) Book Series** brings together research in the areas of distributed computing, systems and software engineering, high performance computing, and service science. This collection of publications is useful for academics, researchers, and practitioners seeking the latest practices and knowledge in this field.

COVERAGE

- Performance Modelling
- Engineering Environments
- Network Management
- Enterprise Information Systems
- Parallel Architectures
- Human-Computer Interaction
- Virtual Data Systems
- Distributed Cloud Computing
- Software Engineering
- Computer Graphics

IGI Global is currently accepting manuscripts for publication within this series. To submit a proposal for a volume in this series, please contact our Acquisition Editors at Acquisitions@igi-global.com or visit: http://www.igi-global.com/publish/.

The Advances in Systems Analysis, Software Engineering, and High Performance Computing (ASASEHPC) Book Series (ISSN 2327-3453) is published by IGI Global, 701 E. Chocolate Avenue, Hershey, PA 17033-1240, USA, www.igi-global.com. This series is composed of titles available for purchase individually; each title is edited to be contextually exclusive from any other title within the series. For pricing and ordering information please visit http://www.igi-global.com/book-series/advances-systems-analysis-software-engineering/73689. Postmaster: Send all address changes to above address.

Titles in this Series

For a list of additional titles in this series, please visit:
http://www.igi-global.com/book-series/advances-systems-analysis-software-engineering/73689

Digital Technologies in Modeling and Management Insights in Education and Industry
GS Prakasha (Christ University, India) Maria Lapina (North-Caucasus Federal University, Russia) and Deepanraj Balakrishnan (Prince Mohammad Bin Fahd University, Saudi Arabia)
Information Science Reference • © 2024 • 320pp • H/C (ISBN: 9781668495766) • US $250.00

The Software Principles of Design for Data Modeling
Debabrata Samanta (Rochester Institute of Technology, Kosovo)
Engineering Science Reference • © 2023 • 318pp • H/C (ISBN: 9781668498095) • US $270.00

Investigations in Pattern Recognition and Computer Vision for Industry 4.0
Chiranji Lal Chowdhary (Vellore Institute of Technology, Vellore, India) Basanta Kumar Swain (Government College of Engineering, Bhawanipatna, India) and Vijay Kumar (Dr B R Ambedkar National Institute of Technology Jalandhar, India)
Engineering Science Reference • © 2023 • 276pp • H/C (ISBN: 9781668486023) • US $270.00

Cyber-Physical System Solutions for Smart Cities
Vanamoorthy Muthumanikandan (Vellore Institute of Technology, Chennai, India) Anbalagan Bhuvaneswari (Vellore Institute of Technology, Chennai, India) Balamurugan Easwaran (University of Africa, Toru-Orua, Nigeria) and T. Sudarson Rama Perumal (Rohini College of Engineering and Technology, India)
Engineering Science Reference • © 2023 • 182pp • H/C (ISBN: 9781668477564) • US $270.00

Cyber-Physical Systems and Supporting Technologies for Industrial Automation
R. Thanigaivelan (A.K.T. Memorial College of Engineering and Technology, India) S. Kaliappan (Velammal Institute of Technology, India) and C. Jegadheesan (Kongu Engineering College, India)
Engineering Science Reference • © 2023 • 444pp • H/C (ISBN: 9781668492673) • US $270.00

IGI Global
PUBLISHER of TIMELY KNOWLEDGE

701 East Chocolate Avenue, Hershey, PA 17033, USA
Tel: 717-533-8845 x100 • Fax: 717-533-8661
E-Mail: cust@igi-global.com • www.igi-global.com

Table of Contents

Detailed Table of Contents

Cryptocurrencies have experienced an unprecedented surge in popularity over the past few years. This surge can be attributed to a multitude of factors, including the unique characteristics and advantages that cryptocurrencies offer. The manuscript highlights the trans-formative nature of accountability within the digital asset business and the ongoing revolution surrounding it. It explores emerging trends and practices that shape the accountability mechanisms in the cryptocurrency market. By critically assessing cryptocurrencies, the manuscript provides readers with a comprehensive understanding of the opportunities and risks in this evolving landscape. Through robust accountability mechanisms, the cryptocurrency market can address challenges such as volatility, investor protection, illicit activities, etc. By adopting an economist's perspective, it explores how cryptocurrencies function within the broader economic structure and the potential impact they have on traditional financial systems, monetary policy, and the overall economy.

This study explores the factors that impact the adoption of blockchain in supply chain financing (SCF). Blockchain's unique features make it a good solution to the current problems in SCF. However, given that both blockchain and SCF are relatively new, there are almost no commercially viable large-scale implementations yet in this area. Research in the factors that drive the adoption of blockchain in SCF, is also scarce. Of the six identified determinants of adoption of blockchain in SCF, the study found four to be significant. Relative advantage, compatibility, organization readiness, and environment readiness influence the adoption of blockchain in SCF. Complexity and technology readiness are insignificant determinants, indicating a technically mature industry capable of handling current blockchain implementations in SCF and associated changes. The authors also found that trust has a mediating effect between compatibility and adoption and between environment readiness and adoption.

For the last few years, rapid digitalization has been observed in the world banking industry, which helped boost global economic growth. At the same time, fraud cases in the banking sector have been increasing immensely. Regulating authorities of banks nationwide have been issuing numerous circulars and guidelines for preventing fraud incidents. However, fraudsters are taking advantage of the digitalization of and shortfalls in the industry, by which the fraudsters easily defraud customers and banks. Hence, it resulted in a worsening of the asset quality of banks and a loss of public trust and confidence in the banking industry. In this regard, banks must be equipped with sophisticated technological tools for fraud identification and preventive measures apart from the conventional systems and procedures since core banking solutions in the banking industry have evolved drastically over the last few years. In this context, this chapter is intended to study the role of blockchain technology and data mining tools in identifying and preventing frauds in specific bank products.

Blockchain has emerged as an important concept at the interface of ICT and higher education. Blockchain is perceived as a revolutionary technology offering a considerable impact of vast magnitude on various sectors since it enables the creation of decentralized applications programmed to run on networks and records sets of data that can be shared securely without third-party mediation. The Blockchain's emphasis on variety in terms of applications may be due to its capacity to build a trusted and decentralized contract environment. The higher education sector is, therefore, a potential user of blockchain technology due to its capacity in allowing stakeholders to validate learning records and identity management. On the other

In an era characterized by rapid technological progress, the persistent challenges of land administration are on the verge of a groundbreaking transformation through the adoption of blockchain technology. Originating with the advent of Bitcoin in 2008, blockchain has emerged as a beacon of hope, promising transparency, trust, immutability, and security in recording transactions. This innovative technology holds immense potential to revolutionize the landscape of land administration in Pakistan, a nation burdened by antiquated paper-based systems, corruption, land disputes, and inefficiencies. Embracing blockchain can offer Pakistan the prospect of an era marked by improved governance, diminished fraud, streamlined record-keeping, and equitable access to vital land information. Nonetheless, the path forward is strewn with challenges, necessitating the establishment of robust legal frameworks, capacity-building initiatives, and the resolution of privacy concerns.

The application of state-of-the-art technologies in functional fields is complex and offers a significant challenge to user and expert teams as well as to technical teams. This chapter presents a mechanism that has been used in a project in the context of digital publications. Ensuring the traceability of digital publications (e-books and e-journals) is a critical aspect of the utmost importance for authors, publishers, and buyers. The SmartISBN project has used blockchain technology to define a protocol for the identification, tracking, and traceability of digital publications. As this was an innovative project that required communication between functional experts (authors, publishers, booksellers, etc.) and technical experts, it was necessary to identify protocols to facilitate communication. This chapter presents the protocol by which the functional tests have been defined and how this has favoured the validation of the project.

Preface

Welcome to the *Handbook of Research on Frameworks for Blockchain Standards, Tools, Testbeds, and Platforms*, a groundbreaking compilation meticulously curated by the esteemed editors, Yanamandra Ramakrishna and Priyameet Keer. In this era of digital transformation, we stand at the precipice of an unparalleled revolution, where the blockchain technology is not merely changing the game; it's rewriting the rulebook. As editors of this comprehensive reference book, we are thrilled to introduce you to a compendium of knowledge that delves deep into the very essence of blockchain, its manifold applications, and the profound implications it holds for the future.

Blockchain technology represents an epochal shift—an evolution away from centralized authority in a massively distributed network. Instead, it heralds a future where trust is dispersed across multiple sources, all in agreement based on algorithms that validate transactions. Furthermore, most blockchain solutions offer an immutable and unalterable record of transactions, a fortress against any form of manipulation, whether from trusted or untrusted sources. Within this technological marvel, "mining" emerges as a fundamental concept. It serves as a decentralized review process for every block in the blockchain, forging consensus without relying on a central authority. It's akin to peer review in a decentralized realm where trust is no longer vested in a single entity.

The rise of Bitcoin, coupled with its growing acceptance among merchants, ushered in a creative resurgence among miners, each striving for rewards in novel ways. In the world of blockchain, Ethereum shines as an open-source, decentralized platform with computational prowess. It transforms basic currency exchange into a value transfer system through a scripting language. Ethereum extends the original ideas behind Bitcoin, enabling a diverse array of applications to thrive on blockchain technology.

Bitcoin, often referred to as the first decentralized autonomous organization (DAO), gave birth to an ecosystem where participants contributed computational power toward a common objective. In Bitcoin, a decentralized protocol provided financial services and rewarded miners, essentially becoming a rudimentary decentralized organization. As the blockchain revolution unfolded, the existing literature was found wanting.

Therefore, this book emerges as both timely and pertinent. Its chapters traverse a broad spectrum of subjects, adding immeasurable value to various stakeholders:

1. To develop models and frameworks for blockchain and its applications.
2. To identify strategies and best practices for blockchain implementation.
3. To analyze real-world case studies and successful examples from across the globe.
4. To propose strategies for implementing virtual currency as a medium of exchange using cryptography.

Our handbook caters to a wide audience, including researchers, industry professionals, academicians, students, policy makers, corporate leaders, financial institutions, investors, and entrepreneurs. With its expansive scope, this book also holds value for those indirectly connected to blockchain and its applications. It is a must-read for undergraduate, graduate, and research-level students.

This book is not just a compendium of information; it's a manifesto for a brighter, blockchain-powered future. Its chapters offer a unique and valuable perspective, authored by experts who have lived and breathed blockchain technology. The array of topics covered includes:

1. A Taxonomy of Digital Assets: The Building Blockchains of Decentralized Finance.
2. Blockchain in Commercial Insurance.
3. Blockchain in Global Trade.
4. Accountability in the Digital Asset Business.
5. Blockchain & Project Management.
6. Blockchain & the Chief Marketing Officer: The Next Era of Marketing.
7. Blockchain & the Chief Financial Officer.
8. Blockchain & the Chief Human Resources Officer.
9. Blockchain and Enterprise Transformation.
10. Introducing Asset Chains: The Future of Supply Chains.
11. Automotive: The Innovation Dilemma of Distributed Ledger Technology.
12. Blockchain Revolution in Higher Education.
13. Blockchain Revolution in Education and Lifelong Learning.
14. Blockchain: The Emerging Platform for Manufacturing 4.0.
15. Blockchain Transformation in Telecommunications.
16. Blockchain Transformation in the Tourism and Hospitality Sector.
17. Distributed Power: How Blockchain will Transform Energy Markets.
18. Reinventing Healthcare on the Blockchain.
19. Web 3 and the Music Industry: A Second Wave of Blockchain Innovation.
20. Blockchain and the Post-Trust World.

We invite you to embark on this journey through the boundless realms of blockchain. This handbook is not just a book; it's a key to unlocking a future where innovation knows no bounds and trust is distributed, secure, and universal. It's a testament to the profound impact of blockchain on our world, and we encourage you to seize this opportunity to gain knowledge and insights that can reshape industries and drive us toward a more prosperous and equitable future.

CHAPTER OVERVIEW

Chapter 1: Accountability Revolution in the Digital Asset Business: Insights From the Cryptocurrency Market

In this chapter, Babita Srivastava of William Paterson University, New Jersey, USA, takes us on an exploration of the cryptocurrency market's transformative nature regarding accountability. With cryptocurrencies gaining unprecedented popularity, this chapter delves into the unique characteristics and advantages that have propelled them into the spotlight. The discussion dissects emerging trends and practices that are shaping accountability mechanisms in the cryptocurrency market. The manuscript critically assesses cryptocurrencies to provide readers with a comprehensive understanding of the opportunities and risks in this dynamic landscape. By examining the economist's perspective, the chapter delves into how cryptocurrencies function within the broader economic structure, shedding light on their potential impact on traditional financial systems, monetary policy, and the overall economy.

Chapter 2: Adoption of Blockchain in Supply Chain Financing

Authored by Sakuntala Rao, Shalini Chandra, and Dhrupad Mathur, this chapter from SP Jain School of Global Management, explores the factors influencing the adoption of blockchain technology in supply chain financing (SCF). As blockchain's unique features hold the promise of solving current SCF challenges, this chapter investigates the determinants that drive its adoption. It uncovers significant factors such as relative advantage, compatibility, organization readiness, and environment readiness that impact the adoption of blockchain in SCF. Moreover, it highlights the mediating role of trust in adoption, shedding light on how trust influences the integration of blockchain in SCF.

Chapter 3: Blockchain Technology and Data Mining Tools for Combating Frauds: With Reference to Banking Sector

In a world witnessing rapid digitalization in the banking sector, this chapter, authored by Satya Sekhar Gudimetla and Naveen Tirumalaraju of GITAM Deemed to be University, India, delves into the increasing challenge of frauds. The chapter underscores the need for banks to equip themselves with sophisticated technological tools to identify and prevent frauds. Focusing on the role of blockchain technology and data mining tools, the authors present a comprehensive approach to address the rising cases of fraud and protect customer trust and confidence.

Chapter 4: Blockchain Implications and Utility for Higher Education

Neeta Baporikar from Namibia University of Science and Technology explores the profound implications of blockchain technology in higher education. By enabling decentralized applications and secure data sharing, blockchain offers substantial benefits for this sector. This chapter delves into how blockchain empowers stakeholders to validate learning records and manage identities. It navigates the potential applications of blockchain in higher education, highlighting the benefits, challenges, and future directions for this transformative technology.

Chapter 5: Blockchain Revolution in Education

Authored by Shankar Subramanian, Amritha Subhayan Krishnan, and Arumugam Seetharaman, this chapter delves into how blockchain technology has the potential to revolutionize higher education. It explores key features, benefits, and challenges and discusses various use cases, including student records management and digital credentialing. The chapter concludes by highlighting the opportunities, limitations, and future directions of blockchain technology in higher education, paving the way for a transformative revolution in the sector.

Chapter 6: Blockchain Revolution in Education and Lifelong Learning

This chapter by Charu Banga and Farhan Ujager from De Montfort University, Dubai, UAE, focuses on the importance of blockchain technology in education and lifelong learning. It discusses various blockchain models applicable to the education sector and their potential to revolutionize traditional education systems and credentialing. The authors highlight blockchain's ability to reduce inequalities and empower stakeholders in the educational ecosystem.

Chapter 7: Geospatial Blockchain Applications for Land Administration in Pakistan

Authored by Munir Ahmad from the Survey of Pakistan, this chapter explores the transformative potential of blockchain technology in land administration in Pakistan. The chapter discusses how blockchain can address long-standing challenges in land administration, such as corruption and inefficiencies. It emphasizes the need for robust legal frameworks and capacity-building initiatives to fully harness the potential of blockchain in this critical domain.

Chapter 8: Mechanism for the Systematic Generation of Functional Tests of Smart Contracts in Digital Publication Management Systems

This chapter, authored by Nicolas Sanchez-Gomez, Javier Gutierrez, Enrique Parrilla, Julian García García, Maria de-Acuña, and Maria Escalona, highlights the application of blockchain technology in digital publication management systems. It presents a mechanism used in the SmartISBN project, which utilized blockchain to ensure the traceability of digital publications. The chapter discusses how functional tests were defined and facilitated communication between functional and technical experts, contributing to the validation of the project.

IN SUMMARY

As we draw the preface of the "Handbook of Research on Frameworks for Blockchain Standards, Tools, Testbeds, and Platforms" to a close, we find ourselves standing at the threshold of a digital frontier marked by profound transformation. The chapters outlined in this preface offer a tantalizing glimpse into the wealth of knowledge, insights, and innovation that await readers within the pages of this comprehensive reference book.

The blockchain revolution is upon us, reshaping industries, economies, and societies. The cryptocurrency market's accountability evolution, as explored in Chapter 1, offers a testament to the transformative power of blockchain. It uncovers the potential to address challenges such as volatility, investor protection, and illicit activities. This chapter reminds us that blockchain's influence extends beyond the digital realm, with repercussions felt throughout the broader economic landscape.

Chapter 2 ventures into the adoption of blockchain in supply chain financing, revealing the factors that drive its implementation. As blockchain and supply chain financing stand at the forefront of innovation, this chapter highlights their intertwined destinies and their capacity to revolutionize trade and commerce.

The battle against fraud in the banking sector takes center stage in Chapter 3, where blockchain technology and data mining tools emerge as powerful allies. This chapter underscores the urgency for technological adaptation to safeguard trust and financial integrity.

Chapters 4 and 5 transport us to the realm of higher education, where blockchain's revolutionary potential is palpable. The implications of blockchain in higher education extend to records validation, identity management, and digital credentialing, promising a future where educational systems are more transparent, secure, and equitable.

Chapter 6 further explores the transformative potential of blockchain in education and lifelong learning, emphasizing its role in reducing inequalities and empowering stakeholders in the educational ecosystem. The promise of innovation in education beckons us to envision a future where knowledge is accessible and secure for all.

The unique application of blockchain in land administration in Pakistan, explored in Chapter 7, represents a paradigm shift in governance and transparency. Blockchain's potential to streamline record-keeping and reduce fraud offers a beacon of hope for a nation burdened by long-standing challenges in land administration.

In Chapter 8, the innovative use of blockchain in digital publication management systems underscores the technology's versatility. By ensuring traceability and transparency, blockchain offers solutions for industries beyond the financial sector, opening new doors for technological innovation.

In conclusion, this preface is a testament to the transformative power of blockchain technology across diverse domains. The chapters collectively form a comprehensive guide that illuminates the potential, challenges, and future trends of blockchain. As we journey deeper into the book, we encourage readers to immerse themselves in the wealth of knowledge it offers, explore the dynamic landscape of blockchain, and imagine the limitless possibilities that await in this digital era.

We extend our deepest appreciation to the distinguished authors who have contributed their expertise and insights to this book. We also thank the readers who embark on this exploration of blockchain's impact on our rapidly evolving world.

It is our sincere hope that the knowledge shared within these pages will inspire and guide you in harnessing the potential of blockchain, ultimately contributing to a brighter and more innovative future.

Warmest regards,

Yanamandra Ramakrishna
School of Business, Skyline University College, Sharjah, UAE

Priyameet Keer
Department of Management Studies, New Horizon College of Engineering, India

Chapter 1
Accountability Revolution in the Digital Asset Business:
Insights From the Cryptocurrency Market

Babita Srivastava
William Paterson University, USA

ABSTRACT

Cryptocurrencies have experienced an unprecedented surge in popularity over the past few years. This surge can be attributed to a multitude of factors, including the unique characteristics and advantages that cryptocurrencies offer. The manuscript highlights the trans-formative nature of accountability within the digital asset business and the ongoing revolution surrounding it. It explores emerging trends and practices that shape the accountability mechanisms in the cryptocurrency market. By critically assessing cryptocurrencies, the manuscript provides readers with a comprehensive understanding of the opportunities and risks in this evolving landscape. Through robust accountability mechanisms, the cryptocurrency market can address challenges such as volatility, investor protection, illicit activities, etc. By adopting an economist's perspective, it explores how cryptocurrencies function within the broader economic structure and the potential impact they have on traditional financial systems, monetary policy, and the overall economy.

INTRODUCTION

One of the most prominent features of cryptocurrencies is their ability to provide a high level of security and resistance to counterfeiting. This is made possible through the underlying technology called blockchain, which is a decentralized

DOI: 10.4018/979-8-3693-0405-1.ch001

and transparent ledger that records all transactions (Alzahrani & Bulusu, 2018). Each transaction is securely linked to the previous one, forming a chain of blocks that are virtually impossible to alter or manipulate. This makes cryptocurrencies highly secure and trustworthy, as every transaction can be independently verified by anyone with access to the blockchain. Furthermore, cryptocurrencies operate in a decentralized manner, meaning they are not issued or regulated by central banks or governments. This decentralization gives individuals greater control over their own finances and removes the need for intermediaries such as banks. Users can send and receive cryptocurrencies directly without the need for a third party, reducing transaction fees and increasing efficiency. The absence of a central authority also makes cryptocurrencies resistant to government intervention and control, providing a level of financial freedom and autonomy. However, the volatility of cryptocurrencies presents a significant challenge. The value of cryptocurrencies can fluctuate dramatically in a short period, driven by market sentiment, speculation, and external factors. This volatility can lead to substantial gains for investors but also carries a high level of risk. It is important to note that investing in cryptocurrencies can be highly speculative, and individuals should exercise caution and conduct thorough research before making any investment decisions (Lapin, 2021). To navigate the cryptocurrency market successfully, it is essential to understand the factors that influence their valuation. Internal factors such as technological advancements, network adoption, and governance structures play a significant role in shaping the value of cryptocurrencies. Additionally, external factors like regulatory developments, geopolitical events, and investor sentiment also have a profound impact on the cryptocurrency market. Moreover, as cryptocurrencies continue to gain traction, the importance of accountability within the digital asset business becomes increasingly evident. The manuscript recognizes this transformative nature and delves into the ongoing revolution surrounding accountability in the cryptocurrency market.

The manuscript highlights the transformative nature of accountability within the digital asset business and the ongoing revolution surrounding it. It explores emerging trends and practices that shape the accountability mechanisms in the cryptocurrency market. By critically assessing the advantages and challenges associated with cryptocurrencies, the manuscript provides readers with a comprehensive understanding of the opportunities and risks in this evolving landscape. Through robust accountability mechanisms, the cryptocurrency market can address challenges such as volatility, investor protection, and illicit activities, fostering trust, stability, and sustainable growth in the industry. The manuscript goes beyond the surface-level examination of cryptocurrencies and delves into the economic implications of these digital assets. By adopting an economist's perspective, it explores how cryptocurrencies function within the broader economic structure and the potential impact they have on traditional financial systems, monetary policy, and the overall economy.

One of the key areas of analysis is the impact of cryptocurrencies on traditional financial systems. Cryptocurrencies challenge the traditional banking model by offering an alternative means of conducting financial transactions. The manuscript explores how this disruptive technology can potentially reshape the financial landscape, from payments and remittances to lending and fundraising. It discusses the potential benefits of increased financial inclusivity, especially for individuals who are unbanked or underbanked, as cryptocurrencies provide them with access to financial services that were previously unavailable. Furthermore, the manuscript examines the implications of cryptocurrencies for monetary policy. Cryptocurrencies are decentralized and independent of central banks, which raises questions about their potential influence on monetary policy tools such as interest rates, money supply, and inflation (Scicchitano, 2020). The manuscript analyzes the potential challenges and opportunities that cryptocurrencies pose to central banks and explores the evolving role of central banks in regulating and adapting to this new financial paradigm. In addition, it also explores the overall economic impact of cryptocurrencies. It considers how the rise of cryptocurrencies can affect macroeconomic factors such as economic growth, employment, and income distribution. It examines the potential benefits of cryptocurrencies in fostering innovation and entrepreneurship, as they provide new avenues for fundraising and capital formation. However, it also highlights the risks associated with cryptocurrencies, such as their potential to facilitate illicit activities and the challenges of effectively integrating them into existing economic frameworks. Essentially, this manuscript offers a comprehensive analysis of the benefits and risks of cryptocurrencies from an economic perspective. By examining their impact on traditional financial systems, monetary policy, and the overall economy, it provides readers with a deeper understanding of the potential implications of cryptocurrencies. Through a critical analysis of these advantages and challenges, readers can develop a comprehensive understanding of the opportunities and risks inherent in these innovative financial instruments. By staying informed about the accountability revolution within the digital asset business, individuals and organizations can navigate the cryptocurrency market with greater confidence and make informed decisions in this rapidly evolving landscape. By understanding the economic implications of cryptocurrencies, readers can gain valuable insights into their potential long-term effects on financial markets and economic stability. This knowledge is crucial for individuals, investors, businesses, and policymakers to make informed decisions regarding cryptocurrencies. It enables them to assess the risks and opportunities associated with this rapidly evolving market and develop strategies to navigate it effectively.

BACKGROUND/LITERATURE REVIEW

Digital assets are quickly becoming normal in today's global economy. As defined by the Internal Revenue Service, digital assets can be seen as "as any digital representation of value which is recorded on a cryptographically secured distributed ledger... Digital assets include (but are not limited to): convertible virtual currency and cryptocurrency, stablecoins and non-fungible tokens (NFTs)" (2023). They are not a fiat currency, which means to say, they are not like what is technically deemed as modern currency such as the coin and paper money of the US. Of all the digital assets, cryptocurrency is the most common one.

According to the definition provided by Kate Ashford [2022], cryptocurrency is highlighted as a digital form of money which is described in relation to blockchain technology. Unlike the United States Dollar or the Euro, whereby they are all centrally managed, the value of a cryptocurrency is not managed or maintained by any central authority. On the other hand, these duties are widely dispersed among the users of cryptocurrency via the usage of the internet. To have a more complete comprehension of cryptocurrencies, one needs also to understand the technology referred to as blockchain. Ashford [2022] describes, "A blockchain is an open, distributed ledger that records transactions in code...Transactions are recorded in 'blocks' that are then linked together on a 'chain' of previous cryptocurrency transactions." It has become quite popular in use since it first came onto the market. Assets that are recorded and tracked in a blockchain network can be tangible, such as a house, car, cash, land, or intangible, such as intellectual property, patents, copyrights, and branding (IBM, 2023). Virtually anything of value can be tracked and traded on a blockchain network.

Cryptocurrency made its debut as Bitcoin in 2008-2009 where its software was made available to the public to mine. Mining is the technical manner in which cryptocurrency gets out to the public, generally in exchange for enabling transactions [Ashford, 2022]. As it had only been mined and never traded, it had no value to start with, so it was traded without any specific values, much more like a barter system than a currency. Since its inception, Bitcoin and other cryptocurrencies have fluctuated in value and some people even fell into scams or other unfortunate circumstances but since 2017, Bitcoin continues to grow and because of this growth, there has been an interest in working with it as a legitimate currency [Marr, 2017]. Due to its growth in value, it has become a very popular investment.

Current research explores various emerging trends and practices that are reshaping the landscape of the digital asset industry, shedding light on how accountability mechanisms are evolving to address the unique challenges presented by cryptocurrencies. It analyzes the current state of accountability within the cryptocurrency market, critically assessing its advantages and challenges. By drawing on a diverse range of sources, including academic research, industry reports, and expert opinions, the manuscript provides a comprehensive analysis of the accountability revolution in the digital asset business. It aims to equip readers with a nuanced understanding of the opportunities and risks presented by these innovative financial instruments. Cryptocurrencies have the potential to revolutionize traditional financial systems by offering numerous benefits (Deepalakshmi et al., 2023). One such advantage is the increased transaction speed compared to traditional banking systems. Cryptocurrency transactions can be processed within minutes, regardless of geographical boundaries, making them ideal for cross-border transactions. This feature can potentially enhance global trade and financial connectivity. Another benefit is the potential for reduced costs. Traditional financial transactions often involve intermediaries such as banks, which charge fees for their services. In contrast, cryptocurrencies enable direct peer-to-peer transactions, eliminating the need for intermediaries and reducing transaction costs. This can particularly benefit individuals in developing countries who may have limited access to traditional banking services. Additionally, cryptocurrencies offer enhanced security through the use of blockchain technology (Frankenfield, 2023). The decentralized and transparent nature of blockchain ensures that every transaction is recorded and verified by multiple participants in the network. This significantly reduces the risk of fraud and tampering, providing users with increased trust and confidence in the system.

However, alongside these benefits, cryptocurrencies also face challenges that necessitate robust accountability mechanisms. The volatility of cryptocurrency prices is a significant concern. Price fluctuations can be rapid and significant, driven by factors such as market speculation, regulatory developments, and investor sentiment. Such volatility can lead to market manipulation and potential financial losses for investors. Therefore, ensuring transparency and accountability in the cryptocurrency market becomes crucial to mitigate risks and protect investors. Furthermore, the absence of centralized regulation in the cryptocurrency market raises concerns regarding investor protection, security breaches, and illicit activities. While decentralized systems offer greater autonomy and freedom, they also require effective mechanisms to address fraudulent activities, money laundering, and cybersecurity threats (achhangani, 2023). Establishing accountability frameworks and regulations that strike a balance between innovation and protection is essential to foster the sustainable growth of the cryptocurrency market.

There are many benefits to the use of blockchains and the use of crypocurrencies. Business runs on information so the faster it's received and the more accurate it is, the better it is for all involved. It tends to provide immediate, shared and completely transparent information stored on an immutable ledger that can be accessed only by permitted network members. The network can track orders, payments, accounts, and production (IBM, 2023).

The benefits of blockchains and digital assets, such as cryptocurrencies, include decentralization, transparency and trust, efficiency and speed, cost reduction, financial inclusion, asset tokenization and finally, innovation. Decentralization in blockchain is a pivotal concept that revolutionizes traditional systems by dispersing control, authority, and data across a network of nodes rather than consolidating it in a single entity or region. This fundamental principle underpins the security and integrity of blockchain technology, thwarting any attempts at transaction tampering or censorship. Moreover, decentralization promotes global accessibility, ensuring that the benefits of blockchain are not confined to specific geographical locations or centralized authorities. The distribution of power in blockchain architecture engenders trust and transparency, as every participant in the network has equal access to the ledger's information. This inclusivity democratizes access to resources and opportunities, leveling the playing field for a diverse range of participants. Consequently, blockchain has emerged as a transformative force across various industries, disrupting conventional paradigms and unlocking new possibilities for innovation and collaboration (Ratta et al., 2021). Within a blockchain, once a transaction is recorded, it cannot be altered or deleted. This provides a high level of transparency and ensures the integrity of the transaction history (Frankenfield, 2023). Transparency is achieved by the provision of a publicly accessible ledger of all transactions. Therefore, this makes it possible for participants to view a list of transaction history, which in turn promotes accountability. The significance of this transparency extends beyond mere record-keeping. It engenders an environment of trust among participants, as they can rely on the veracity of the information presented. This has far-reaching implications for financial systems, where trust is paramount. Blockchain's transparency is a cornerstone in its promise to revolutionize not only how transactions are conducted, but also how trust is established in the digital realm (Narayanan et al., 2016).

Blockchains also allow for faster transactions. They can significantly reduce transaction settlement times, particularly in cross-border transactions. This is a game-changer for industries where speed is crucial. It also allows parallel processing. This technique enables the system to handle multiple transactions which in turn boosts transaction speed (Scherer, 2017). Blockchain technology also relies on a low latency network infrastructure. Faster internet connections as well as well-distributed nodes have been proven to cut down latency and thus optimize transaction speed and validation. Another way it increases speed is through Automated Smart contracts, which are self-executing contracts with predefined rules. They automatically execute actions when conditions are met, streamlining complex transactions and reducing the need for intermediaries. With that streamlining process, it leads to cost reductions.

There are several ways in which blockchains reduce cost. Firstly, through the elimination of intermediary fees. Traditional financial transactions often involve fees for various intermediaries. With blockchains, direct peer-to-peer transactions can eliminate or drastically reduce these fees (Frankenfield, 2023). Secondly, blockchain transactions can be more cost-effective, especially for international transfers. This is particularly significant for businesses operating globally (Fauzi et al., 2020). And finally, there is a reduction of administrative costs. Enhancements such as smart contracts, self-executing contracts can automatically carry out several administrative tasks, and thus doing away with the need for human effort. For instance, the system can automatically initiate payments and enforce contracts. Other factors that cut down costs include asset tokenization, decentralization of finance, collaboration and data sharing (Wilkie & Smith, 2021). Tokenization allows assets to be divided into smaller, tradable units. It creates fractional ownership. This enables broader participation in investments and unlocks new opportunities for smaller investors. Illiquid assets like real estate or fine art can also become more liquid through tokenization. This can lead to greater market efficiency and accessibility. Therefore, the representation of physical assets as token in either utility, payments and security tokens on a blockchain technology makes it very convenient to manage, divide and trade assets. This leads to enhanced saving of costs (Kharitonova, 2021). Blockchains can also provide access to financial services for individuals in regions without traditional banking infrastructure. This can empower people who were previously excluded from the global economy. Around the world, there are billions of individuals without access to traditional banking services. Blockchain technology has the potential to bring financial services directly to these populations (Mougayar, 2016). This not only empowers individuals but also stimulates economic growth in historically marginalized regions. Blockchain technology is poised to be a global force for financial inclusion, reshaping the financial services landscape for the betterment of all (Mougayar, 2016).

Finally, blockchains enable transparency and traceability in supply chains and can therefore, increase the effectiveness of Supply Chain Management. This can be crucial in industries like pharmaceuticals or luxury goods to combat counterfeiting and ensure product authenticity. Another innovative use are the Blockchain-based voting systems, which have the potential to revolutionize elections by providing a secure and transparent platform. This could increase trust in electoral processes by the public, which has been under increased scrutiny as of late.

Before any new system or technology can be implemented, one must consider the risks involved, just as one does the benefits. It should be considered simultaneously in its implementation to avoid issues. Though many have been quick to adopt it into their business plans and general usage, there are significant challenges that need to be overcome when using digital assets and the technology used to manage them. Firstly, scalability is a major challenge when it comes to digital assets since it involves handling a large number of transactions with many users and at the same time, keeping its efficiency and performance. Scalability challenges are often caused by the localized existence of a blockchain in which every transaction must be registered and verified by various networks. Scalability is effected via throughput Limitations. Some blockchains face challenges in handling a high volume of transactions quickly. This can lead to congestion and slower processing times. In addition, the confirmation process may be delayed because of many users, especially when the demand is high. Also high fees are a factor facing scalability. During periods of high demand, blockchain networks can become congested, resulting in delayed transaction confirmations. Many users running the same network cause flooding, hence causing inconvenience to many customers and costly to the company.

Different blockchain networks often operate independently. This lack of interoperability hinders seamless communication and collaboration between them (MOUGAYAR, 2016). This absence of interoperability has tangible implications for asset transfers, data exchange, and transactions across disparate blockchain platforms. Each blockchain network speaks its own unique "language," employing distinct protocols, consensus mechanisms, and smart contract standards. As a result, attempting to facilitate transactions or share data between these networks can be akin to trying to bridge a linguistic divide without a translator. This fragmentation of the blockchain landscape inhibits the potential for fluid and efficient cross-platform operations. It leads to a scenario where assets and information become confined within their respective blockchains, limiting their accessibility and utility in a broader ecosystem. Efforts are underway to address this challenge, with various projects and initiatives focused on developing interoperability solutions. These endeavors seek to create bridges or protocols that enable different blockchains to communicate and interact seamlessly. By establishing common protocols and standards, these interoperability solutions aim to break down the barriers that currently hinder cross-blockchain collaboration.

Proof-of-work (PoW) blockchains, a foundational technology in the world of digital assets, have drawn attention for their substantial energy consumption. The process of validating and recording transactions on a PoW blockchain requires miners to perform complex calculations, necessitating significant computational power. This computational intensity leads to a considerable expenditure of electricity, which in turn raises environmental concerns. The growing recognition of the environmental impact of PoW blockchains has prompted a concerted effort to explore and implement more sustainable consensus mechanisms (Fauzi et al., 2020). These mechanisms aim to maintain the integrity and security of the blockchain while minimizing its energy footprint. In the context of cryptocurrency mining, participants engage in a competitive process to solve intricate mathematical puzzles. The first miner to successfully solve the puzzle is rewarded with newly minted cryptocurrency coins or transaction fees. This competitive nature further escalates the energy demands of the process. As miners strive to outperform one another, they continually invest in more powerful hardware and employ increased computational resources, exacerbating the overall energy consumption. Regrettably, the extensive energy usage associated with cryptocurrency mining contributes to higher emissions, which directly impact the environment. The release of greenhouse gases, a byproduct of the energy-intensive mining process, adds to the cumulative environmental stresses that are contributing to the ongoing challenges of climate change. Efforts are underway to explore alternative consensus mechanisms, such as Proof-of-Stake (PoS) and Proof-of-Authority (PoA), which are designed to drastically reduce the energy requirements of blockchain networks (Narayanan et al., 2016). These sustainable approaches are becoming increasingly important as society grapples with the need for both technological innovation and responsible environmental stewardship.

There are legal uncertainties revolving such a new and fast changing technology. The regulatory landscape for blockchain and digital assets is still evolving. This can create uncertainty for businesses and users regarding compliance requirements (Fauzi et al., 2020). Since many cryptocurrencies are used worldwide, every country has its regulations and laws to comply with. This becomes a challenge because there is no benchmark for global regulation of cryptocurrency. This affects the consistency of cryptocurrency. Meeting Anti-Money Laundering (AML) and Know Your Customer (KYC) regulations can be challenging, especially for decentralized platforms. This is because cryptocurrency is usually untraceable and provides a clear platform for money laundering and financing illegal activities. Although measures have been put to fight back against these vices it's still a challenge since many users are in control of their accounts and hence can leave the hint of their intentions. This is a major challenge to digital assets and can be a threat globally.

Another threat is in regards to the security of digital assets. Smart contracts are executed automatically and are immutable. Flaws in their code can lead to security breaches and financial losses (Fauzi et al., 2020). This occurs because the buyers and sellers execute their contracts individually and one may acquire sensitive information or funds because it's easier to hack without being traced. the smart contract is vulnerable since it uses foreign sources of data which is easily compromised. In addition, these contracts are usually written in complex computer languages which causes inconvenience to the user with basic knowledge. Blockchains that rely on Proof-of-Work consensus mechanisms are vulnerable to 51% attacks, where a single entity controls the majority of computational power (Fauzi et al., 2020). This raises a lot of security concerns because hackers can easily access personal data while the users think is an added security. The attacks are higher compared to the control measures hence raising security concerns to a threat level. On top of outside threats, there are also basic human errors to consider. Handling and managing private keys and wallets can be complex and potentially risky, especially for non-technical users.

Losing access to a wallet can result in permanent loss of assets. Many first-time users can be conned due to unskilled management of their private accounts and may end up sharing sensitive information hence suffering Cyber attacks. Mistakes in transactions (e.g., sending funds to the wrong address) can be irreversible, leading to potential loss of assets. Little or no experience by the users can lead them to make mistakes by making a transaction with the wrong users and scammers leading to losses. Most cryptocurrency transactions cannot be reversed hence it becomes a major challenge and it is hard to know who to trust in the cryptocurrency business.

Many potential users and businesses are unfamiliar with blockchain technology and its potential applications. Bridging this knowledge gap is crucial for broader adoption. Many users lack a clear understanding of cryptocurrency because of its complex nature. This then makes them vulnerable and can easily be scammed. In addition, little education can cause misinformation to the users leading to losses of assets. The presence of numerous blockchains and digital assets, each with its unique features, can lead to confusion for potential adopters due to the fragmentation of the market. Since there are many markets with different currencies, the cryptocurrency price fluctuates posing a challenge for traders to implement their exchange without expecting huge losses. In addition, lack of standard technology and different laws and regulations leads to the executing of business difficult due to confusion and inconveniences.

MAIN FOCUS OF THE CHAPTER

The transformative nature of accountability with digital assets, and most particularly on blockchain technology, marks a very critical aspect in terms of its value proposition. Blockchain therefore has the ability to bring a newfound revolution of accountability through several ways. First, the technology ensures immutable recordkeeping which ensures transparency, traceability, transparency, security and reliability to all participants (Yu et al., 2018). Second, the decentralization of control and resources reduces risk because a failure at one point in the system does not affect the others (Da Xu et al, 2018). Therefore, this makes it hard for a single entity to manipulate the system. Third, this system is useful in management of supply chains (Queiroz et al., 2020) This is possible through the ability to track and monitor goods in transit. Fourth, the technology is able to facilitate transactions from any vantage point on the globe with a considerable reduction of intermediaries. This reduces operation costs and in turn optimizes accountability and other forms of efficiency.

Regardless of the challenges blockchains and digital assets may present, they are becoming more and more common place. It is impossible to deny that there are several emerging trends and ways in which blockchain technology and digital assets are being used. Besides cryptocurrencies, there is another form of digital asset that emerged over the last few years. Non-Fungible Tokens (NFTs) are a groundbreaking development in the world of digital assets which stand out for their exclusivity and indivisibility. NFTs are distinct digital assets that cannot be exchanged one-for-one with any other token, in contrast to fungible tokens, such as cryptocurrencies, where each unit is interchangeable with another of the same sort. Because of their special quality, they are perfect for denoting ownership of distinctive goods or material. their characteristic has found many uses, especially in the fields of digital art, collectibles, and gaming (Rajput, 2023). The specificity of each NFT enables verified ownership of a particular digital item, whether it be a piece of digital art or a rare item in a virtual game. This ownership is transparently and immutably recorded on the blockchain, providing both creators and consumers with enhanced security and trust in the provenance of the digital asset. The arrival of NFTs has not only disrupted traditional methods of ownership and asset management in the digital realm but has also provided new avenues for artists and creators to monetize their work in a direct and secure manner. NFTs, however, have waned in usage over the last year or so, showcasing the volatility and spontaneity of some emerging cryptocurrencies.

Central Bank Digital Currencies (CBDCs) represent a significant shift in the global financial environment, as various central banks are actively studying the viability of introducing their own digital currencies, no doubt hoping to get ahead of the market on the use of digital assets. CBDCs are a government-backed and controlled type of digital currency that functions as a digital counterpart to traditional fiat money. They are positioned to provide various benefits, including better payment system efficiency, lower costs connected with currency creation and circulation, and more transparency in financial transactions. Furthermore, CBDCs have the potential to increase financial inclusion by providing a larger population with safe and accessible digital financial services. However, their implementation creates complicated regulatory and privacy concerns that politicians and central banks must carefully address. The exploration of CBDCs reflects a convergence of traditional finance and emerging blockchain technology, signifying a pivotal moment in the evolution of monetary systems worldwide.

Just like digital assets, blockchain technologies are also constantly in flux. Decentralized Finance, often known as DeFi, is a disruptive paradigm in the financial ecosystem. DeFi, which is based on blockchain technology, aims to reinvent and reconstruct traditional financial institutions such as lending, borrowing, and asset trading. DeFi runs on decentralized systems, as opposed to traditional financial frameworks, which are frequently centralized and entail many middlemen. Individuals now have unprecedented power and autonomy over their financial assets and transactions as a result of this fundamental change (Rajput, 2023). The elimination of traditional financial intermediaries such as banks, credit agencies, or payment processors allows for more direct, peer-to-peer connections. As a result, consumers get greater freedom, lower expenses, and increased security in managing their financial concerns. DeFi is a pillar in the changing financial technology landscape because it gives the person direct authority over their financial assets and activities, marking a major move away from traditional, centralized financial systems.

Layer 2 solutions represent a pivotal advancement in blockchain technology, addressing inherent limitations related to scalability and transaction throughput. These are secondary protocols or frameworks that are constructed atop foundational blockchains, like Bitcoin or Ethereum, with the explicit aim to expedite transaction processing and thereby ameliorate issues of network congestion. Noteworthy implementations include the Lightning Network for Bitcoin and Optimism and zkSync for Ethereum (Rajput, 2023). The Lightning Network, for example, enables high-speed, low-cost transactions by creating off-chain payment channels that only interact with the main blockchain for opening and closing the channels. Similarly, Ethereum's Layer 2 solutions like Optimism employ Optimistic Rollups to bundle multiple transactions into a single one, effectively reducing the data stored on-chain and improving transactional efficiency. zkSync uses zk-Rollups to achieve the same goal but adds zero-knowledge proofs for enhanced security and privacy. The advent of these Layer 2 solutions not only mitigates existing bottlenecks but also paves the way for more scalable, efficient, and adaptable blockchain networks. These enhancements are crucial for blockchain technology to sustain a growing user base and diversifying application scenarios, thereby realizing its full transformative potential.

Decentralized Autonomous Organizations (DAOs) and Web3 herald a paradigm change in the design and administration of digital ecosystems. A decentralized version of the internet called Web3 is being developed, and its main goal is to give consumers more control over their data and online activities. In a similar vein, DAOs operate as organizational entities with governance structures encoded directly into transparent and immutable computer programs. Unlike traditional organizations that often have centralized authority figures or decision-making bodies, DAOs are collectively governed by their membership, free from the undue influence of a central governing entity (Guida, 2023). These digitally-encoded rules facilitate transparent decision-making and democratic governance, thereby fostering an ecosystem that is intrinsically resistant to single points of failure or control. By reducing the need for intermediaries and centralized entities, both Web3 and DAOs have the potential to revolutionize not just the infrastructure of the internet, but also the very mechanisms by which organizations function and make decisions. Together, they offer a promising glimpse into a future where decentralization and community-led governance are not merely theoretical constructs, but practical, functioning realities.

To mitigate and overcome the challenges of blockchains and the digital assets used, there are several ways in which the industry is changing and creating blockchain technologies. The future of blockchain technology is in interoperability and cross-chain technology, which aims to eliminate communication and collaboration barriers across various blockchain networks. These initiatives play a crucial role in broadening the use and value of blockchain technology. Developers may take use of the distinctive properties of many networks to create more extensive and adaptable apps by allowing different blockchains to interact. This is especially important since different blockchains each have their own advantages and disadvantages, and cross-chain interoperability can reduce these drawbacks while maximizing their advantages. Additionally, interoperability makes it easier for various blockchain ecosystems to be integrated, creating a more unified and linked digital environment. Wide-ranging effects include improved cross-border payment systems as well as new applications for supply chain management and decentralized finance.

The combination of blockchain technology and the Internet of Things (IoT) is a strong synergy that has the potential to generate significant improvements in security, transparency, and operational efficiency. IoT is defined by the interconnection of various devices and sensors, which frequently deal with sensitive data and important operations. The powerful security characteristics of blockchain, such as cryptographic encryption and immutability, can reinforce the IoT ecosystem by protecting data integrity and minimizing risks. It facilitates secure data sharing and transactions between IoT devices, guaranteeing that information is both tamper-proof and traceable, boosting network trust. The role of blockchain in third-generation security cannot be emphasized; it offers a crucial line of defense against evolving dangers and flaws in the IoT environment (Rajput, 2023).

Regarding the environmental impact digital assets have, especially with consideration of mining, the pursuit of sustainable and environmentally conscious blockchain solutions is gaining substantial traction as the energy consumption of blockchain networks comes under heightened scrutiny. With the proliferation of blockchain technologies, particularly those relying on energy-intensive Proof-of-Work (PoW) consensus mechanisms, concerns about their environmental impact have grown. As a response, there is a notable push within the blockchain community to develop more sustainable consensus mechanisms and energy-efficient blockchain solutions. These innovations aim to reduce the carbon footprint of blockchain networks while maintaining their security and functionality. Transitioning from PoW to alternatives like Proof-of-Stake (PoS) or delegated PoS, which require significantly less energy, is a prominent example. This sustainability-driven shift not only addresses environmental concerns but also aligns blockchain technology with broader efforts to combat climate change and promote eco-friendly practices. It exemplifies the adaptability and responsiveness of blockchain developers and stakeholders to evolving environmental and societal priorities in their quest to make blockchain technology more sustainable and responsible.

Privacy-preserving technologies constitute a crucial frontier in the evolution of blockchain systems, particularly as concerns about data security and confidentiality continue to mount. These technologies, such as zero-knowledge proofs and privacy coins, are engineered to augment the privacy and confidentiality of transactions and data stored on blockchains. Zero-knowledge proofs, for instance, allow parties to verify the truth of a statement without revealing any specific information about the statement itself. This groundbreaking cryptographic technique enables confidential transactions while maintaining transparency and security. Privacy coins, on the other hand, are cryptocurrencies designed with a primary focus on concealing transaction details and user identities. These innovations are instrumental in addressing privacy concerns that have arisen with the increasing prevalence of transparent and traceable blockchains. By providing enhanced confidentiality, privacy-preserving technologies empower individuals and organizations to safeguard sensitive information and transactional data, striking a balance between transparency and privacy within the blockchain ecosystem.

The tokenization of assets represents a groundbreaking shift in the way we perceive and manage real-world assets, such as real estate, art, and stocks, by digitizing them and recording their ownership on a blockchain. This innovative trend holds the potential to revolutionize traditional financial markets by allowing these tangible assets to be represented as digital tokens. One of the key advantages of asset tokenization is the facilitation of fractional ownership, whereby these tokens can be divided into smaller, tradable units. Due to the democratization of investing options, more people, including those with low starting money, may take part in asset ownership. Additionally, because these digital tokens can be purchased and traded more easily than their physical equivalents, it adds liquidity to usually illiquid markets. The tokenization of assets changes the landscape of asset management and trade in the digital era by streamlining the transfer of ownership and opening up new avenues for investment and market efficiency.

Blockchain technology and artificial intelligence (AI) together represent a promising new frontier that has the potential to provide useful applications in a variety of industries. In industries like healthcare, supply chain management, and financial services, this technological integration is particularly notable (Rajput, 2023). Innovative solutions are produced when the data analysis, machine learning, and predictive modeling capabilities of AI are combined with the inherent security and transparency of blockchain. Blockchain and AI in healthcare can improve patient data management by guaranteeing the confidentiality, integrity, and interoperability of medical records. To increase transparency and streamline procedures in the supply chain, AI-driven analytics may be seamlessly combined with blockchain traceability. Furthermore, blockchain assures trust and transparency in financial transactions, while AI-powered algorithms can enhance investing methods. These industries might undergo a transformation thanks to the synergy between AI and blockchain, which would enable data-driven insights, security, and efficiency in previously unimaginable ways.

The rise of governance tokens and community-led initiatives represents a sea change in the landscape of blockchain technology and decentralized platforms. Governance tokens are cryptographic tokens that allow users to actively engage in a blockchain project's decision-making and development processes. This movement is based on the decentralization concept, since it allows the community of users and token holders to have a direct and important part in setting the platform's future path (Rajput, 2023). Users obtain voting rights by owning governance tokens, allowing them to propose and vote on crucial issues such as protocol updates, tokenomics modifications, and other governance-related topics. This democratic method not only encourages users to feel a feeling of ownership, but also assures that choices are taken collaboratively, reducing the possibility of centralized control. Finally, governance tokens represent the decentralization ethos, making blockchain projects more inclusive and responsive to their communities' different needs and goals.

We must also look into the impact these new technologies will have on our economic structure. In an economic structure, cryptocurrency can be attributed to several roles. First, it is a medium of exchange and supports financial transactions between persons and business entities. Some online commercial platforms accept cryptocurrency as a mode of payment. Second, it can be used as a unit or store of value. Cryptocurrencies such as part Bitcoin can act as a digital store of value and a leeway against inflation and economic fluctuations. Cryptocurrencies have sparked attraction from speculative investors who anticipate high returns. Market dynamics such as price volatility and the potential for price increases have driven persons and organizations to invest heavily on cryptocurrency. Third, cryptocurrency some cryptocurrencies such as Ethereum has the ability to create smart contracts. These contracts can execute predefined agreements when some conditions are met. On financial systems, blockchain as a digital asset is poised to infuse several efficiencies such as enhancement of security, transparency and accountability, facilitation of trade internationally, tokenization of assets and a seamless management of supply chains. Therefore, blockchain technology is seen as a gamechanger in all financial transactions.

In terms of policy implication on organizations, this technology is continuing to drive businesses to adopt innovative methodologies in their daily operations. Therefore, the technology has the potential to significantly impact policy across many areas of application due to its unique characteristics such as immutability, transparency, security and management efficiencies. However, it has to be noted that while there are several advantages that are attributed to the technology, there are also several challenges such as integration with existing systems, scalability and regulatory compliance. In addition, the technology is dynamically evolving and therefore its widespread adoption in policy domains calls for several considerations.

The impact of blockchain technology on microeconomics and macroeconomics is a very multifaceted concept and is subject to change based on adoption levels and use cases. On macroeconomic, the technology can heavily impact monetary policies, the stability of financial systems, international trade and innovation. In terms of microeconomics, blockchain is deemed to lead to several efficiencies such as cost reduction, security of financial transactions, transparency, easy access to capital, data privacy and supply chain efficiencies.

SOLUTIONS AND RECOMMENDATIONS

From an economic perspective, the technology is poised to bring several efficiencies such as transparency and trust, efficiency and reduction of costs, data integrity and security, ownership and decentralization. In terms of shortfalls, the technology can be attributed to several challenges such as scalability, uncertainties with regulation, and incompatibility with the existing systems. Digital assets include three characteristics that are advantageous in a currency: they are difficult to earn, restricted in quantity, and simple to verify. Economists believe that cryptocurrencies have a long way to go before it can fulfill all of the requirements for the role of money. A unit of account, a medium of exchange, and a store of value are all functions that money performs. Countries that have shown a willingness to accept cryptographic networks have reaped economic gains in the form of increased innovation, investment, and employment. Other countries, have either not wholly embraced it or banned it outright, such as China.

In order for digital assets to be utilized fully within the economic space, it is understood that regulations will need to be put into place that don't necessarily disrupt the market too much but rather, enhance it. It is a pressing issue with global implications, knowing how regulations manifest in the digital asset markets is considerably valuable (Griffith & Clancey-Shang, 2023). In their paper, Griffith and Clancey-Shang (2023), make a study on how the 2021 Chinese Ban on cryptocurrency lead to changes to the crypto market. Their results showed that there was a significant value drop after the announcement of their policy and volatility increased but the effects were temporary. However, the carbon emissions associated with bitcoin mining dropped when the ban was announced and shot back up once the mining migrated to Kazakhstan, which is less environmentally efficient. Essentially, regulations or a direct ban "by a country with a significant crypto market presence can destabilize the crypto market, and cause adverse environmental effects. However, even with highly stringent enforcement measures, the long-term effectiveness of crypto regulations is questionable without an effective monitoring mechanism" (Griffith & Clancey-Shang, 2023). With that being said, in order for the digital asset market to be viable, the big players in that market should be careful with how to regulate the market and do so to allow it to flourish and stabilize, as much as a currency can be stabilized. There are substantial benefits for allowing digital assets to create economic gains and advantages. Two of the commercial advantages are access to new demographics as well as technological efficiency in the administration of the treasury, advantages that may be realized by embracing cryptocurrency as a kind of digital asset. Digital assets can have a positive impact on the economy ensuring that businesses are able to thrive under difficult situations.

FUTURE RESEACH DIRECTIONS/IMPLICATIONS

More research will need to be done on digital assets and the financial implications of regulations and its impact on the digital asset markets. As noted by Ngwakwe (2023), "(t)he uncertainty and seemingly attendant crypto investment jittery emerged recently as some crypto companies such as Binance and Coinbase came under the Securities and Exchange Commission (SEC) regulatory scrutiny" (p.96). Actions such as those made by the SEC, affect the acceptability of digital assets and its usage. The lawsuit can either have a negative impact, such as making investors and operators less inclined to utilize the technology as well as regulatory uncertainties, or a positive impact, where it can determine how digital assets can improve. Since digital assets and blockchain technology is still an evolving technology, its immediate adoption by organizations from so many years of reliance on conventional systems is subject to more research and consideration. For instance, more research has to be channeled to areas of concern enlisted above (Interoperability, security, control and privacy).

There is a growing number of software applications and tools that make the usage of digital assets easier and bring them closer to the attention of the general public. Because these digital assets are entirely decentralized, trade may take place unrestrictedly in any country in the world. This is an additional advantage of using something like cryptocurrency. The use of technology will make possible a financial revolution that will result in an increased sense of financial connection, empowerment, and enablement for all people. Through that business and people who transact frequently will be catered for. As it is a constantly evolving technology and practice, there is still positive innovation and improvements happening in real-time. There is constant improvement to address the issues presented with the usage of blockchains and digital assets. As businesses continue to use them, they will also find ways to improve them.

CONCLUSION

In conclusion blockchain technology is viewed by many as the gamechanger in financial transactions. Cryptocurrencies have posed a challenge to the traditional banking model by offering an alternative means of conducting financial transactions. Since its market debut however, cryptocurrencies have experienced an unprecedented surge in popularity over the past few years, with an ever-growing number of digital currencies being actively traded in various markets. One of the most prominent features of cryptocurrencies is their ability to provide a high level of security and resistance to counterfeiting. This article explored various emerging trends and practices that are reshaping the landscape of the digital asset industry, shedding light on how accountability mechanisms are evolving to address the unique challenges presented by cryptocurrencies.

The transactions associated with blockchain technology and cryptocurrencies are mechanized, digitized, and recorded on a ledger that is invulnerable to manipulation on the part of individuals, organizations, or governments. It not only gives the people more power and independence, but it also reduces the likelihood that they will be taken advantage of or corrupted in any way. One cannot succeed in interfering with the system. In a society that is rapidly becoming more digital, the social need to interact with people in other countries is increasingly manifesting itself in the form of financial necessities. Cryptocurrencies have an advantage here over more conventional forms of financial transaction, which are incapable of doing this task. Over the course of time, company owners will be able to help expand options to save, invest, and move money across international boundaries, which will, in turn, reframe global business processes.

REFERENCES

Achhangani. (2023, June 7). *Three challenges in cryptocurrency regulation*. Atlantic Council. https://www.atlanticcouncil.org/blogs/econographics/three-challenges-in-cryptocurrency-regulation/

Ashford, K. (2022). What is Cryptocurrency? *Forbes*. https://www.forbes.com/advisor/investing/cryptocurrency/what-is-cryptocurrency/

Deepalakshmi, M. U.s, L., S, S., P, S., & K, Y. (2023). Awareness of Cryptocurrency - An Empirical Study. *Innovation in Economy & Policy Research, 4*(1), 46–51. https://matjournals.co.in/index.php/JEPR/article/view/2686

Fauzi, M. A., Paiman, N., & Othman, Z. (2020). Bitcoin and Cryptocurrency: Challenges, Opportunities and Future Works. *The Journal of Asian Finance. Economics and Business, 7*(8), 695–704. doi:10.13106/jafeb.2020.vol7.no8.695

Frankenfield, J. (2023, February 4). *Cryptocurrency Explained With Pros and Cons for Investment*. Investopedia. https://www.investopedia.com/terms/c/cryptocurrency.asp

Griffith, & Clancey-Shang, D. (2023). Cryptocurrency regulation and market quality. *Journal of International Financial Markets, Institutions & Money, 84*, 101744–. doi:10.1016/j.intfin.2023.101744

Guida, P. (2023, September). Council Post: The State Of DAOs And What That Can Mean For Web3. *Forbes*. https://www.forbes.com/sites/forbesfinancecouncil/2022/10/14/the-state-of-daos-and-what-that-can-mean-for-web3/?sh=39711e9e7f37

IBM. (2023). *What is blockchain technology?* IBM. https://www.ibm.com/topics/blockchain

Internal Revenue Service. (2023). *Digital Assets*. IRS. https://www.irs.gov/businesses/small-businesses-self-employed/digital-assets

JEL classification: G20, G21, G28. (2022, September). *The Financial Stability Implications of Digital Assets*. Federal Reserve Bank Of New York. Www.newyorkfed.org. https://www.newyorkfed.org/research/staff_reports/sr1034

Kharitonova, A. (2021, March). Capabilities of Blockchain Technology in Tokenization of Economy. In *1st International Scientific Conference" Legal Regulation of the Digital Economy and Digital Relations: Problems and Prospects of Development"(LARDER 2020)* (pp. 28-32). Atlantis Press. 10.2991/aebmr.k.210318.006

Lapin, N. (2021, December 23). Explaining Crypto's Volatility. *Forbes*. https://www.forbes.com/sites/nicolelapin/2021/12/23/explaining-cryptos-volatility/?sh=33ab79027b54

Marr, B. (2017). A Short History of Bitcoin and Crypto Currency Everyone Should Read. *Forbes*. https://www.forbes.com/sites/bernardmarr/2017/12/06/a-short-history-of-bitcoin-and-crypto-currency-everyone-should-read/?sh=1b53ac3f3f27

Mougayar, W. (2016). *The Business Blockchain: Promise, Practice, and Application of the Next Internet Technology*. Wiley.

Narayanan, A., Bonneau, J., Felten, E., Miller, A., & Goldfeder, S. (2016). *Bitcoin and Cryptocurrency Technologies: A Comprehensive Introduction*. Princeton University Press.

Ngwakwe, C. (2023). Emerging Regulatory Challenges on The Value and Future Of Cryptocurrency Exchange Business. Acta Universitatis Danubius. *Juridica, 19*(2).

Rajput, M. (2023, April 28). Top 15 Blockchain Technology Trends to Follow in 2023. *Mind Inventory*. https://www.mindinventory.com/blog/blockchain-development-trends/

Ratta, P., Kaur, A., Sharma, S., Shabaz, M., & Dhiman, G. (2021). Application of blockchain and internet of things in healthcare and medical sector: Applications, challenges, and future perspectives. *Journal of Food Quality*, *2021*, 1–20. doi:10.1155/2021/7608296

Scherer, M. (2017). *Performance and scalability of blockchain networks and smart contracts*.

Scicchitano, M. (2020, December 12). *How Cryptocurrencies May Impact the Banking Industry*. Wolf & Company, P.C. https://www.wolfandco.com/resources/insights/how-cryptocurrencies-may-impact-the-banking-industry/

Seth, S. (2021, August 25). *Central Bank Digital Currency (CBDC)*. Investopedia. https://www.investopedia.com/terms/c/central-bank-digital-currency-cbdc.asp

Wilkie, A., & Smith, S. S. (2021). Blockchain: speed, efficiency, decreased costs, and technical challenges. In The emerald handbook of blockchain for business (pp. 157-170). Emerald Publishing Limited. doi:10.1108/978-1-83982-198-120211014

KEY TERMS AND DEFINITIONS

Accountability Mechanisms: Creating a set of standards by which to judge and criticize the object in question and figuring out the effects and consequences of those standards, should they be implemented.

Bitcoin: A type of digital currency that can be used at a global scale online that is verified through a network and recorded in a digital ledger.

Blockchain Technology: A digital network that contains blockchains in a database that can be public, private or built by several organizations all at once.

Blockchain: A digital ledger that is distributed peer to peer worldwide that is linked together as a series of records, or blocks.

Cryptocurrency: Digital currency which is used virtually and used as both a currency and a virtual accounting system that is exchanged via a computer network and managed via a digital wallet.

Digital Assets: Anything of perceived value that is a digital product and can be stored digitally.

Sustainable Growth: A level of growth at which an entity can realistically maintain without coming across major issues.

Chapter 2
Adoption of Blockchain in Supply Chain Financing

Sakuntala Rao
S.P. Jain School of Global Management, Bangalore, India

Shalini Chandra
https://orcid.org/0000-0002-7808-4617
S.P. Jain School of Global Management, Bangalore, India

Dhrupad Mathur
S.P. Jain School of Global Management, Dubai, UAE

ABSTRACT

This study explores the factors that impact the adoption of blockchain in supply chain financing (SCF). Blockchain's unique features make it a good solution to the current problems in SCF. However, given that both blockchain and SCF are relatively new, there are almost no commercially viable large-scale implementations yet in this area. Research in the factors that drive the adoption of blockchain in SCF, is also scarce. Of the six identified determinants of adoption of blockchain in SCF, the study found four to be significant. Relative advantage, compatibility, organization readiness, and environment readiness influence the adoption of blockchain in SCF. Complexity and technology readiness are insignificant determinants, indicating a technically mature industry capable of handling current blockchain implementations in SCF and associated changes. The authors also found that trust has a mediating effect between compatibility and adoption and between environment readiness and adoption.

DOI: 10.4018/979-8-3693-0405-1.ch002

INTRODUCTION

This section provides the justification for the research and introduces the research model.

The Euro Banking Association (EBA) defined SCF as 'The use of financial instruments, practices and technologies to optimise the management of processes for working capital and liquidity tied up in the supply chain collaborating business partners' (Jansen, Beyer, & Taschner, 2018, p. 7). According to Strategic Treasurer (2021), SCF has been gaining importance in recent years. It is especially useful during times of high or fluctuating interest rates; in conditions of onerous compliance requirements, in cross border trade; and where there are large networks of suppliers and financers. However, traditional SCF has several issues, including too much paperwork, multiplicity and duplication of information and the need for reconciliation, as there are too many systems capturing piecemeal information (instead of an end-to-end system), a need for a common communication system, lack of trust and opportunities for fraud.

Blockchain is taking the world by storm. The concept was based on the seminal whitepaper by Satoshi Nakamoto (2008). In this system, all transactions are verified and stored in a block. Each block is linked to the previous block, thereby creating a chain. Hence, the term 'blockchain'. The transactions are time stamped, and this prevents anyone from altering the ledger (Tapscott & Tapscott, 2016).The key blockchain characteristics are a distributed database, peer-to-peer (P2P) transmission, transparency with pseudo-anonymity, irreversibility of records and computational logic (Tapscott & Tapscott, 2017). Blockchain is still, however, in the early stage in terms of theory, methods and empirical work. Scholars only started publishing articles on this topic, in 2014 (Frizzo-Barker et al., 2020).

The review of the existing literature showed that more research is needed on blockchain in SCF. Some examples are set out in Table 1.

Given the above, we chose the adoption of blockchain in SCF as our research topic.

The subject of this research was the adoption of blockchain in SCF at an enterprise level. Accordingly, information system (IS) theories of technology adoption were examined, particularly at the organization level. The diffusion of innovations (DOI) and technology-organization-environment (TOE) theories of adoption were identified as the most appropriate for this research. A combination of the two theories was used to provide the theoretical framework for this research. Thus, a model was developed wherein six determinants, namely, relative advantage, compatibility, complexity (from the DOI theory), technology readiness, organization readiness, and environment readiness (from the TOE theory), influence the adoption of blockchain in SCF.

Table 1. Identified gaps in the research on adoption of blockchain in supply chain financing (SCF)

Gap	Reference
Future research: impact of blockchain on SCF, barriers for adoption and motivation required for adoption.	Parkhi (2021)
Blockchain is relatively new, both technically and practically, in the field. Further research into the adoption of blockchain, including field surveys, is needed.	Rijanto (2021)
Adoption of blockchain in SCF is in its infancy.	Rijanto (2021)
Blockchain and SCF combination details are rarely mentioned. Future research: how to get core enterprises to join the SCF blockchain. In addition, quantitative research on the impact of blockchain on SCF.	Li, Zhu, Zhang and Yu (2020)
Future research: other areas of SCF. In addition, how blockchain resolves trust and commitment issues.	Dong, Chen, Shi and Ng (2021)
The database Scopus (as of 22 July 2020) had 915 publications with the phrases 'Supply Chain' and 'Blockchain' but only 70 with 'Supply Chain + Finance + Blockchain'. Therefore, more research is required in this area as well as in the area of sustainable SCF.	Bal and Pawlicka (2021)
Adoption of blockchain by organizations is limited. There are inconsistent results in previous studies, as no mediating variable was considered. In addition, most of the research is on the technical side.	Malik, Chadhar, Vatanasakdakul and Chetty (2021)
The promising but immature state of blockchain begs the question whether blockchain in identity management in organizations is practical or just hype. More research is needed, especially using a quantitative approach to technology-organization-environment.	Mulaji and Roodt (2021)
The adoption of this technology remains low. Furthermore, barriers to adoption have been identified by only a few studies.	Choi, Chune, Seyha and Young (2020)

The literature review identified trust as a key factor impacting the adoption of technology. Bahmanziari, Pearson and Crosby (2003) defined trust as a leap of faith due to the lack of complete information when adopting a new technology. Lippert and Davis (2006) suggested that greater technology adoption and internalisation are by-products of trust, both technology-related trust and interpersonal trust. Obal (2013) surveyed 134 SaaS users and concluded that pre-existing inter-organizational trust influences the adoption of disruptive technologies.

However, we did not come across research that combined trust with the TOE and DOI theories and looked at the role of trust as a mediating variable (MV) in the adoption of technology, particularly, in the adoption of blockchain in SCF. Accordingly, this research included the examination of trust as an MV between the independent variables (IVs) derived from the TOE and DOI theories and the dependent variable (DV), that is, the adoption of blockchain in SCF. Trust was included in the research objectives, the research questions, the hypotheses and the research model. The focus of this research was the adoption of blockchain in SCF. With this in mind, the research aim, objectives, questions and hypotheses were developed.

Research Aim

- Determine the perceptions of SCF and blockchain technology professionals regarding the core factors influencing the decision to adopt blockchain in SCF.

Research Objectives

- Establish the factors that influence the adoption of blockchain in SCF.
- Determine the role of trust in this process.

Research Questions

- RQ1: What are the factors that positively influence the adoption of blockchain in SCF?
- RQ2: What are the factors that negatively influence the adoption of blockchain in SCF?
- RQ3: What is the role of trust in this process?

Research Hypotheses

- H1: The perception of relative advantage (RA) of blockchain positively impacts the adoption of blockchain in SCF (AD).
- H2: The compatibility (CO) of blockchain positively impacts AD.
- H3: The complexity (CX) of blockchain negatively impacts AD.
- H4: Technology readiness (TR) positively impacts AD.
- H5: Organization readiness (OR) positively impacts AD.
- H6: Environment readiness (ER) positively impacts AD.
- H7: Trust (TS) positively mediates the relationship between RA and AD.
- H8: TS positively mediates the relationship between CO and AD.
- H9: TS negatively mediates the relationship between CX and AD.
- H10: TS positively mediates the relationship between TR and AD.
- H11: TS positively mediates the relationship between OR and AD.
- H12: TS positively mediates the relationship between ER and AD.

Figure 1. Research model

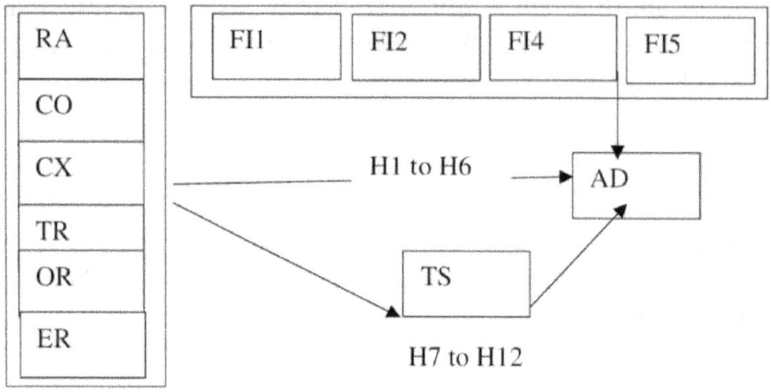

LITERATURE REVIEW

The research included an extensive literature review. Given the scarcity of peer-reviewed literature on the adoption of blockchain in SCF, the literature review was extended to include supply chain management as well as other areas, such as finance and manufacturing. The literature review also included "grey literature". The findings of the literature review were synthesised with the use of coding, and the findings were contextualised to SCF. More than 300 articles spread over the years 1998 to 2022 were reviewed. Given that both SCF and blockchain are fairly nascent, more than 65% of these articles were published in the years 2017–2022.

The literature review focussed on technology in supply chain management (SCM), SCF (need, types, current technology, advantages, current issues), blockchain (meaning, types, application in SCM and SCF, features, advantages, drawbacks, conditions for implementation, adoption, and theories of technology adoption).

An example of how the literature review findings were summarised is shown below in Table 2.

Before blockchain implementation, the legacy infrastructure, political and regulatory requirements, trust and the partner ecosystem should be considered. Furthermore, it is important that the necessary expertise and networks are in place. Significant investment is needed to go from proof of concept to implementation of scale. Blockchain implementation also requires security, ecosystem management, data management, legacy system remediation and integration with systems of record (Gartner, 2019). Blockchain in SCM requires a collaborative effort, potentially even a consortium among key stakeholders. There are four transformation requirements, namely, a business model, information model platforms, business process standards

Table 2. Features of blockchain

Area	Features	Reference
Supply chain financing	Decentralization, stability, security, anonymymity and non-tampering.	Du, Chen, Xiao, Yang and Ma (2020)
Supply chain financing in banking	Trust, reduction in financial costs and optimising processes.	Safiullin, Elshin and Abdukaeva (2020)
Supply chain financing	Decentralization, traceability, tamper proof and smart contracts.	Sun, He and Su (2021)
Supply chain financing	Peer-to-peer network, consensus, permissions and smart contracts.	Chen et al. (2020)
Supply chain financing	Decentralization, tamper proof, traceability and maintainability.	Wang (2021)
Supply chain financing	Cryptography, distributed storage, consensus mechanisms and smart contracts. Smart contract characteristics are decentralization, autonomy, verifiability and information sharing.	Zhang, Li and Jiang (2021)
Supply chain financing	Decentralized, immutable and transparent.	Li, Han, Crespi, Minerva and Sun (2021)

and data transfer operators (Korpela, Hallikas, & Dahlberg, 2017). It is important to solve the problems of data collection, integration and display before implementing blockchain in SCF (Zhang et al., 2021).

METHODOLOGY

Given the nature of the topic and its stage of evolution, a quantitative approach was followed, using a hypothetico-deductive research approach. This provided a scientific basis for validating theories by formulating hypotheses and testing them. The survey method was adopted for this research, rather than the case study method, as there are currently no successful implementations of blockchain in SCF at scale in India.

After conducting the literature review, the DV, IVs, MV and CVs were identified. This was followed by a literature synthesis with appropriate contextualisation and encoding, where we identified the axial and selective codes. We have explained each of the axial codes, contextualised to the adoption of blockchain in SCF, as shown in Table 3. Axial codes are also known as independent subvariables (SVs).

This research used a combination of the DOI and TOE theories. Therefore, the groupings for this research were relative advantage, compatibility and complexity from the DOI theory and technology readiness, organization readiness and environment readiness from the TOE theory. These groups were used as the IVs or *selective codes*

Table 3. Description of the independent sub-variables

Independent Sub-Variable	Description	Reference
Alignment with Vision	The vision in supply chain financing is to increase liquidity of all participants in the supply chain and to do this at the lowest possible cost, especially in a scenario of high interest rates and lack of liquidity. This includes leveraging the creditworthiness of the large buyers in the supply chain to get better rates for suppliers, who are often SMEs, and for the financing for tail-end suppliers who normally cannot get financing (deep financing). In order to fulfil this vision to the utmost extent, it is important to take away the information asymmetry currently prevalent in the supply chain financing ecosystem and foster trust among all the participants. Blockchain provides the answer and helps to turn this vision into reality.	Choi (2020)
Consensus	Blockchain in its truly decentralized form uses a consensus mechanism to record transactions in the blockchain. The most commonly used consensus mechanism is proof of work. The blockchain has several nodes, and each node can record the transaction on the blockchain. In order for a node to be the one to enter the transaction, it has to show 'Proof of Work'. Since all nodes in the system are competing to be the one to enter the transaction, there is a massive use of computing power and electricity in this process, and throughput or the number of transactions that can be entered suffers. Various alternatives are being proposed to overcome these issues including 'Proof of Stake'; however, these alternatives also have some attendant problems.	Beck, Müller-Bloch and King (2018)
Cost	The cost of implementing and running blockchain in supply chain financing.	Chod, Trichakis, Tsoukalas, Aspegren and Weber (2020)
Culture	It is critical that the culture of the organization is such that people are open to implementing new technologies, with a high risk tolerance. It should also be a culture that fosters inter-departmental co-operation because a number of departments are involved in the implementation of blockchain in supply chain financing, including IT, Finance, Accounting and Supply Chain Management. Change management is key to overcoming any resistance to change.	Bhardwaj, Garg and Gajpal (2021)
Decentralization	To leverage the true power of blockchain, it needs to be permissionless and on a public blockchain with true decentralization. The permissionless blockchain provides peer-to-peer transmission with no single entity controlling the blockchain. This decentralization poses a lot of challenges from a business model perspective, as the company needs to move away from a centralized business model and cede control. Hence, the current enterprise pilots are largely on private blockchains, which still have some form of centralized control over the data, the participants or the platform. Thus, these are efficiency plays rather than truly disruptive ones.	Furlonger and Uzureau (2019)
Efficiency	Blockchain is considered efficient. It speeds up transactions because all stakeholders use the same database, thereby eliminating disputes and the need for reconciliation. It is easy and cost-efficient to implement, especially if a permissionless version is used and existing blockchain infrastructure can be utilised.	Disparte (2017)
GIGO (garbage-in-garbage-out)	The reason GIGO is an issue with blockchain is that there is no control over transactions in the physical world, leading to potentially inaccurate data getting onto the blockchain. This is referred to as 'the last-mile problem', and it is currently being worked on. It is hoped that this is resolved in the near future with the use of a combination of technologies, such as Internet of Things or Oracle (a trusted off-chain data source that smart contracts can reference to execute a transaction or action on blockchain). Three approaches can overcome this problem. Passive identifiers based on physical properties (e.g. Everledger), active identifiers, such as serial number or QR code or embedded Internet of Things device, and active crypto identifiers, which combine established technologies such as near-field communication devices and public key cryptography, facilitate direct interaction of a physical object and blockchain.	Tucker and Catalini (2018)
Government	Government is a key stakeholder in the supply chain financing ecosystem. Regulatory certainty is key to the growth of any innovation. Government readiness includes having regulations in place that govern the blockchain environment in supply chain financing as well as the policies and standards around digital financing, non-bank financing and a completely paperless environment, including the legitimacy of smart contracts. In this regard, an attempt has been made by the National Standards Authority of Australia to standardise blockchain and distributed ledger technology. This is called ISO/TC 307. Cross-border regulations as well as laws relating to data protection and privacy, such as the EU's Data Protection Regulation, are important.	Rieger, Lockl, Urbach, Guggenmos and Fridgen (2019)

continued on following page

Table 3. Continued

Independent Sub-Variable	Description	Reference
Infrastructure Readiness	Infrastructure readiness refers to the availability of the hardware and software needed to implement blockchain. This implies a high degree of computerisation and computing power.	Clohessy and Acton (2019)
Integration	Technology readiness can also be increased through integration of blockchain with the existing legacy systems (mainly enterprise resource planning) of all the participants. This is important in order to prevent the multiplicity of several parallel systems resulting in inefficiencies in terms of data entry and reconciliation.	Wu, Cegielski, Hazen and Hall (2013)
Interoperability	Interoperability is important, both at the protocol level and the ontology (shared vocabulary) level. There are several versions of blockchain on platforms such as Hyperledger and Ethereum, and, if the ecosystem is to grow, it is important that there is interoperability between all these.	Tapscott, Iansiti, Lakhani and Tucker (2019)
Inter-Organization Trust	Supply chain financing involves several stakeholders outside the organization, such as buyers, vendors and providers of finance. It is important to create and foster trust among all the participants.	Frizzo-Barker et al. (2020)
Intra-Organization Trust	Supply chain financing involves several stakeholders within the organization, that is, multiple departments such as Finance, IT and Supply Chain Management. It is important to create and foster trust among all these participants.	Di Vaio and Varriale (2020)
Market	Market refers to the market in which the stakeholders of the supply chain operate. Market structure and dynamics are key. If the market is highly competitive and if competitors are looking to leverage technology solutions, this will add impetus to adopt new technology. The market also needs facilitating factors, such as information and blockchain model platforms, consultants in this field, business process and information standards and lack of constraints in the bill market.	Jensen, Hedmanand Henningsson (2019)
Partners	Partners are key stakeholders in the supply chain financing ecosystem. These include all buyers, vendors and financiers in the supply chain. Partner readiness includes security controls, data availability, user training, technical support skills and internet penetration. An ecosystem strategy is required in order to onboard as many partners as possible and create a 'network effect'. This should include governance to foster a collaborative partnership, methods to verify/limit risks and distribute costs and any incentives required.	Bender, Burchardi and Shepherd (2019)
Scalability	The current lack of scalability of blockchain adds to its complexity. Given the consensus mechanisms (e.g. proof of work), as well as storage requirements of the blockchain, the permissionless version of the blockchain is currently not a scalable solution. Several solutions to scalability are currently being worked on, including sharding data link layers to off-chain state channels, increases to block size, different consensus mechanisms or side chains to speed up transaction times. Vitalik Buterin (co-founder of Etherium) talked about a trilemma, meaning how blockchain can have at most two out of three properties – decentralization, scalability and security. Blockchain has not yet demonstrated its ability to solve complex problems at scale.	Ganeriwalla, Casey, Shrikrishna, Bender and Gstettner (2019)
Security	Blockchain is considered secure, as it is immutable and tamper proof and provides data permanency. Once a transaction is entered on the blockchain, it cannot be altered. With its cryptography, blockchain also complies with the EU's General Data Protection Regulation, which states that 'both the keys and data should remain with the data owner'.	Grover, Kar, Janssen and Ilavarasan (2019)
Smart Contracts	Smart contracts are another feature, particularly of the Ethereum blockchain. They were originally defined by Nick Szabo as 'computerised transaction protocol that executes the terms of a contract'. They are a distributed software application, written in a language such as solidity, that runs across several computers with built-in business rules and deal terms that execute automatically, even among untrusted partners, when the deal terms are met. Since pre-approved logic is built into the blockchain, as long as all partners have opted in, payments can be made immediately following the transfer of asset ownership. At least two criteria need to be fulfilled for smart contracts to create significant value: no ambiguity in terms of the contract and successful execution needs to be objectively and easily measurable.	Kandaswamy and Furlonger (2018)

continued on following page

Table 3. Continued

Independent Sub-Variable	Description	Reference
Technology Skills	It is important to have the relevant technology skills within the organization to implement blockchain. This includes internet skills, data transfer skills and an ability to train people as required. It also includes blockchain competency, especially from an enterprise perspective.	Hackius and Petersen (2017)
Tokenization	Tokenization refers to issuing a 'token' or digital unit that can be used as an information unit to facilitate interoperability or as a unit of currency to incentivise partners to join the blockchain ecosystem. This kind of token will grow in value as the network grows, thereby benefiting all. A token can be split and used to get funding from several different sources, or several tokens can be consolidated and used to securitise loans.	Furlonger and Uzureau (2019)
Top Management Support	Top management support includes their support, advocacy and participation. Leadership characteristics and attitude towards change are key. Top management support is critical for any large organizational initiative, especially if it fundamentally changes the way the organization works. It is also needed to get the financial and other resources required for the project.	Yin (2021)
Traceability	Blockchain also facilitates traceability, which takes away the information asymmetry currently plaguing supply chain financing and reduces the risk of fraud. Blockchain provides digitisation of all transactions and records as well as time stamped chronological capture and storage. This provides transparency and auditability. It also helps in establishing the provenance of a product in the supply chain. There are three key flows in each supply chain, that is, product, data and money, and the blockchain can provide traceability in all these areas.	Chong, Lim, Hua, Zheng and Tan (2019)
Trust in Government	The stakeholders need to trust the government in the country or countries in which the organization operates. The organization needs to trust that the government's policies and regulations will be supportive of blockchain in supply chain financing.	Choi et al. (2020)
Trust in Technology	The stakeholders need to trust in the blockchain technology. This can be fostered by the presence of established proof of concepts and scalable models of blockchain in supply chain financing, thus creating the necessary 'halo effect'. Institutional trust diminishes as blockchain becomes more prevalent in establishing power of work as a trust mechanism.	Yin (2021)

in the research model. Each of the selective codes, contextualised to the adoption of blockchain in SCF, are explained in Table 4.

The literature review yielded a lot of information about the features of blockchain, especially as it applied to the adoption of blockchain in SCF. This information was further clarified and analyzed through literature synthesis. Five industry experts with expertise in both blockchain and SCF were contacted and were asked to group these features into seven groups: relative advantage, compatibility, complexity, technology readiness, organization readiness, environment readiness and trust. The final grouping that was used in our research was based on the consensus of these experts. This is shown in the table 5.

The literature review identified firm age, size, location and experience as control variables (CVs). Some authors considered these variables to be CVs, while others viewed them as independent variables (IVs). As our survey respondents included people working for firms of different ages, sizes, locations and experience, we aimed to isolate the impact of these variables when considering the hypotheses

Table 4. Description of the independent variables (selective codes)

Category of IV	Theory	Description	Ref
Relative Advantage	DOI	The perceived advantage of blockchain over existing technologies such as enterprise resource planning in solving the issues that currently plague supply chain financing, such as paper-based systems, information asymmetry and lack of trust.	Lundblad (2003)
Compatibility	DOI	How blockchain will meet existing social and cultural values, previously introduced ideas and client needs as well as how it is compatible with other blockchains.	Lundblad (2003)
Complexity	DOI	The complexity that blockchain will bring into the business model and the supply chain financing process of the organization. Complexity makes a system difficult to use and may deter some of the companies from becoming early adopters of the innovation, at least until the complexities are resolved with the passage of time.	Lundblad (2003)
Technology Readiness	TOE	How ready the organization is from a technology perspective to implement blockchain in supply chain financing.	Malik et al. (2021)
Organization Readiness	TOE	How ready the organization is from an organization perspective (excluding the technology aspect covered above) to implement blockchain in supply chain financing.	Malik et al. (2021)
Environment Readiness	TOE	How ready the organization is from an environment perspective (including all stakeholders outside the organization, such as government, market and partners) to implement blockchain in supply chain financing.	Malik et al. (2021)

Key: DOI = Diffusion of Innovations, TOE = Technology, Organization, Environment.

A survey questionnaire was drafted based on the consensus of the experts as outlined above. It checked whether the respondent had an awareness of blockchain and SCF. If the answer to either of these questions was 'No', the survey was aborted. This ensured that only respondents with an awareness of both blockchain and SCF participated in the survey.The questionnaire used a 7-point Likert scale for each answer.The survey instrument was developed using various constructs for each of the IVs, based on past research and adapted to the context of adoption of blockchain in SCF. This included constructs for each of the IVs, in order to enable the respondent to provide a yes or no answer. There were no open-ended questions in this part of the questionnaire.

A pilot study was then conducted. The pilot study was sent to 30 respondents, of whom 20 responded. The pilot study was used to confirm the validity of the

Table 5. Experts' responses to variables grouping

Experts' Responses to Variables Grouping							
Sl	***Variable***	***Expert 1***	***Expert 2***	***Expert 3***	***Expert 4***	***Expert 5***	***Majority***
1	Alignment with Vision	OR	OR	CO	Trust	OR	OR
2	Consensus	CX	CX	CX	OR	CX	CX
3	Cost	RA	RA	OR	TR	RA	RA
4	Culture	OR	OR	OR	OR	OR	OR
5	Decentralisation	RA	ER	ER	CO	CO	ER
6	Efficiency	RA	RA	RA	RA	RA	RA
7	GIGO (Garbage-in-garbage-out)	TR	CO	CO	OR	TR	CO
8	Government	ER	ER	ER	ER	ER	ER
9	Infrastructure Readiness	TR	TR	OR	TR	TR	TR
10	Integration	CX	TR	TR	CX	TR	TR
11	Interoperability	CX	CX	CX	CX	TR	CX
12	Inter-organisation Trust	TS	TS	ER	TS	ER	TS
13	Intra-organisation Trust	CO	CO	OR	CO	OR	CO
14	Partners	CX	CO	CO	TS	CO	CO
15	Market	ER	ER	CO	ER	RA	ER
16	Scalability	CX	CX	CX	CX	CX	CX
17	Security	CX	TS	TS	OR	CX	TS
18	Smart Contracts	RA	RA	RA	RA	RA	RA
19	Technology Skills	TR	TR	TR	TR	TR	TR
20	Tokenisation	TS	ER	CO	ER	CX	ER
21	Top Management Support	CO	OR	OR	CO	OR	OR
22	Traceability	RA	RA	RA	RA	RA	RA
23	Trust in Government	ER	ER	ER	ER	ER	ER
24	Trust in Technology	TS	TS	TS	TS	TR	TS

Key: RA = Relative advantage, CO = Compatibility, CX = Complexity, TR = Technology readiness, OR = Organization readiness, ER = Environment readiness, TS = Trust.

The last column shows the final grouping

contents of the questionnaire. In addition, it was used to confirm that the way the survey was administered was appropriate.

After the pilot study, the main study was conducted. The purpose of the main study was to produce the fundamental set of empirical data that could be used to verify the structural integrity of the conceptual model and all the hypotheses. Accordingly, in the main study, all the hypotheses and variables in the research model were tested for the occurrence of causal relationships in order to either substantiate or negate each hypothesis.

The survey questionnaire was sent to over 500 respondents. Given the need to get at least 240 responses (given that there were 24 SVs) and the fact that the target respondent needed to be aware of both blockchain and SCF, the task of collecting responses was subcontracted to a company called Lucid. Lucid is a niche provider of such services to academia globally. The researcher was involved in all stages of the data collection, including drafting the questionnaire and putting the questionnaire onto

SurveyMonkey. The researcher had several meetings with Lucid to clearly specify the targeted respondent profile, geographical locations and ethical considerations. Given the constraints of time and cost, it was decided to focus on the main English-speaking areas, namely, the US, the UK, Singapore and India. However, given that these regions are the largest users of technology, including blockchain, in SCF in the English-speaking world, the researcher found that this limitation did not detract from the validity of the sample and research findings. We finally received a total of 249 valid responses from across the globe.

DATA ANALYSIS

This section sets out the analysis of the data received from the survey. The objective of data analysis is to obtain appropriate information to confirm or negate the hypotheses arrived at by the literature review.

Structural equation modelling (SEM) is a flexible and powerful multivariate path analysis technique for investigating the relationships between IVs or measured variables and dependent or latent constructs (Hair, Ringle, & Sarstedt, 2011). Each relationship in the model is connected to a predefined hypothesis. The relationship is tested to check on the presence, and to determine the magnitude, of a causal relationship. SEM is best suited to test confirmatory research based on theory and requires the researcher to design the research approach with precision (Hair, Hollingsworth, Randolph, & Chong, 2017).

Partial least squares (PLS) path modelling is regarded as the most fully developed variance-based SEM and is the preferred statistical tool for IS studies and organizational research (Hair et al., 2017). There are two sets of linear equations in PLS path models: the outer model and the inner model. The outer model is also called the measurement model. It specifies the relations between a construct and its observed indicators. The inner model is also called the structural model. It specifies the relationships between the constructs (Henseler, Ringle & Sarstedt, 2014).

The results of the survey questionnaire were analyzed using ADANCO 2.3.1, which is a stand-alone commercial partial least squares structural equation modelling (PLS-SEM) application with a graphical user interface. It was used to test the 12 hypotheses presented earlier in this chapter as well the measurement and structural models. The following measures were tested. Measurement model: construct reliability (Jöreskog's rho and Cronbach's alpha), scale validity (convergent validity, using average variance extracted [AVE] and loadings; discriminant validity, using the Fornell–Larcker criterion; and inter-construct correlations and validating scale through cross-loadings) and indicator multicollinearity through the variance inflation factor (VIF). Structural model: path coefficients; coefficient of determination (R^2); testing of hypotheses; and direct, indirect and total effect inference.

Measurement Model Results

Hair, Hult and Ringle (2021) stated that the goal of the measurement model is to ensure reliability and validity of the construct measures. This validates the suitability of their inclusion in the path model.

Jöreskog's rho and Cronbach's alpha can be used to evaluate the scale of construct reliability. Jöreskog's rho is calculated on the weights instead of parallel correlations among the variables in SEM; hence, it is considered to be a superior consistency measure to Cronbach's alpha (Demo, Neiva, Nunes, & Rozzett, 2012).For the validity of a construct, the value of the Jöreskog's rho is required to be greater than 0.70. Our model fulfilled this condition, as the Jöreskog's rho values of all constructs ranged between 0.7882 and 0.8960, demonstrating the validity of the constructs. Burgess and Steenkamp (2006) stated that the minimum acceptable value of Cronbach's alpha is 0.60. A construct is highly reliable if this value is above 0.70. Our model fulfilled this condition, as the Cronbach's alpha values of all constructs were above 0.60 (0.6061–0.8269), demonstrating the validity of the constructs.

Hair et al. (2011) stated that validity refers to the degree to which the tool measures what it claims to measure. A test cannot be considered valid if it is not reliable. However, reliability alone is not enough for validity. Therefore, the test of validity is conducted after the constructs' reliability has been established by the previous tests. There are several different ways to test validity. We used convergent validity, discriminant validity and validating scale through cross-loadings.

Hair, Hult, Ringle and Sarstedt (2014) stated that convergent validity detects whether the measures of a construct are more correlated with others within the same construct than with the measures of another construct. The AVE values of all the constructs in our model ranged from 0.5549 to 0.7417. As these values are greater than the threshold of 0.50, they indicate convergent validity.

Hair et al. (2014) stated that discriminant validity is the extent to which a construct is distinct from other constructs. This is both in terms of the extent to which indicators represent only a single construct as well as how much a construct correlates to other constructs. When two constructs that are conceptually different are also statistically different, discriminant validity is said to be achieved. Discriminant validity can be established in several ways, two of which are the Fornell–Larcker criterion and inter-construct correlations.

The Fornell–Larcker criterion states that the AVE of a construct should be greater than its squared correlations with all other constructs in the model (Fornell & Larcker, 1981, as cited in Hair et al., 2014). In our model, the AVE of the construct is greater than its squared correlations with all other constructs. This is true for all the constructs in the model, including the four CVs (FI1, FI2, FI4, FI5). Hence, the model meets the Fornell–Larcker criterion of discriminant validity.

The estimated correlations between constructs are contained in the matrix of inter-construct correlations (Henseler, 2017). The inter-construct correlations provide the basis for understanding the possibility of developing multiple regression models. Voorhees, Brady, Calantone and Ramirez (2016) specified that the inter-construct correlations must be noticeably less than 1 to establish discriminant validity. In our model the inter-construct correlations are noticeably less than 1 for all the constructs in the model, including the four CVs (FI1, FI2, FI4, FI5). This once again confirms the discriminant validity of the measurement model.

The validity of a model can be established through cross-loadings, which confirm the coherent formation of the constructs (Hair et al., 2014). Each indicator should load highest on the construct it is intended to measure (Hair, Sarstedt, Ringle, & Mena, 2012). We removed RA1 (cost) and ER2 (tokenization) because their cross-loadings were not valid.The loadings are higher than their cross-loadings on all other constructs, confirming the validity of the instrument, without any cross-loading, and the clear construction of the constructs.

Based on these tests, we can reasonably conclude that the model passed the convergent, discriminant and cross-loading tests of validity and shows good validity and reliability.

Collinearity arises when two indicators are highly correlated. It is called multicollinearity when more than two indicators are involved (Hair et al., 2014). As a result of high multicollinearity in the measurement model, an indicator can become redundant or non-significant (Hair et al., 2011). Multicollinearity can be identified through tolerance and its reciprocal, that is, the VIF. The higher the VIF, the higher the degree of multicollinearity.Henseler, Ringle and Sinkovics, (2009) stated that a VIF greater than 10 reveals a critical level of multicollinearity, while Hair et al. (2011) stated that the preferred level for VIF is less than 5. The model displayed a low degree of multicollinearity among all SVs. All the SVs' VIF values were less than 1.93, well below the value of 5, proving the low degree of multicollinearity.

Structural Model Results

Henseler et al. (2009) stated that 'reliable and valid outer model estimations permit an evaluation of the inner path model estimates' (p. 303). Once the measurement model is validated, the proposed hypotheses are tested using the structural model. The structural or inner model specifies the relationships between the constructs, taking into account the relationships among latent variables (Götz, Liehr-Gobbers, & Krafft, 2010).

The coefficient of determination (R^2) quantifies the proportion of a DV's variance that is explained by the IVs. R^2 ranges in value from 0 to 1 (Benitez, Henseler, Castillo, & Schuberth, 2020).

The R^2 of the DV, which is AD, is 0.507 (Figure 2). This indicates that, in the model, 50.7% of the variance in the DV is explained by the influencing factors. This denotes moderate explanatory power (Ansari, Muhideen, Das, Butt, & Wei, 2018).

Figure 2. Coefficient of determination (R2) (see separate file)

Note: RA = Relative advantage, CO = Compatibility, CX = Complexity, TR = Technology readiness, OR = Organization readiness, ER = Environment readiness, TS = Trust, AD = Adoption of blockchain in supply chain financing, FI1 = Firm age, FI2 = Firm size, FI4 = Firm location and FI5 = Firm experience.

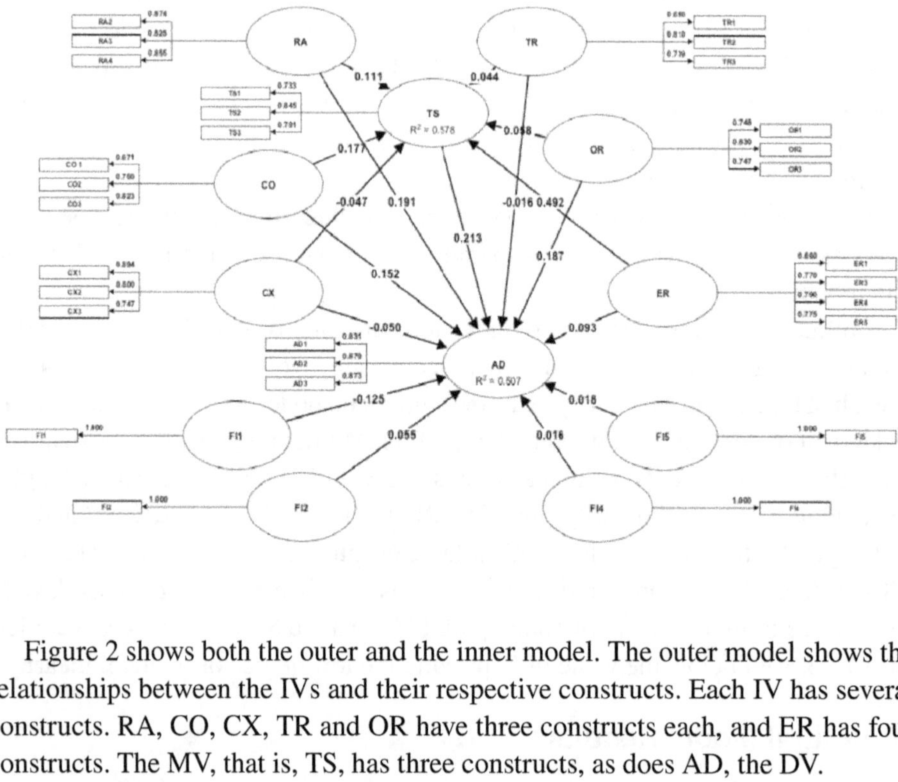

Figure 2 shows both the outer and the inner model. The outer model shows the relationships between the IVs and their respective constructs. Each IV has several constructs. RA, CO, CX, TR and OR have three constructs each, and ER has four constructs. The MV, that is, TS, has three constructs, as does AD, the DV.

The inner model shows the relationships between the IVs (RA, CO, CX, TR, OR and ER) and the DV (AD), both directly and through the MV (TS). It also shows the relationships between the CVs (FI1, FI2, FI4 and FI5) and the DV (AD). The path coefficients are set out in Table 6 for ease of reference.

A bootstrapping method (Henseler, Ringle, & Sarstedt, 2015) was used to model the unknown population data.The significance of relationships between the various

Table 6. Path coefficients to TS and AD

Path	Path Coefficient
RA to TS	+0.111
CO to TS	+0.177
CX to TS	−0.047
TR to TS	+0.044
OR to TS	+0.058
ER to TS	+0.492
RA to AD	+0.191
CO to AD	+0.152
CX to AD	−0.050
TR to AD	−0.016
OR to AD	+0.187
ER to AD	+0.093
TS to AD	+0.213
FI1 to AD	−0.125
FI2 to AD	+0.055
FI4 to AD	+0.016
FI5 to AD	+0.018

Note: RA = Relative advantage, CO = Compatibility, CX = Complexity, TR = Technology readiness, OR = Organization readiness, ER = Environment readiness, TS = Trust, AD = Adoption of blockchain in supply chain financing. FI1 = Firm age, FI2 = Firm size, FI4 = Firm location and FI5 = Firm experience.

A '+' indicates a positive relationship and a '−' indicates a negative or inverse relationship.

constructs in the model can be determined by t-values. Two-tailed tests measured at 10%, 5% and 1% significance levels were used in this research (Hair et al., 2011). The reliability of each hypothesis was evaluated using the t-values and p-values of the IVs and the DV. Six direct and six indirect relationships were tested in this study, a total of 12 hypotheses.

Table 7 shows that four direct hypotheses are supported, one at the 99% confidence level (H1, relating to the impact of RA on AD) and three at the 95% confidence level (H2, H5 and H6, relating to the impact of CO, OR and ER on AD). Two direct hypotheses, highlighted in bold in the table, (H3 and H4, relating to the impact of CX and TR on AD) are not supported.

As described earlier in this chapter, this research explored the mediating effect of TS between the six IVs (RA, CO, CX, TR, OR and ER) and the DV (AD) resulting in six hypotheses i.e. H7 to H12. It was found that TS mediated the relationship between CO and AD and between ER and AD.

Table 7. Total effect inference of direct hypotheses

Effect	Original coefficient	Mean value	Standard error	t-value	p-value (2-sided)	Significant
			Standard bootstrap results			
RA -> AD	0.2144	0.2161	0.0825	2.5986	0.0094	Yes at 99% confidence level
CO -> AD	0.1895	0.1922	0.0878	2.1580	0.0310	Yes at 95% confidence level
CX -> AD	-0.0604	-0.0529	0.0690	**-0.8748**	**0.3817**	No
TR -> AD	-0.0065	-0.0005	0.0697	**-0.0931**	**0.9259**	No
OR -> AD	0.1990	0.1940	0.0804	2.4747	0.0134	Yes at 95% confidence level
ER -> AD	0.1984	0.1940	0.0874	2.2694	0.0233	Yes at 95% confidence level

Note: RA = Relative advantage, CO = Compatibility, CX = Complexity, TR = Technology readiness, OR = Organization readiness, ER = Environment readiness and AD = Adoption of blockchain in supply chain financing.

This research included four CVs. These are FI1 (firm age), FI2 (firm size), FI4 (firm location), and FI5 (firm experience). Only the CV FI1 is significant at the 95% confidence level. The other three CVs, that is, FI2, FI4 and FI5, have non-significant results. Thus, they do not have an impact on AD.

We started with 12 hypotheses, of which six were direct and six were indirect. This section presented the evaluation of the hypotheses. The results are summarised in Table 8.

Table 8. Results of the evaluation of the direct and indirect hypotheses

H No.	Hypothesis	Result of Evaluation
H1	The perception of relative advantage (RA) of blockchain positively impacts the adoption of blockchain in SCF (AD).	Supported
H2	The compatibility (CO) of blockchain positively impacts AD.	Supported
H3	The complexity (CX) of blockchain negatively impacts AD.	Not supported
H4	Technology readiness (TR) positively impacts AD.	Not supported
H5	Organization readiness (OR) positively impacts AD.	Supported
H6	Environment readiness (ER) positively impacts AD.	Supported
H7	Trust (TS) positively mediates the relationship between RA and AD.	Not supported
H8	TS positively mediates the relationship between CO and AD.	Supported
H9	TS negatively mediates the relationship between CX and AD.	Not supported
H10	TS positively mediates the relationship between TR and AD.	Not supported
H11	TS positively mediates the relationship between OR and AD.	Not supported
H12	TS positively mediates the relationship between ER and AD.	Supported

LIMITATIONS AND FUTURE RESEARCH

This section summarises the key limitations of our research as well as avenues for future research. While this research made a sincere effort to analyze the factors impacting the adoption of blockchain in SCF, it cannot claim to be exhaustive. Accordingly, it is important to highlight the limitations of this study to provide a context for the research and to provide future researchers with meaningful input for their work.

1. **Grey literature:** Both blockchain and SCF are fairly new phenomena, and there is limited peer-reviewed literature on this topic. Therefore, we were forced to review grey literature (non-peer-reviewed articles) for this research. However, we exercised due diligence by ensuring that the source of this literature was legitimate and respected, for example, sites and publications of Gartner, E&Y, Strategic Advisor and The Blockchain Research Institute.
2. **Research design:** This research was based on a positivist, cross-sectional design. We adopted a hypothetico-deductive approach with a reductionist stance, designed to comprehend the causal effects of an identified set of variables by analyzing data collected through a survey of various stakeholders.

This research method is generally preferred to arrive at a conclusive set of results. However, an approach based on an inductive design may have led to a deeper understanding of the subject.

3. **Theories:** We used the TOE and DOI theories augmented by trust as a theoretical lens for our research. Other theories can also be used, such as the technology acceptance model (TAM) and the unified theory of acceptance and use of technology (UTAUT), focusing on individuals' adoption characteristics, or newer theories, such as the game theory, the sensemaking theory, the force field theory, the resource-based view or the information processing theory.
4. **Variables:** We grouped the variables in this research into six categories, namely, relative advantage, compatibility, complexity, technology readiness, organization readiness and environment readiness. Each of these groups is vast, meriting further individual investigation.
5. **Trust:** We used trust as an MV in our research. But trust itself is a vast area of study, with extensive literature covering several dimensions and theories.
6. **Other mediating variables:** While we used trust as an MV in our research, there are other MVs that can be used, for example, risk.

7. **Moderating effect possibilities:** We had no moderating variables in our model. Future research may include moderating variables to add to the richness of the research in this area.
8. **Other control variables:** We used four CVs in the model (firm age, firm size, firm location and firm experience), of which only firm age was found to be significant. There could be other CVs that can be used in future research, for example, industry.
9. **Sample coverage:** Given the constraints of time and cost, our sample was largely from English-speaking geographical areas such as the US, the UK, Singapore and India. Future research can expand to other parts of the world, including non-English-speaking countries, for example, China, where there is a lot of activity in this area.

In addition to some of the areas for future reserch mentioned above, there are several areas for future research in this fast-growing area. Some of those areas are mentioned below:

1. **Additional variables:** Future research could unearth additional variables that impact the adoption of blockchain in SCF. This is particularly true as the technology matures and the use cases scale, potentially reducing the significance of trust and increasing the importance of variables such as interoperability.
2. **Case studies:** As this area matures and several implementations of blockchain in SCF become at scale, future researchers could focus on conducting in-depth analyses of both successful and failed implementations. This will help to understand the factors that drive a successful implementation as well as factors that lead to failure.
3. **Evolution of blockchain technology:** Blockchain technology is fairly recent and, like all IS innovations in their infancy, is constantly evolving to reveal new possibilities. As an example, there are several solutions currently being worked on to solve the problem of scalability of blockchain. In the future, these advancements may make it viable for companies to use public blockchains even in sensitive commercial areas such as SCF. Accordingly, as blockchain evolves, the factors impacting its adoption in SCF will also evolve, providing fresh possibilities for future researchers.
4. **Consortium:** The true value of blockchain in SCF will come into play when industry-wide consortia start to adopt it, which will result in a set of new challenges and factors that will impact the adoption of blockchain in SCF. These include true decentralization, governance, interoperability and tokenization. Co-opetition (co-operation among competitors) will become a key strategy.

Compliance of all parties in a consortium is critical to its success. Furthermore, there could be a vast difference between implementation in a consortium and that in SMEs. Future researchers will find this is a rich arena for their research.

5. **Blockchain with other technologies:** Another fascinating area for future research is the use of blockchain with other technologies, such as artificial intelligence (AI), internet of things (IoT), machine learning (ML) and robotic process automation (RPA). This scenario will give rise to a new set of factors that will impact the adoption of blockchain in SCF.

CONCLUSION

The study has several implications for theory as well as for practice in the area of blockchain in SCF. Ours is one of the first studies to look at the factors impacting the adoption of blockchain in SCF. It is also one of the first studies to do this using the lens of two theories of technology adoption (the DOI and TOE theories). It is based on respondents covering the major English-speaking regions which have adopted blockchain in SCF (US, UK, Singapore, India), thereby contributing to the global applicability of our research. Our research does have some limitations which have been covered earlier in this chapter along with areas for future research.

We conclude this chapter by reiterating that this research comes at an opportune moment, as it identifies significant considerations that influence the adoption of blockchain in SCF by organizations. It provides a useful knowledge foundation to a vast selection of people in various roles in the process of making adoption a practical reality. There is, of course, a lot of scope for future research on this fascinating and constantly changing topic.

REFERENCES

Ansari, A. A., Muhideen, S., Das, N., Butt, A. R., & Wei, S. (2018). *North American Academic Research.* Linkedin.

Bahmanziari, T., Pearson, J. M., & Crosby, L. (2003). Is trust important in technology adoption? A policy capturing approach. *Journal of Computer Information Systems, 43*(4), 46–54.

Bal, M., & Pawlicka, K. (2021). Supply chain finance and challenges of modern supply chains. *LogForum, 17*(1), 71–82. https://doiorg.spjain.idm.oclc.org/ 10.17270/ J.LOG.2021. 525.

Beck, R., Müller-Bloch, C., & King, J. L. (2018). Governance in the blockchain economy: A framework and research agenda. *Journal of the Association for Information Systems, 19*(10), 1020–1034. https://doi-org.spjain.idm.oclc.org/ 10.17705/ 1jais.00518.

Bender, J. P., Burchardi, K., & Shepherd, N. (2019). Capturing the value of blockchain. Boston Consulting Group, 9.

Benitez, J., Henseler, J., Castillo, A., & Schuberth, F. (2020). How to perform and report an impactful analysis using partial least squares: Guidelines for confirmatory and explanatory IS research. *Information & Management*, *57*(2), 103168. doi:10.1016/j. im.2019.05.003

Bhardwaj, A. K., Garg, A., & Gajpal, Y. (2021). Determinants of blockchain technology adoption in supply chains by small and medium enterprises (SMEs) in India. *Mathematical Problems in Engineering*, *2021*, 1–14. doi:10.1155/2021/5537395

Burgess, S. M., & Steenkamp, J. B. E. (2006). Marketing renaissance: How research in emerging markets advances marketing science and practice. *International Journal of Research in Marketing*, *23*(4), 337–356. doi:10.1016/j.ijresmar.2006.08.001

Chen, J., Cai, T., He, W., Chen, L., Zhao, G., Zou, W., & Guo, L. (2020). A blockchain-driven supply chain finance application for auto retail industry. *Entropy (Basel, Switzerland)*, *22*(1), 95. doi:10.3390/e22010095 PMID:33285870

Chod, J., Trichakis, N., Tsoukalas, G., Aspegren, H., & Weber, M. (2020). On the financing benefits of supply chain transparency and blockchain adoption. *Management Science*, *66*(10), 4378–4396. doi:10.1287/mnsc.2019.3434

Choi, D., Chune, Y. C., Seyha, T., & Young, J. (2020). Factors affecting organizations' resistance to the adoption of blockchain technology in supply networks. *Sustainability (Basel)*, *12*(21), 8882. doi:10.3390u12218882

Choi, T. M. (2020). Supply chain financing using blockchain: Impacts on supply chains selling fashionable products. *Annals of Operations Research*. doi:10.100710479-020-03615-7

Chong, A. Y. L., Lim, E. T., Hua, X., Zheng, S., & Tan, C. W. (2019). Business on chain: A comparative case study of five blockchain-inspired business models. *Journal of the Association for Information Systems*, *20*(9), 9. doi:10.17705/1jais.00568

Clohessy, T., & Acton, T. (2019). Investigating the influence of organizational factors on blockchain adoption: An innovation theory perspective. *Industrial Management & Data Systems*, *119*(7), 1457–1491. doi:10.1108/IMDS-08-2018-0365

Demo, G., Neiva, E. R., Nunes, I., & Rozzett, K. (2012). Human resources management policies and practices scale (HRMPPS): Exploratory and confirmatory factor analysis. *BAR - Brazilian Administration Review*, *9*(4), 395–420. doi:10.1590/S1807-76922012005000006

Di Vaio, A., & Varriale, L. (2020). Blockchain technology in supply chain management for sustainable performance: Evidence from the airport industry. *International Journal of Information Management*, *52*, 102014. https://doiorg.spjain.idm.oclc.org/10.1016/j.ijinfomgt.2019.09.010. doi:10.1016/j.ijinfomgt.2019.09.010

Disparte, D. (2017). Blockchain could make the insurance industry much more transparent. *Harvard Business Review*, 2–5.

Dong, C., Chen, C., Shi, X., & Ng, C. T. (2021). Operations strategy for supply chain finance with asset-backed securitization: Centralization and blockchain adoption. *International Journal of Production Economics*, *241*, 108261. doi:10.1016/j.ijpe.2021.108261

Du, M., Chen, Q., Xiao, J., Yang, H., & Ma, X. (2020). Supply chain finance innovation using blockchain. *IEEE Transactions on Engineering Management*, *67*(4), 1045–1058. doi:10.1109/TEM.2020.2971858

Euro Banking Association Working Group on Electronic Alternative Payments. (2016). *Applying cryptotechnologies to trade finance*. Information Paper.

Frizzo-Barker, J., Chow-White, P. A., Adams, P. R., Mentanko, J., Ha, D., & Green, S. (2020). Blockchain as a disruptive technology for business: A systematic review. *International Journal of Information Management*, *51*, 102029. https://doi-org.spjain.idm.oclc.org/10.1016/j.ijinfomgt.2019.10.014. doi:10.1016/j.ijinfomgt.2019.10.014

Furlonger, D., & Uzureau, C. (2019). The 5 kinds of blockchain projects (and which to watch out for). *Harvard Business Review*, 2–6.

Ganeriwalla, A., Casey, M., Shrikrishna, P., Bender, J. P., & Gstettner, S. (2019). Does your supply chain need a blockchain? *The Boston Consulting Group.*

Götz, O., Liehr-Gobbers, K., & Krafft, M. (2010). Evaluation of structural equation models using the partial least squares (PLS) approach. In V. E. Vinzi, W. W. Chin, J. Henseler, & H. Wang (Eds.), *Handbook of Partial Least Squares* (pp. 691–711). Springer Berlin Heidelberg. doi:10.1007/978-3-540-32827-8_30

Grover, P., Kar, A. K., Janssen, M., & Ilavarasan, P. V. (2019). Perceived usefulness, ease of use and user acceptance of blockchain technology for digital transactions – Insights from user-generated content on Twitter. *Enterprise Information Systems, 13*(6), 771–800. https://doi-org.spjain.idm.oclc.org/10.1080/ 17517575. 2019.1599446.

Hackius, N., & Petersen, M. (2017). Blockchain in logistics and supply chain: Trick or treat? In *Proceedings of the Hamburg International Conference of Logistics* (HICL) (pp. 3–18). Epubli.

Hair, J., Hollingsworth, C. L., Randolph, A. B., & Chong, A. Y. L. (2017). An updated and expanded assessment of PLS-SEM in information systems research. *Industrial Management & Data Systems, 117*(3), 442–458. doi:10.1108/IMDS-04-2016-0130

Hair, J. F., Ringle, C. M., & Sarstedt, M. (2011). PLS-SEM: Indeed a silver bullet. *Journal of Marketing Theory and Practice, 19*(2), 139–152. doi:10.2753/MTP1069-6679190202

Hair, J. F., Sarstedt, M., Ringle, C. M., & Mena, J. A. (2012). An assessment of the use of partial least squares structural equation modeling in marketing research. *Journal of the Academy of Marketing Science, 40*(3), 414–433. doi:10.100711747-011-0261-6

Hair, J. F., Tomas, G., Hult, M., & Ringle, C. M. (2021). Partial least squares structural equation modeling (PLS-SEM) using R. OAPEN.

Hair, J. F. J., Hult, M. T. G., Ringle, C. M., & Sarstedt, M. (2014). A primer on partial least squares structural equation modeling (PLS-SEM). *Sage (Atlanta, Ga.).* doi:10.1108/EBR-10-2013-0128

Henseler, J. (2017). Bridging design and behavioral research with variance-based structural equation modeling. *Journal of Advertising, 46*(1), 178–192. doi:10.108 0/00913367.2017.1281780

Henseler, J., Ringle, C. M., & Sarstedt, M. (2014). A new criterion for assessing discriminant validity in variance-based structural equation modeling. *Journal of the Academy of Marketing Science, 43*(1), 115–135. doi:10.100711747-014-0403-8

Henseler, J., Ringle, C. M., & Sarstedt, M. (2015). A new criterion for assessing discriminant validity in variance-based structural equation modeling. *Journal of the Academy of Marketing Science, 43*(1), 115–135. doi:10.100711747-014-0403-8

Henseler, J., Ringle, C. M., & Sinkovics, R. R. (2009). The use of partial least squares path modeling in international marketing. *Advances in International Marketing*, *20*, 277–319. doi:10.1108/S1474-7979(2009)0000020014

Jansen, J., Beyer, H-M, & Taschner, A. (2018). Supply chain finance in SMEs: A comparative study in the automotive sector in Germany and The Netherlands. *Logistiek: tijdschrift voor toegepaste logistiek*, (5), 59-81.

Jensen, T., Hedman, J., & Henningsson, S. (2019). How TradeLens delivers business value with blockchain technology. *MIS Quarterly Executive*, *18*(4), 221–243. https://doi-org.spjain.idm.oclc.org/10.17705/2msqe.00018. doi:10.17705/2msqe.00018

Kandaswamy, R., & Furlonger, D. (2018). Gartner report: Pay attention to these 4 types of blockchain business initiatives. *Gartner, Stamford, CT, USA, Tech. Rep., Mar.*

Korpela, K., Hallikas, J., & Dahlberg, T. (2017, January). Digital supply chain transformation toward blockchain integration. In *Proceedings of the 50th Hawaii International Conference on System Sciences*. Scholar Space. 10.24251/HICSS.2017.506

Li, D., Han, D., Crespi, N., Minerva, R., & Sun, Z. (2021). Fabric-SCF: A blockchain-based secure storage and access control scheme for supply chain finance. *arXiv preprint* arXiv:2111.13538.

Li, J., Zhu, S., Zhang, W., & Yu, L. (2020). Blockchain-driven supply chain finance solution for small medium enterprises. *Frontiers of Engineering Management*, *7*(4), 500–511. doi:10.100742524-020-0124-2

Lippert, S. K., & Davis, M. (2006). A conceptual model integrating trust into planned change activities to enhance technology adoption behaviour. *Journal of Information Science*, *32*(5), 434–448. doi:10.1177/0165551506066042

Lundblad, J. P. (2003). A review and critique of Rogers' diffusion of innovations theory as it applies to organizations. *Organization Development Journal*, *21*(4), 50–64. https://www.proquest.com/scholarly-journals/review-critique-rogers-diffusion-innovation/docview/197971687/se-2

Malik, S., Chadhar, M., Vatanasakdakul, S., & Chetty, M. (2021). Factors affecting the organizational adoption of blockchain technology: Extending the technology–organization–environment (TOE) framework in the Australian context. *Sustainability (Basel)*, *13*(16), 9404. doi:10.3390u13169404

Mulaji, S. S. M., & Roodt, S. S. (2021). The practicality of adopting blockchain-based distributed identity management in organizations: A meta-synthesis. *Security and Communication Networks*, *2021*, 1–19. Advance online publication. doi:10.1155/2021/9910078

Nakamoto, S. (2008). *A peer-to-peer electronic cash system*. Bitcoin. https://bitcoin.org/bitcoin. pdf,

Obal, M. (2013). Why do incumbents sometimes succeed? Investigating the role of interorganizational trust on the adoption of disruptive technology. *Industrial Marketing Management*, *42*(6), 900–908. doi:10.1016/j.indmarman.2013.05.017

Rieger, A., Lockl, J., Urbach, N., Guggenmos, F., & Fridgen, G. (2019). Building a blockchain application that complies with the EU General Data Protection Regulation. *MIS Quarterly Executive*, *18*(4), 263–279. https://doi-org.spjain.idm.oclc.org/10.17705/2msqe.00020. doi:10.17705/2msqe.00020

Rijanto, A. (2021). Business financing and blockchain technology adoption in agroindustry. *Journal of Science and Technology Policy Management*, *2*(2), 215–235. doi:10.1108/JSTPM-03-2020-0065

Rijanto, A. (2021). Blockchain technology adoption in supply chain finance. *Journal of Theoretical and Applied Electronic Commerce Research*, *16*(7), 3078–3098. doi:10.3390/jtaer16070168

Safiullin, M. R., Elshin, L. A., & Abdukaeva, A. A. (2020). An empirical assessment of the impact of blockchain technologies on the effectiveness of the supply chain development. *International Journal of Supply Chain Management*, *9*(4), 887–892.

Shilpa Parkhi, K. M. (2021). Blockchain enabled technology platform for enhancing supply chain financing for SME's. *Psychology and Education Journal*, *57*(9). doi:10.17762/pae.v57i9.2689

Sun, R., He, D., & Su, H. (2021). Evolutionary game analysis of blockchain technology preventing supply chain financial risks. *Journal of Theoretical and Applied Electronic Commerce Research*, *16*(7), 2824–2842. doi:10.3390/jtaer16070155

Tapscott, D., Iansiti, M., Lakhani, K. R., & Tucker, C. (2019). *Blockchain: The insights you need from Harvard Business Review*. Harvard Business Review Press.

Tapscott, D., & Tapscott, A. (2016). *Blockchain revolution: how the technology behind bitcoin is changing money, business, and the world*. Penguin.

Tapscott, D., & Tapscott, A. (2016). The impact of the blockchain goes beyond financial services. *Harvard Business Review*, 2–5.

Tapscott, D., & Tapscott, A. (2017). Blockchain could help artists profit more from their creative works. *Harvard Business Review*, 2–5.

Treasury Technology Analyst Report. (2021). Straticic Treasurer. www.strategictreasurer.com

Tucker, C., & Catalini, C. (2018). What Blockchain Can't Do. *Harvard Business Review*, 2–4.

Voorhees, C. M., Brady, M. K., Calantone, R., & Ramirez, E. (2016). Discriminant validity testing in marketing: An analysis, causes for concern, and proposed remedies. *Journal of the Academy of Marketing Science*, *44*(1), 119–134. doi:10.100711747-015-0455-4

Wang, Y. (2021). Research on supply chain financial risk assessment based on blockchain and fuzzy neural networks. *Wireless Communications and Mobile Computing*, *2021*, 2021. doi:10.1155/2021/5565980

Wu, Y., Cegielski, C. G., Hazen, B. T., & Hall, D. J. (2013). Cloud computing in support of supply chain information system infrastructure: Understanding when to go to the cloud. *The Journal of Supply Chain Management*, *49*(3), 25–41. https://www.proquest.com/scholarly-journals/cloud-computing-support-supply-chain-information/docview/1467435391/se-2?accountid=162730. doi:10.1111/j.1745-493x.2012.03287.x

Yin, W., & Ran, W. (2021). Theoretical exploration of supply chain viability utilizing blockchain technology. *Sustainability (Basel)*, *13*(15), 8231. doi:10.3390u13158231

Zhang, T., Li, J., & Jiang, X. (2021). Analysis of supply chain finance based on blockchain. *Procedia Computer Science, 187*(2021), 1–6. https://doi.org/doi:10.1016/j.procs.2021.04.025

KEY TERMS AND DEFINITIONS

Blockchain: Blockchain is a relatively new technology which was first used as the underlying technology for the cryptocurrency bitcoin. It is a system where data is stored in a series of blocks based on cryptography. These blocks are linked by a chain, hence the term blockchain. Blockchain has several advantages including security, privacy, immutability and decentralization. It aims to inspire trust in the system thereby enabling disintermediation. It is also called the internet of value or the internet of money.

Supply Chain Financing (SCF): In SCF, the buyers and suppliers in a supply chain enter into agreements to finance supplies to generate working capital benefits for both parties. The finance can be provided by the parties themselves or by banks or other financial institutions. SCF can either be buyer centric, where the buyer gets funded based on his accounts payable or AP, or supplier centric where the supplier gets funded based on his accounts receivable or AR.

Trust: Trust in the context of adoption of a disruptive technology like blockchain refers to the ability to take a leap of faith, particularly given the lack of complete information as the technology is relatively new. Trust can have various facets including trust in technology, trust in government, intra-organizational trust or inter-organizational trust.

Chapter 3
Blockchain Technology and Data Mining Tools for Combating Fraud:
With Reference to the Banking Sector

Satya Sekhar Venkata Gudimetla
https://orcid.org/0000-0001-5171-065X
GITAM University, India

Naveen Tirumalaraju
https://orcid.org/0000-0002-0596-4517
GITAM University, India

ABSTRACT

For the last few years, rapid digitalization has been observed in the world banking industry, which helped boost global economic growth. At the same time, fraud cases in the banking sector have been increasing immensely. Regulating authorities of banks nationwide have been issuing numerous circulars and guidelines for preventing fraud incidents. However, fraudsters are taking advantage of the digitalization of and shortfalls in the industry, by which the fraudsters easily defraud customers and banks. Hence, it resulted in a worsening of the asset quality of banks and a loss of public trust and confidence in the banking industry. In this regard, banks must be equipped with sophisticated technological tools for fraud identification and preventive measures apart from the conventional systems and procedures since core banking solutions in the banking industry have evolved drastically over the last few years. In this context, this chapter is intended to study the role of blockchain technology and data mining tools in identifying and preventing frauds in specific bank products.

DOI: 10.4018/979-8-3693-0405-1.ch003

INTRODUCTION

The banking sector plays a vital role in every nation's development, and it is the critical field that ensures the nation's decent GDP growth and empowers many sectors of society. The banking sector is the intermediary channel between producers and consumers, providing resources for both. For the past two decades, substantial digital transformation has happened in the core banking system in the global banking industry. At the same time, fraudsters took advantage of the same and defrauded the banks as well as customers of the banks by observing the shortfalls in the industry. Despite vast technology gradation in the banking industry, banks' fraud cases have risen yearly. Therefore, banks' asset quality has been the worst hit due to the high provisions set aside. This leads to banks losing public trust and confidence. In the current scenario, banks must be equipped with technology defense for fraud identification and preventive measures apart from the manual systems and procedures. Blockchain technology and Data mining tools play a vital role in identifying different frauds in banking.

This paper is presented in four sections: i) review of empirical studies with a focus on banking sector, blockchain technology and data mining tools, ii) conceptual background of block chain technology and data mining tools, iii) fraud detection mechanism and iv) findings and conclusion.

OBJECTIVES OF STUDY

- To make aware of various online scams/frauds related to products of banking sector.
- To study the role of blockchain technology tools in identifying and preventing fraud.

RESEARCH METHODOLOGY

We have analyzed various modus operandi of fraud prevention mechanism, case studies, operational experiences, and a review of empirical studies, to address the objectives of this paper.

REVIEW ON EMPIRICAL STUDIES

This literature review is based on systematic review of empirical studies using key words viz., Blockchain technology, fraud detection, data mining tools and frauds in banking sector.

STUDIES ON BANKING SECTOR

In the current period of globalization, digital banking has occupied a prominent place in the present century. Online crimes are also increasing along with technology. To arrest the same to a certain extent, specific preventive measures must be adopted, i.e., to find out the source of the crime, recruit skilled employees, and adopt preventive measures, i.e., educate the customers (More et al., 2015).

Financial statement-type fraud affects the economy worldwide, and effective measures should be employed in detecting and preventing the said type of fraud. Further it is to be noted that fraud detection techniques should be updated continuously over time and identify criminal strategies (Renu Chaudhary, 2013). It should be noted that banks must implement sophisticated fraud preventive measures to build customer trust; without the above checks, it is difficult to build customer trust and increase business (Suh and Han, 2002). A research study by Sharma and Brahma (2000) revealed that the causes of many frauds are due to the negligence of the bank's supervisory staff. Further, it was stated in the study that supervisory staff at the branch level need to control the above types of fraud.

The banks are directed by the 'Uniform Customs and Practice (UCP)' concerning 'Letter of Credit (LC)'; upon full compliance with the requirements, banks should honor payment to the seller. However, it was disclosed that banks must obey the UCP guidelines despite being presented with counterfeit documents. Further, it was recommended preventive measures for banks in dealing with such fraudulent activities in the 'LC' transactions (CheHashim et al., 2014). In a research study of data relating to financial fraud cases from 2009 to 2019, it was revealed that the SVM technique is the most widely used technique for fraud detection and that most data mining techniques are used in the banking and insurance field in the financial sector (Khaled et al., 2021).

Jae-Sung Lee (2020) stressed the importance of letters of credit transactions and preventive measures. Since there is a possible fraud occurrence in some of the L/C transactions, he recommended adding some countermeasure material to the unification rules of L/Cs. Fraudulent transactions cannot surpass accumulated guarantees and guarantees as each transaction must be made by a group of miners. With moderate data storage and administrative systems, hacking, and breach are all possible, but the widespread blockchain compliance mechanism prevents this. The blockchain technology works in detecting various types of fraud, such as rating fraud, deceitful gaining fraud, insurance fraud, and other fraudulent scams, and it was further mentioned ten different areas where blockchain application has made an impact that people faces counterfeit problems in financial transactions (Rakshit et al 2022).

STUDIES ON BLOCKCHAIN TECHNOLOGY

Blockchain Technology (BCT) is a visionary innovation that takes the banking sector on another path, and the transactions are more secure, agile, cost-effective, and transparent. They suggested that pragmatic research can be undertaken soon to assess the evolution of Bitcoin Technology in India when compared to other developing countries (Gupta and Gupta, 2018).

Many financial institutions are searching for the potential of blockchain technology and the same to overcome the challenges that remain not least regulatory and security issues. It was discussed that blockchain technology can replace existing technology for transferring payments and security. Also, it provides a round-the-clock payment service on a real-time basis (Barnes, 2015).

Blockchain technology in the financial sector maintains data integrity, allows banks to track every transaction in real time, and allows transactions in the public domain. It can identify the customer's trustworthiness before entering into a business contract. They have mentioned that blockchain technology will gain more importance in the financial sector soon (Mohdjaval et al, 2022). It was found that recognizing fraudsters is not easy as fraudsters can act tactically to cover themselves, and also the research explored the possible strengths and limits of blockchain-grounded systems under two different goals: bad-mouthing and ballot-stuffing (Yuanfeng and Dan, 2016).

Blockchain technology is described as "Intermediary free platform" and it plays a vital role in the financial sector (Rashikala et al., 2023). It can transform the banking industry to another level when used in operations, reducing costs and increasing operational efficiencies. Further, it eliminates third-party intervention, making banking more transparent and efficient (Malkar Vinod Ramchandra et al., 2022).

A comparative analysis of the present banking system and the future banking system with blockchain technology was discussed by Gandhi, Rupali, et al. (2019). It was mentioned that extensive research is required to explore further the activities that happen in the banking industry on a real-time basis, and it is the biggest challenge for regulators and decision-makers. They proposed a design for incorporating blockchain technology in the banking system to study the viability of blockchain technology in the banking system.

The Institute for Development and Research in Banking Technology (IDRBT) (2017) mentioned that intensive research has been happening to identify the potential areas, and also emphasized the several features of blockchain like the applications, primary subject, advantages, trials, and prospects of blockchain technology in the Indian Banking Sector.

Blockchain technology can be used for efficient results in various sectors viz., agriculture, banking, health care, education and aviation (Kanika Agarwal et al.

2022). A peer-to-peer business transaction model based on blockchain technology, for safe and secure transaction is ensured through a business process modeling and intelligent contracts (Reza Toorajipour et al. 2014).

Banks use blockchain for their payments especially cross-border payments with consensus algorithms. Cross border payments are faster and less expensive and need decentralized ledger without intermediaries. Online transactions are impossible without identity verification. Blockchain create it possible securely reuse identity verification. In this case we need consensus algorithm which provide more secure than others (Thulya, 2020).

One of the advantages for the banking industry is to maintain a fraud-free environment in the banking industry through blockchain technology, and it also improves the efficiency of the bank's working conditions. Further, it eliminates the intermediaries in the bank's daily operational activities and helps maintain records digitally, allowing the provision of environmentally friendly service. By using blockchain technology, banks can prevent fraud incidents. This study focused on the importance of blockchain's role in preserving natural resources. Also, the expenditure incurred for safeguarding records will be reduced by adopting blockchain technology. Some of the banks have carried out immense research work in the field of blockchain technology to obtain the maximum benefits from it (Meenakshi and George, 2018).

Mallesha and Haripriya (2019) stated that the blockchain technology, transactions in banking can be secured and unaltered as the shape of banking in India has changed to an advanced stage. Also, blockchain technology can eliminate third-party needs to prevent fraud.

Challenges and opportunities in blockchain implementation in the banking industry were discussed by Cocco, Pinna, et al. (2017), and they mentioned the potential aspect of adopting this emerging technology. They have mentioned three derived benefits from this emerging technology, i.e., "operating efficiency," "economic efficiency," and "proficient service."

The World Economic Forum (WEF) assessed that more than USD 1.4 billion has been invested in blockchain technology. Further, they have stated that this technology has revolutionized banks' clearing (payments) and credit information systems. It was mentioned that implementing blockchain technology in banks will eliminate the third-party/mediators' concept. Further, they have stated that it also encourages the development of "multi-center" scenarios, which helps the banking industry achieve operational efficiency. Several regulatory compliances and technical aspects have to be clear before implementing the technology into banking applications (Rega and Riccardi, 2017).

There is a need for intensive research is required to overcome the issues faced by the banks in the adoption of blockchain technology (Hossein et al., 2019). The

Banking sector has yet to be used extensively despite blockchain technology's high potential in the industry. The main advantages discussed using the said technology are more security, mechanization, and decentralized networks, which are the main contributors to future banking (Salah and Haitham, 2020).

Yusof, Munir, et al. (2018) have studied the factors influencing Malaysian banking institutions' behavioral intention to adopt blockchain technology. The authors used primary data to define the objectives, and the methodology adopted for their research was to obtain data from 149 respondents from banks in five states through a questionnaire. Key determinants such as social influence, facilitating condition, effort and performance expectancy with the use of technology, and a unified theory of acceptance have been adopted for their study. Out of the four key determinants, only Effort Expectancy displays an inconsequential relationship with the behavioral intention to adopt blockchain technology.

STUDIES ON DATA MINING TOOLS

The data mining tools are having edge over conventional methods, which require a lot of workforces, are expensive, and are inaccurate (Fahd Sabry et al., 2023). Further, blockchain technology could push the banking sector into new growth avenues. It is noted that the banking sector in China is facing revenue-generating issues due to interest spread variations and financial innovations; the efficiency of the banking sector will be improved by using blockchain applications. They have concluded that regulatory and technical matters must be resolved before integrating blockchain technology into the Banking sector (Ye and Chen, 2016).

A new data mining technique known as "CARDWATCH" is a fraud discovery mechanism for credit cards. It is based on a neural network learning section and provides a connection to multiple commercial databases. A high fraud detection rate is the output results attained from the said detection model. The model displayed high accuracy and huge processing speed in fraud recognition but has a limitation that requires a separate network for each customer (Aleskerov et al, 1997).

Mandeep Kaur (2018) explained that fraud numbers have been increasing recently, and the figure is more extensive in number in PSBs compared to the PVBs as the advances part is high in PSBs. The paper explains the instrument of cheats identified through data mining methods.

RekhaBowmik (2008) stated some data mining techniques for handling fraud detection. The author mentioned a few data mining algorithms: statistics-related, rule-based, and decision tree algorithms. The author implemented the Bayesian classification method for detecting insurance fraud in the automobile industry.

In his study, Madan (2015) found that security control measures needed to be complied with under the following heads, i.e., internal checks, Demand Drafts section, cheque book issue department, loans and advances, deposit account and internal branch accounts. He discussed that banks should concentrate on fraud prevention techniques and enable an effective mechanism to investigate all fraud cases. The primary reason behind the high incidence of Fraud in Indian public and private sector banks was a failure in the regulatory supervision system. Auditors have failed to perform their duties effectively, so many frauds are not known. He further discussed that all banks should share the methods and procedures adopted by the fraudsters in different reported scams so that they can be arrested in the future course. It is suggested that the regulatory members collaborate by sharing databases and inputs to prevent fraud.

ONLINE SCAMS AND BANKING RELATED FRAUDS

The impact of online scams and banking related frauds explored from various empirical studies are presented here:

There are four channels for online banking: ATMs, Credit Cards, Net-banking, and Mobile Banking. It is found that there are various types of card frauds viz., credit card fraud, debit card fraud, lost or stolen card, card skimming, chargeback fraud, and card not present fraud. Card skimming is a fraud in which fraudsters obtain customers' card details by installing skimmers in ATMs. Jagtap (2014) study reveals that 38% of the customers are still non user of online banking because of low safety level, risk of fraud and no guidance for operation. It was also observed that in spite of being educated customers are unwilling to use online banking as they feel it is unsafe to use. Another research survey finds that 24% of respondents believe using credit cards is unsafe, while 29% believe mobile banking is unreliable (Komal and Rani, 2012).

The financial loss in the banking sector is huge across the globe both in terms of combating cyber-attacks and on development of systems, so that such attacks need to be prevented in the future (Raghavan and Prathiban, 2014). It is evident that the banking sector is now facing security threats and due to online scams and technology-based frauds, like: phishing, cash transfer fraud, impersonation, call-centre fraud, credit card fraud, debit card fraud, spoofing website fraud etc. Sometimes the fraudster attempts to obtain confidential information from a telephonic call or sending a fake link, which includes ATM PIN, one-time password, user ID, or any other details. The research result shows that there is a sharp rise in phishing data in India; it might be due to increase in launching of phishing sites and rise complaints relating to phishing (Singh, 2007). A rough estimate reveals that nearly 80% of all fraud cases involved amounts less than Rs. one lakh while on an aggregated basis; the amount involved in such cases was only around 2% of the total transactions (Chakraborty, 2013). A report on Top 100 banking frauds is published by Central Vigilance Commission, India in 2017, categorizes the frauds in various sections like: Fixed Deposits, Demand Loan, letter of comfort, discounting of cheques across industries viz., Gems and Jewelry, Agro, Aviation, and Manufacturing (Bhasin, 2018). The overall incidents of fraud (involving Rs 1 lakh and above) recorded by banks/FIs grew by 28 percent by volume and 159 percent by value during 2019-20. (Gurmeet Singh and Simanpreet Kaur, 2023).

EVOLUTION OF BLOCKCHAIN TECHNOLOGY

Blockchain technology has a history of over three decades. The origin started by scientists Stuart Haber and W. Scott Stornetta (1991), who attempted to maintain a backup of digital documents and added time stamps and chains to safeguard the previously stored information. In 1992, they brought the concept of Merkle trees to store more information in a single block. In 2004, Hal Finney obtained reusable proof of work (RPOW), and the idea has positively contributed to the environment as it reduced the impact on the environment due to bitcoin mining and helped the mining process more effectively. In 2008 a hash cash algorithm for Bitcoin using blockchain technology is developed by Satoshi Nakamoto (2008).

DISTRIBUTED LEDGER TECHNOLOGY (DLT)

Investors can invest in digital assets like Bitcoin and Non-Fungible Tokens (NFT), facilitating liquidity. The assets accumulated by digital finance cannot be traced because of the distributed ledger system, as it is a digital ledger that stores data/records in blocks and is connected; the same is spread across multiple nodes/computers/organizations. Anyone who is an authorized person at respective nodes/network can have access to the distributed ledger. Multiple people can access the ledger simultaneously, so any alterations in the data alert participants in the network. Hence, the distributed ledger system is the most secure. Blockchain is one of the types of distrusted ledger systems.

DLT is maintained through network agreement conventions and deals with remarkable security highlights. Blockchain is proposed to dispose of the requirement for an outsider mediator regarding the exchange of significant worth or information between two gatherings. It alludes explicitly to the mechanical framework and conventions that permit the concurrent access, approval, and refreshing of records that describe appropriated forms. It operates on a computer network that spans multiple organizations or locations. It securely stores data using cryptography, and cryptographic keys and signatures restrict access to authorized users. The innovation additionally makes an unchanging data set, and that implies data, once put away, can't be erased, and any updates are for all the time for any family down the line.

This design addresses a massive change in how data is accumulated and conveyed by moving record-keeping from a solitary, legitimate area to a decentralized framework in which all essential substances can see and alter the record. Thus, any remaining elements can see who is utilizing and changing the record. This straightforwardness of DLT gives the members an elevated degree of trust and dispenses with the opportunity of deceitful exercises happening in the record. Like this, DLT eliminates the requirement for elements utilizing the record to depend on a confided-in focal power that controls the record or an outside, outsider supplier to play out that job and go about as a check against control.

There are three types of distributed ledger system viz., i) Private, ii) Public and iii) Consortium, explained below:

- Public: This type of ledger system can be accessed by anyone, and no permission is required for any modifications/alterations; however, consensus protocol validates the transactions. This type of ledger system has no single controller/network administrator. Blockchain is one of the types of public distributed ledger systems.
- Private: This ledger system is a dedicated network created by particular organizations for their activities. This system consists of one or a few entities that control the web and require permission to access it. The private type is much faster than the public ledger system as it requires less electrical computational.
- Hybrid: It is a combination of features belonging to public and private blockchains by which they can choose what data type is accessible.
- Consortium: This type of ledger system is similar to a hybrid one. However, the basic difference is that a consortium ledger system is private and belongs to a particular group of members/organizations.

BLOCKCHAIN- LEVELS AND SCALE OF OPERATION

Any block of a chain contains data with the following structures: data, previous block hash, and hash data and previous hash (Iansiti et al. 2017).

Blockchain is the principal register that stores and records all prior dealings and activities, validating the title of all currency units at any time. Blockchain has a finite length and contains a limited number of transactions—similar copies of the blockchain store each block of the crypto currency's software network. Cryptocurrency miners run the distributed server, which continually records and validates cryptocurrency transactions.

Proof of work (PoW) and proof of stake (PoS) are consensus algorithms. An explanation of work is the type of validation that authenticates the transaction as it confirms particular results done by nodes (Li, Wenting et al., 2017). A cryptocurrency transaction is finalized once linked to the blockchain, usually within minutes. If the transaction is settled, then it is irreversible. Unlike traditional payment processors like PayPal and credit cards, most crypto management has no built-in refund or chargeback functions. This is an exception to some newer crypto management with rudimentary refund features. Pan et al. (2011) analyzed that fraudsters take advantage of the existing model of financial markets and defraud customers. The study describes a theoretical context for the study of fraud in the financial sector. It highlighted that the number of scams has been augmented due to the usage of the fraud triangle.

BLOCKCHAIN IN BANKING

Blockchain can change the banking industry to be more effective as it impacts the various functionalities in banks. It can reduce costs by implementing intelligent contracts as intermediary concepts can be eliminated. Further, transaction costs can be minimized between interbank transactions and also ttransactions can be done in real-time, so the time taken between the transactions will be reduced drastically, e.g., international transactions.

Banks can maintain a secured transaction mechanism due to the distributed ledger technology. The data stored in the distributed ledger can be tracked by all authorized members; hence, permission is required from the authorized members if any alteration is to be made in the record. Therefore, fraudsters cannot tamper with the records under any circumstances as there is no single server concept. Data recorded in the ledger can be accessed by every authorized member; hence, any infringement in the data is easily identifiable by the other users. Therefore, fraudsters cannot tamper with the records under any circumstances. Data tampering/alteration is impossible with blockchain applications, and it supports fraud detection and prevention. Suppose any attempt made for a data breach by a fraudster will automatically prevent the action in real time.

DATA MINING IN BANKING

Earlier, banks depended mainly on manual decision-making in their daily operational activities, leading to more time-consuming, error-prone, and fraud-prone business activities. Over the last few years, vast technological upgrades have occurred, and every bank has been using data mining tools in their daily operations activities.

Banks can generate leads for their business growth based on historical and current data. Further, the data mining tools helps in selecting appropriate customers for on boarding products based on their bio-data, and monitoring customer transactions and identifying the transaction patterns, whether legitimate or illegitimate. Nowadays, banks have a separate division for online transaction monitoring cells to monitor fraudulent transactions exclusively using data mining tools.

FRAUD DETECTION BY BLOCKCHAIN TECHNOLOGY

Figure 1 shows linkage can bring out the anomalies in the transactions. The fraud perpetrator can be any of the four parties, i.e., exporter or importer, staff of any

Figure 1.

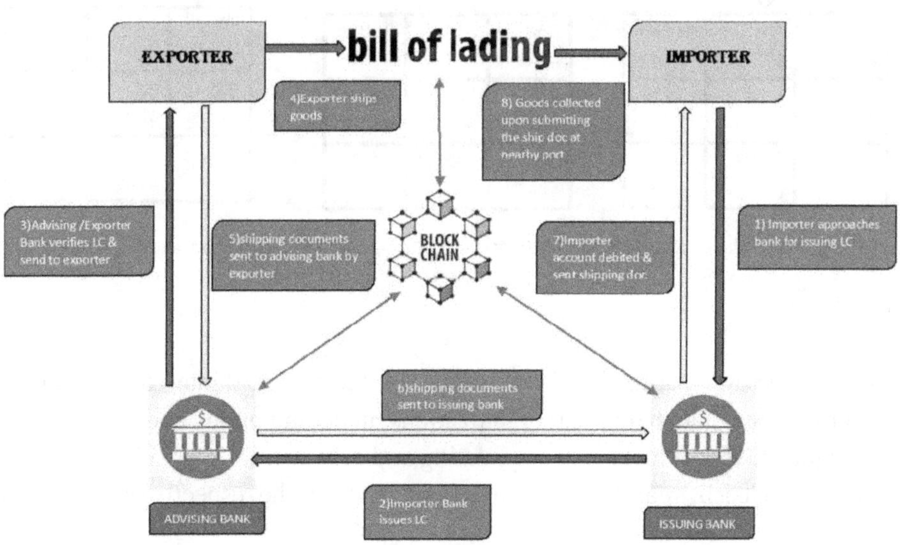

bank. We can see that blockchain connects the principal intermediaries in the above LC process; here, the issuing bank is located in one country, and the advising bank is located in another country so that banking regulators can act on behalf of the respective banks during the initial stage of implementation of blockchain technology.

Figure 2 shows that the third link/node is the customs department of the respective country so that the information about the goods shipped and the authenticity of the transaction can be visible clearly between the intermediaries. By implementing the above process, we can eliminate LC fraud. Hybrid or Consortium type of Blockchain technology can be used in the above process. The above picture denotes the transaction between two countries; likewise, all country's banking regulators' customs HQs will be brought under blockchain for fraud-free international trade.

Figure 2.

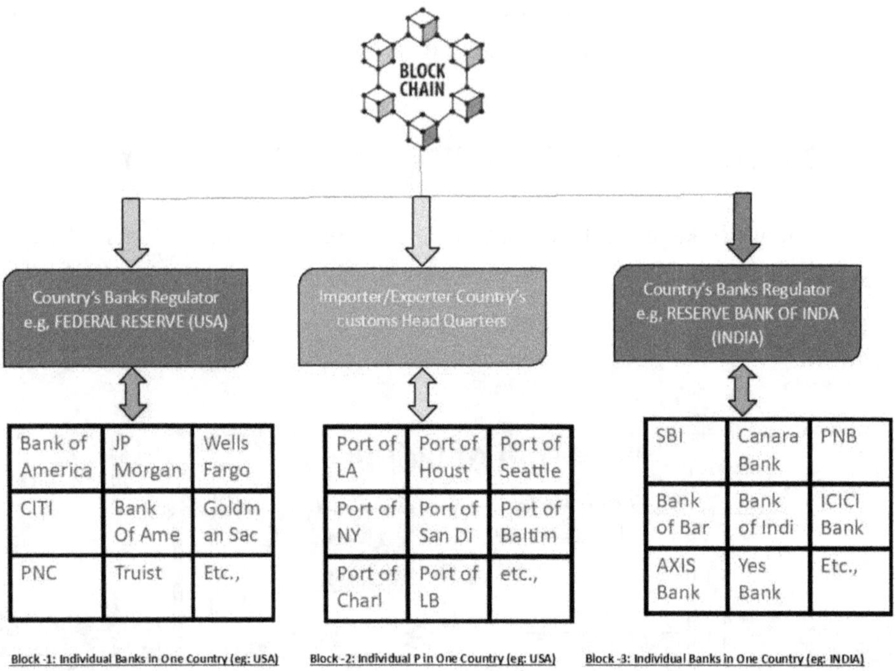

Figure 3 shows that the blockchain connects the principal intermediaries in the above BG process; all banks and organizations, including public and private, are to be brought under the blockchain. Regulating authority can act as a node on behalf of the banks, and each organization has a separate node, or the respective state industry

Figure 3.

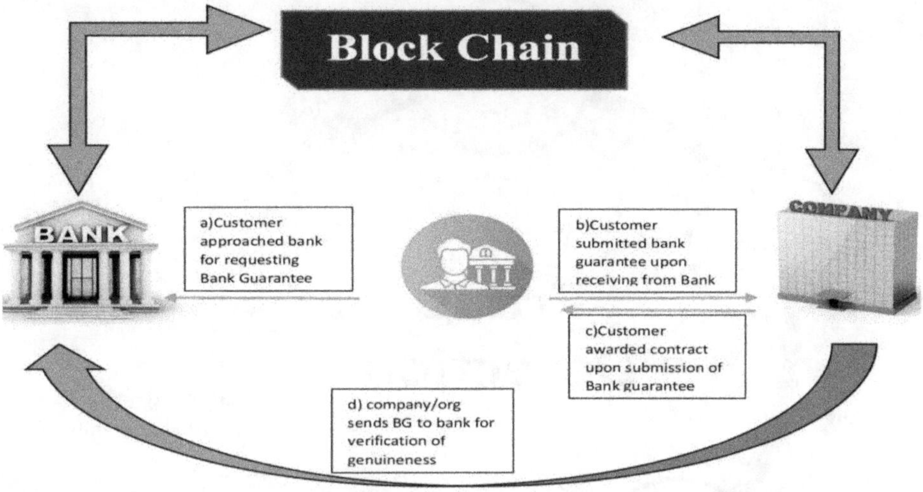

board can act as a node on behalf of the organizations. Either Hybrid or Consortium type of Blockchain technology can be used in the above process.

Figure 4 shows the process of eliminating transfer frauds. Nowadays, banks adopt the conventional methods for identifying the end use of the funds by using MIS reports or activity-related related by observing the nature of transactions. Auto block by system or message trigger from the system is not available in most banks for blocking fraudulent transactions. Hence, banks must be equipped with sophisticated data mining tools for identifying fraudulent transactions from genuine dealings, and this process segregates a list of transactions into two classes, namely fraudulent and authentic.

IMPLEMENTATION OF BLOCKCHAIN TECHNOLOGY IN KYC

In the current scenario, customer KYC procedure in banks is done individually by each bank or any other financial institution, and identity proofs like Passport, AADHAR (National Identity), Voter Identification card, and Ration card, etc. (e.g., Country-India) are to be validated separately and cross-checked with third party website. By doing this, banks face significant time consumption. Further, in some cases, banks opened accounts without verifying the genuineness of KYC particulars since fraudsters submitted fabricated KYC documents for opening bank accounts. In this regard, a private blockchain should be made by a bank regulating authority exclusively for KYC particulars. Further, customer data privacy will be safeguarded

Figure 4.

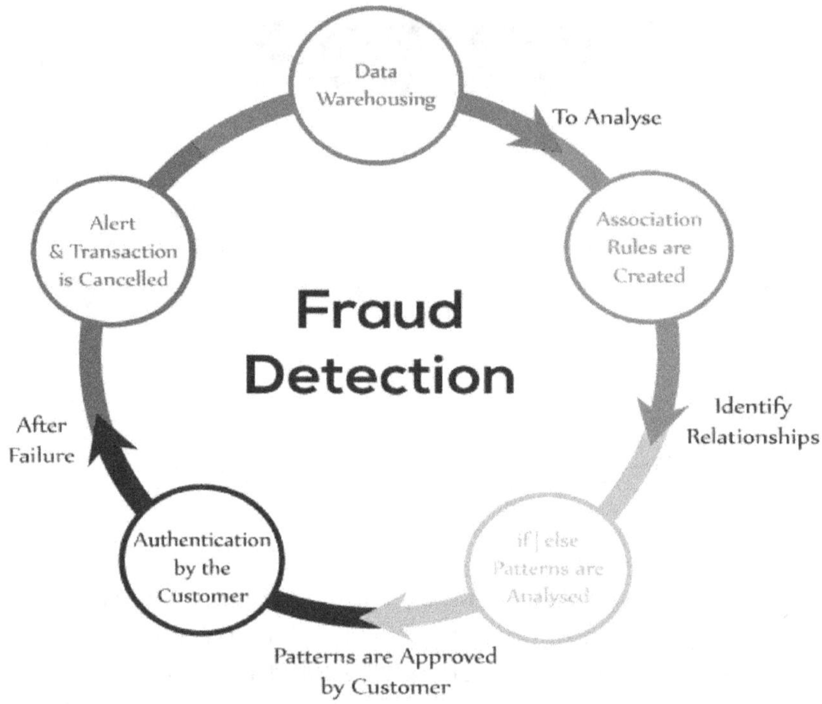

since it is a private blockchain. Once the customer's KYC details are recorded in the block blockchain, they will be sufficient for their future use in any financial institution. Further, customers need not carry KYC documents once registered with the blockchain; thereby, it is impossible to access/unauthorized usage by fraudsters.

LETTER OF CREDIT AND BANK GUARANTEE

Advanced tools like Blockchain technology implementation in the global banking sector, especially in developing countries, is complex as it requires a lot of regulatory compliance, skilled manpower, infrastructure, and additional capital. In the present scenario, Blockchain technology and data mining tools can be implemented in a stage-wise manner, and it would be beneficial to use the following products at the initial stage so that regulatory authorities can bring all banks under a single umbrella. Further, international trade transactions are more prone to credit risk due to a lack of limited geographical extent, hence, blockchain technology plays a vital role in monitoring international trade transactions (especially in Letter of credit or documentary credit and bank guarantees). Financial institutions have to ascertain the creditworthiness of both parties before issuing the letter of credit as it shows the party's genuineness & existence in the business. Further, financial institutions have enough confidence to get their finance back. All the above checks are from the customer/applicant point of view and it is to be done manually and further, due diligence to be ensured step-wise. Also, there are plenty of incidents of fraud reported in letters of credit transactions globally, which were done by staff of either LC issuing or advising banks. From this point of view, financial institutions' internal control mechanism comes into the picture for ensuring fraud-free transactions. In this regard, blockchain adoption can prevent and alert all the types of frauds perpetrated by external persons (customer/third party) or insiders (bank staff), and deployment of blockchain mechanism can prevent letters of credit fraud and make fraud-free international trade transactions.

- **Letter of Credit:** Documentary credit is a facility in which the bank guarantees the exporter/seller on behalf of the importer/buyer to make payment once the terms and conditions of the Letter of credit have been fulfilled. This process includes Buyer (importer), Issuing Bank (Buyer's bank), Advising Bank (seller's bank), and Seller (exporter). Letter of credit has played an essential role in international trade for the past few years; as per recent statistics, global trade reached 25.3 Trillion dollars in the year 2022, and the transaction settlement depends on documentary credit as it provides an assurance for both Buyer as well as seller those who are unknown to each other. However, this facility has become dangerous to banks recently as many fraudulent activities took place in this process. Any parties involved in the Letter of credit transaction may defraud others. During the 1990s, Madhavpatel shook many Gulf regions, Europe, and Indian-based banks, and many banks opened LCs in favor of foreign companies (including his own company, solo industries) for importing metals. However, he has diverted the same for his mining activities.

A Chinese firm named "HONTOP" (one of the firms attached to Chinese refiner WANDA holding group) has obtained a letter of credit finance from CIMB, a Malaysian bank to purchase 4,76,000 barrels of crude oil from Sugiah energy international (also called as Aeturnum Energy International Pvt Ltd). Later, it was supposed to be sold to "BP", a UK-based oil firm by HONTOP. Upon the bills invoice submitted by Sugiah, CIMB paid the amount. The same was raised on BP for payment by the CIMB, it apparently informed that the payment was not received for the cargo. After investigating the matter, it was revealed that documents submitted to the CIMB were fabricated. In this transaction, the victim is the CIMB bank and the accused fraudsters involved in the transaction are HONTOP (Financial Times,2020).

In another case, Zenrock Commodities, a Singapore-based oil trader is the mediator between the crude oil transaction between Socar Trading, a firm that pertains to Azerbaijan Republic, and Total Oil Trading (France). Socar Trading obtained 'Letter of credit' finance from Hong Kong Shanghai Banking Corp (HSBC) to deliver the cargo to Total Oil Trading, subsequently, the bank approached Total Oil Trading for payment, however, the firm reportedly said that it had already paid the dues to Zenrock. Subsequently, it was revealed that Zenrock has sold the same cargo to Gold Base (a Singapore-based firm) with the same documents shown to HSBC. In this transaction, Zenrock is the fraudster and the victim is the Hong Kong Shanghai Banking Corp (HSBC) (S&P Global, 2020).

- **Bank Guarantee:** It is a type of facility that the bank that provides a guarantee to the beneficiary (third party) on behalf of the bank's customer that the bank would pay the beneficiary if the applicant (customer) is failed to repay his debts or perform his contract, it depends on the type of guarantee. The fraud perpetrator can be any of the four parties, i.e., customer, bank staff, or company persons. Kompass Infrastructure Private Limited has obtained multiple Bank guarantees from Union Bank of India (Indian Bank) worth Rs.15 crores; based on this, a few companies supplied raw materials to him. Beyond the abovementioned limit, new bank guarantees were not to be issued to the above party as per extant guidelines. Later, the party submitted fake BGs in the bank name and obtained materials. Similarly, he has received new BGs by submitting fake letters from companies to banks to return the existing BGs. Here, banks and as well companies were defrauded.

A Recent example, Chandigarh Municipal Corporation, India filed a police case about the fabricated bank guarantee documents submitted by Sanjay Sharma during April, 2023 one of the directors of M/s Pashchatya Entertainment Private Limited, and others of Delhi for allegedly submitting three number of false bank guarantees amounting to Rs 1.65 crore. Several members including bank employees have been arrested in the fake bank guarantee racket. The main theme behind the fake bank guarantee racket is one of the accused opened bank accounts in the name of relatives and other friends, that submitted bids in the name of their relatives for parking tender and transferred the toll collected amount to subsidiary company accounts and alternatively, it is a money laundering concept.

Role of Blockchain Technology in Letter of Credit Transactions

For Financial Institutions, a letter of credit transaction is mainly based on the compliance of the documentation, and the same is well known to fraudsters, so they are encashing millions of US dollars by cheating banking institutions vide submitting forged documents (like bill of lading, invoices), since, banks are doing millions of transactions globally on each day based on the documentary evidence. Further, fraudsters are using the fraudulent amount for illegal purposes like money laundering, terror financing, drug trafficking, and other financial crimes. Due to the increase in technology and global financial criminals, numerous frauds have taken place during the last few years and the count is going on. At this juncture, red flags are to be identified in the letter of credit transaction and exercise.

RED FLAGGED ACCOUNT (RFA)

The Reserve Bank of India (RBI) has issued guidelines for dealing with loan frauds, in these circulars, different indicative signals are provided by the RBI to be considered as Early Warning Signals (EWS) to alert the officials about some wrongdoing in the account, which may turn later into fraud. EWS enables the officials at all levels to monitor their accounts.

Thus, the concept of a Red Flagged Account (RFA) is also being introduced in the current framework as an important step in fraud risk control. An RFA is one where a suspicion of fraudulent activity is thrown up by the presence of one or more EWS. These signals in a loan account should immediately put the bank on alert regarding wrongdoing which may ultimately turn out to be fraudulent.

Almost, all the banks adopted similar kinds of fraud detection approaches in their regular operations. Every bank in India has an exclusive fraud prevention wing and vigilance set up are there to look into the matter for detecting frauds and issued guidelines to mitigate the fraud incidents in banks' daily business.

CENTRAL FRAUD REGISTRY

The registry has been created with the prime objective to enable timely identification, control, and mitigation of fraud risk and for carrying out due diligence during the credit sanction process. RBI has set up an online searchable database of frauds reported by banks and which contains fraudulent borrower details. Fraud can never be eliminated from the business entirely simply because collusion can always overcome normal organizational control. To combat, fraud needs a different and fresh approach that will need to cover all aspects of the fraud cycle.

SAFETY MEASURES TO CUSTOMERS

Customers should be aware about phishing websites often pass hand-in-hand with phishing emails. Phishing emails can link to a duplicate website designed to borrow login credentials or prompt one to install malware. Customers should not deploy software or log in to a website except you are one hundred percent sure it is not a fake one. Phishing websites can also appear as subsidized effects on search engines or in-app marketplaces used by cell gadgets. Be cautious not to download a fake app or click a subsidized link to a phony website (au bank, 2023). In addition to fake mails, prize giveaway scams trick customers into taking action or offering facts about themselves, for instance, imparting a call, dealing with, emailing, and making contact with a number to claim a prize. This could allow a hacker to try and use the data to gain access to money owed by impersonating you (Federal Trade Commission, 2023).

Card fraud is the type of fraud where fraudsters use theft card data to gain financial benefits. Various types of card fraud are credit card fraud, debit card fraud, lost or stolen card, card skimming, chargeback fraud, and card not present fraud. Card skimming is a fraud in which fraudsters obtain customers' card details by installing skimmers in ATMs. A skimmer is a device that records customer card details, including PIN, when he inserts the card into an ATM. Chargeback fraud is an intentional act committed by the customer to claim a refund from the issuing bank despite having received benefits from the purchase (St. Pauls Chambers, 2023). Further, Fraudsters open fictitious accounts with stolen information/identity of actual customers to gain financial benefits. This activity will defraud banks and existing customers. The main reason for this fraud is that the fraudster obtained the help of existing customers illegitimately. In addition to this, customers must be aware of fake telephonic call, fax, email, or messenger is used as a medium for fraud by funds transfer, and fraudsters pretend/bluff them as a well-known person and request a wire transfer.

Customer should know that there are cases of unusual execution of a fraud email, where the sender transmits a message claiming that they have hacked into your laptop and is running it through remote computer protocol. The sender says that a key logger has been established and that your internet cam was used to file you doing something you may not need others to realize approximately. Hence, the customer should not open unknown links and should delete fake mails. Further, there are chances of impersonation to attract the customers. The impersonator then replies to it with a comply with-up message or name to motion - like an unfastened giveaway - using an account that looks nearly identical to the original poster or creator. This makes it look like the actual individual is pronouncing it. Alternatively, impersonators may try to use these equally fake bills to trick others via personal or direct messages into taking a few movements to defraud or compromise.

Customers should be aware about fake mobile apps. And be cautious about what packages you put in for your devices, especially for people who request administrator entry. Additionally, please make sure to double-take a look at the fact that the application you are downloading is not a faux one; it is impersonating a valid one you have used in the past (Checkpoint, 2023). Last, but not the least, customers should be aware of 'Credential stuffing' is a type of cyber fraud in which fraudsters gain access to the victim login of one company/organization by using victim credentials (user name/password) of another organization and multiple combinations of user name and passwords for gaining access. Generally, fraudsters obtain stolen data from many organizations through the dark web. The main reason for the credential stuffing discussion is that most people use the same/similar username and password for multiple login accesses. It is also called a brute force attack (Owasp, 2023).

CONCLUSION

This chapter highlights various issues about online scams and frauds relating to banking sector. It also focuses on how the blockchain technology eliminates the fabrication of record concepts used mainly by fraudsters in opening bank accounts for money laundering purposes. Advanced tools like blockchain technology provide a fraud-free platform for international trade transactions, as it is challenging to monitor international trade transactions with the existing manual of instructions in respective countries. Data mining tools identify fraudulent transactions in the banking sector and are extensively helpful in Anti-money laundering activity. Governments and BASEL should form a committee with industry experts for implementing blockchain technology in the Global Banking sector.

The advantage of tools is they eliminate middle persons or private entity intervention in financial transactions between two parties. In developing countries, the banking industry has witnessed many changes over the past century, and we can see the changes in a phased manner. Implementing new technologies in a single stretch is impossible due to insufficient infrastructure, enough capital, a knowledgeable workforce, and many statutory obligations. Hence, banking regulators and governments should collectively put efforts to revamp the technology in the banking industry, especially in Letter of credit, Bank guarantee transactions, and customer KYC at the initial stage. In this chapter also focuses on precautions to be taken by customers to face online frauds and scams like phishing websites, fake emails, card skimming, fake mobile applications, prize giveaway scams and impersonation etc. Hence, banks, investors and government can take advantage of blockchain technology and data mining tools to combat frauds and scams.

REFERENCES

Agrawal, K., Aggarwal, M., Tanwar, S., Sharma, G., Bokoro, P. N., & Sharma, R. (2022). An Extensive Blockchain Based Applications Survey: Tools, Frameworks, Opportunities, Challenges and Solutions. *IEEE Access : Practical Innovations, Open Solutions*, *10*, 116858–116906. doi:10.1109/ACCESS.2022.3219160

Aleskerov, E., Freisleben, B., & Rao, B. (1997). CARDWATCH: A neural network-based database mining system for credit card fraud detection. *Proceeding of the IEEE/IAFE on Computational Intelligence for Financial Engineering*. IEEE. 10.1109/CIFER.1997.618940

Bhasin, T. M. (2018). Analysis of Top 100 Bank Frauds. Central Vigilance Commission India, New Delhi.

Bhowmik, R. (2008). Data Mining Techniques in Fraud Detection. *Journal of Digital Forensics, Security and Law*, *3*(2). doi:10.15394/jdfsl.2008.1040

Cai, Y., & Zhu, D. (2016). Fraud detections for online businesses: A perspective from blockchain technology. *Financial Innovation*, *2*(1), 1–10. doi:10.118640854-016-0039-4

Cocco, L., Pinna, A., & Marchesi, M. (2017). Banking on blockchain: Costs savings thanks to the blockchain. [Internet.]. *Future Internet*, *25*(9), 25. www.mdpi.com/journal/futureinternetFuture. doi:10.3390/fi9030025

Dan, B. (2015). Blockchainmanoeuvres: applying Bitcoin's technology to banking. *The Banker*. https://www.thebanker.com/Transactions-Technology/Technology/Blockchain-manoeuvres-applying-Bitcoin-s-technology-to-banking?ct=true, 25.06.21

Gandhi, H., More, R., & Patil, N. (2019). A blockchain in banking application. *Global Journal for Research Analysis*, *8*(4), 265–276.

Guo, Y., & Liang, C. (2016). Blockchain application and outlook in the banking industry. *Financial Innovation*, *2*(1), 24. doi:10.118640854-016-0034-9

Gupta, A., & Gupta, S. (2018). Blockchain technology: Application in the Indian banking sector. *Delhi Business Review*, *19*(2), 89–94. doi:10.51768/dbr.v19i2.192201807

Haber, S., & Stornetta, W. S. (1991). How to time-stamp a digital document. *Journal of Cryptology*, *3*(2), 99–111. doi:10.1007/BF00196791

Hassani, H., Huang, X., & Silva, E. (2019). Big Data and Climate Change. *Big Data and Cognitive Computing*, *3*(1), 12. doi:10.3390/bdcc3010012

Hayati, Y., Mai, F. M., Badrul, M., & Zulnurhaini, Z. (2018). Behavioral intention to adopt blockchain technology: Viewpoint of the banking institutions in Malaysia. *International Journal of Advanced Scientific Research and Management*, *3*(10), 368–377.

IDRBT. (2017). *Applications of Blockchain Technology to Banking and Financial sectors in India*. Institute for Development and Research in Banking Technology.

Jagtap, V. (2014). To Study Perception of Educated and Working Group of customers towards E - Banking in Thane Region. *Abhinav International Monthly Refereed Journal of Research in Management and Technology.*, *3*(7), 29–35.

Sabry Esmail, F., Kamal Alsheref, F., & Elsayed Aboutabl, A.Fahd Sabry Esmail. (2023). Review of loan fraud detection process in the banking sector using Data Mining Techniques. *International Journal of Electrical and Computer Engineering Systems*, *14*(2), 229–239. Advance online publication. doi:10.32985/ijeces.14.2.12

Singh, G., & Kaur, S. (2023). Bank Frauds Reported In India: A Case Study. *Journal of Pharmaceutical Negative Results*, *14*(2), 304–309.

Chaudhary, R. (2013, September). Data Mining Tools To Detect Financial Fraud. [IJERT]. *International Journal of Engineering Research & Technology (Ahmedabad)*, *2*(9).

CheHashim, R., & Mahdzan, N. S.Rosmawani CheHashim and Nurul Shahnaz Mahdzan. (2014). Fraud in letter of credit transactions: The experience of Malaysian bankers. *International Journal of Law, Crime and Justice*, *42*(3), 224–236. doi:10.1016/j.ijlcj.2014.01.008

Iansiti, M., & Lakhani, K. (2017). The Truth About Blockchain. *Harvard Business Review*, *95*, 118–127.

Javaid, M., Haleem, A., Singh, R., Suman, R., & Khan, S. (2022). A review of Blockchain Technology applications for financial services. *Bench Council Transactions on Benchmarks, Standards and Evaluations, 2*(3). . doi:10.1016/j.tbench.2022.100073

Kaur, M. (2018). A Study on Current Frauds Trends in the Indian Banking Industry and Its Detection Using Data Mining Algorithms. [June.]. *International Journal of Computer Engineering In Research Trends*, *5*(6), 177–186.

Al-Hashediand, K. & Magalingam, P. (2021). Financial fraud detection applying data mining techniques: A comprehensive review from 2009 to 2019. *Computer Science Review, 40*. doi:10.1016/j.cosrev.2021.100402

Komal & Rani. (2012). Progress of Banking India: Customers' perspectives. *Business Intelligence Journal.*, *5*(1), 28–40.

Lee, J. S. (2020, November). *Journal of Korea Trade*, *24*(7), 73–92.

Li, W., Bohli, J., & Ghassan, K. (2017). *Securing Proof-of-Stake Blockchain Protocols*. (pp. 297-315). Springer. . doi:10.1007/978-3-319-67816-0_17

LalBhasin, M. (2015). An Empirical Study of Frauds in the Banks. *European Journal of Business and Social Sciences*, *4*(7), 1–12.

Mallesha, C., & Hari Priya, S. (2019, July – September). A Study on blockchain technology in the banking sector. *International Journal of Advanced Research in Commerce, Management and Social Science*, *2*(03), 123–132.

Meenakshi, K., & George, A. R. (2018). Green banking through blockchain. *International Journal of Research and Analytical Reviews*, *1*(12), 212–220.

More, D. M. M., & Nalawade, M. P. J. D. K. (2015). Online banking and cyber-attacks: The current scenario. *International Journal of Advanced Research in Computer Science and Software Engineering*, *5*(12), 743–749.

Nakamoto, S. (2008). *Bitcoin: A Peer-to-Peer Electronic Cash System*. Bitcoin. https://bitcoin.org/bitcoin.pdf

Palihapitiya, T. (2020). *Blockchain in Banking Industry*. University of Moratuwa.

Pan, G., Seow, P. S., Suwardy, T., & Gay, E. (2011). Fraud: A Review and Research Agenda. *Journal of Accountancy Business and the Public Interest*, *10*, 138–178.

Raghavan A.R. & Parthiban, L. (2014). The effect of cybercrime on a Bank's finances. *International Journal of Current Research and Review, 2*(2), 173-178.

Rakshit, A. & Kumar, S. (2022). Fraud Detection: A Review on Blockchain. *International Research Journal of Engineering and Technology (IRJET), 9*(1).

Ramchandra, M. V., Kumar, K., Sarkar, A., & Kr, S. (2022). Assessment of the impact of blockchain technology in the banking industry. *Materials Today: Proceedings, 56*(4), 2221-2226. .(https://www.sciencedirect.com/science/article/pii/S2214785321075763) doi:10.1016/j.matpr.2021.11.554

Rega, F. G., & Riccardi, N. (2018). *Blockchain in the banking industry: an Overview*. (White Paper). Research Gate. https://www.researchgate.net/profile/Federico-Rega/publication/327601993_Blockchain_in_the_banking_industry_an_Overview/links/5bfefaeaa6fdcc1b8d49f252/Blockchain-in-the-banking-industry-an-Overview.pdf

Singh, N. P. (2007). Online Frauds in Banks with Phishing. *Journal of Internet Banking and Commerce*, *12*(2).

Suh, B., & Han, I. (2002). Effect of trust on customer acceptance of Internet banking. *Electronic Commerce Research and Applications*, *1*, 247-263. . doi:10.1016/S1567-4223(02)00017-0

Swan, M. (2018). *Smart Network Field Theory: The Technophysics of Blockchain and Deep Learning*. SSRN. doi:10.2139/ssrn.3262945

Toorajipour, R., Oghazi, P., Sohrabpour, V., Patel, P. C., & Mostaghel, R. (2022). Block by block: A blockchain-based peer-to-peer business transaction for international trade. *Technological Forecasting and Social Change*, *180*, 121714. doi:10.1016/j.techfore.2022.121714

Weerawarna, R., Miah, S. J., & Shao, X. (2023). *Emerging advances of blockchain technology in fiancé: a content analysis*. PersUbiquitcomput. doi:10.100700779-023-01712-5

KEY TERMS AND DEFINITIONS

Blockchain: It is an immutable, cryptographic, distributed, consensus-driven ledger. It is a software protocol for the instantaneous transfer of money and other forms of value via the Internet. It is a system of linking blocks in a chain format that stores data and is chronologically consistent. Because one cannot delete or modify the chain without consensus from the network.

Crowdfunding: Crowdfunding is a way of raising debt and equity with a collective effort of multiple investors through an internet-based platform.

Cryptocurrency: It is an encrypted, decentralized digital currency transferred between peers and confirmed in a public ledger via a process known as mining. This is also known as Digital currency.

Crypto-Wallet: It stores the private key needed to unlock funds from the investor's wallet address on the blockchain.

Decentralized Financial Transactions (DeFi): DeFi is an economic paradigm that leverages distributed ledger technologies to offer services such as lending, investing, or exchanging crypto assets like cryptocurrency, smart contracts, bitcoin, etc., without relying on a traditional centralized intermediary.

Digital Currency: It is also known as Crypto Currency. It is an encrypted, decentralized digital currency transferred between peers and confirmed in a public ledger via a process known as mining. Digital currencies are issued by private developers and denominated in their unit of account. They are obtained, stored, accessed, and transacted electronically and are neither denominated in any sovereign currency nor issued or backed by any government or central bank.

Digital Finance: This term is used to describe the usage of technologies in the financial services industry. It includes various products, applications, processes, and business models that have transformed the traditional way of providing banking and financial services.

Distributed Ledger Technology: The technological infrastructure and protocols that allow simultaneous access, validation, and record updating in an immutable manner across a network that's spread across multiple entities or locations.

Forward Contract: Sales and purchase of currency where currencies are delivered at a future date at a rate mentioned in the agreement.

Chapter 4
Blockchain Implications and Utility for Higher Education

Neta Baporikar
https://orcid.org/0000-0003-0676-9913
Namibia University of Science and Technology, Namibia & SP Pune University, India

ABSTRACT

Blockchain has emerged as an important concept at the interface of ICT and higher education. Blockchain is perceived as a revolutionary technology offering a considerable impact of vast magnitude on various sectors since it enables the creation of decentralized applications programmed to run on networks and records sets of data that can be shared securely without third-party mediation. The Blockchain's emphasis on variety in terms of applications may be due to its capacity to build a trusted and decentralized contract environment. The higher education sector is, therefore, a potential user of blockchain technology due to its capacity in allowing stakeholders to validate learning records and identity management. On the other hand, higher education may be understood as a system that includes, among others, two major stakeholders, higher education institutions, (HEIs) and students. Adopting a systematic literature review and thematic content analysis, this chapter aims to understand the blockchain implications and utility in higher education.

INTRODUCTION

Blockchain is defined as a ledger of decentralized data that is securely shared. Blockchain technology enables a collective group of select participants to share data. With blockchain cloud services, transactional data from multiple sources can

DOI: 10.4018/979-8-3693-0405-1.ch004

be easily collected, integrated, and shared. Data is broken up into shared blocks that are chained together with unique identifiers in the form of cryptographic hashes. Blockchain provides data integrity with a single source of truth, eliminating data duplication and increasing security. In a blockchain system, fraud and data tampering are prevented because data can't be altered without the permission of a quorum of the parties. A blockchain ledger can be shared, but not altered. If someone tries to alter data, all participants will be alerted and will know who make the attempt.

Blockchain has emerged as an important concept at the interface of ICT and higher education. Blockchain is perceived as a revolutionary technology offering a considerable impact of vast magnitude on various sectors since it enables the creation of decentralized applications programmed to run on networks and records sets of data that can be shared securely without third-party mediation. The Blockchain's emphasis on variety in terms of applications may be due to its capacity to build a trusted and decentralized contract environment. The higher education sector is, therefore, a potential user of blockchain technology due to its capacity in allowing stakeholders to validate learning records and identity management. On the other hand, higher education may be understood as a system that includes, among others, two major stakeholders, Higher Education Institutions (HEIs) and students (Baporikar, 2016; 2017b; Baporikar, & Sony, 2020). Adopting a systematic literature review and thematic content analysis this chapter aims to understand the blockchain implications and utility in higher education.

LITERATURE REVIEW

Blockchain technology is an advanced database mechanism that allows transparent information sharing within a business network. A blockchain database stores data in blocks that are linked together in a chain. Blockchain technology is also known as distributed ledger technology. It allows participants to secure the settlement of transactions, achieve the transaction, and transfer of assets at a low-cost (Tschorsch and Scheuermann 2016). Blockchain is not only a new type of internet infrastructure based on distributed applications but also a new type of supply chain network. Essentially, blockchain is a distributed network of computers (nodes) used to maintain the source of information sharing. A blockchain is a decentralized, distributed and public digital ledger that is used to record transactions across many computers so that the record cannot be altered retroactively without the alteration of all subsequent blocks and the consensus of the network. To study more about blockchain, its underlying technology, here are some important definitions.

- **Decentralized trust:** The key reason that organizations use blockchain technology, instead of other data stores, is to provide a guarantee of data integrity without relying on a central authority. This is called decentralized trust through reliable data.
- **Blockchain blocks:** The name blockchain comes from the fact that the data is stored in blocks, and each block is connected to the previous block, making up a chainlike structure. With blockchain technology, you can only add (append) new blocks to a blockchain. You can't modify or delete any block after it gets added to the blockchain.
- **Consensus algorithms:** Algorithms that enforce the rules within a blockchain system. Once the participating parties set up rules for the blockchain, the consensus algorithm ensures that those rules are followed.
- **Blockchain nodes: Blockchain** blocks of data are stored on nodes—the storage units that keep the data in sync or up to date. Any node can quickly determine if any block has changed since it was added. When a new, full node joins the blockchain network, it downloads a copy of all the blocks currently on the chain. After the new node synchronizes with the other nodes and has the latest blockchain version, it can receive any new blocks, just like other nodes. There are two main types of blockchain nodes: full nodes store a complete copy of the blockchain and lightweight nodes only store the most recent blocks, and can request older blocks when users need them.

TYPES OF BLOCKCHAIN

There are four main types of blockchain networks: public blockchains, private blockchains, consortium blockchains and hybrid blockchains explained briefly below:

- **Public blockchain:** A public, or permission-less, blockchain network is one where anyone can participate without restrictions. Most types of crypto currencies run on a public blockchain that is governed by rules or consensus algorithms.
- **Private Blockchain:** A private blockchain also referred as permissioned allows organizations to set controls on who can access blockchain data. Only users who are granted permissions can access specific sets of data. E.g. Oracle Blockchain Platform is a permissioned blockchain.
- **Consortium Blockchain:** A blockchain network where the consensus process (mining process) is closely controlled by a preselected set of nodes or by a preselected number of stakeholders.

- **Hybrid Blockchain:** A hybrid blockchain is a unique type of blockchain that derives its features from public and private blockchains. It's a blend of both blockchains; the public and private aspects of the hybrid blockchain work hand-in-hand.

As Bitcoin and other crypto currencies have been picking up steam, focus has turned to blockchain – the underlying distributed ledger technology (DLT) that powers these digital currencies. Blockchain technology is simple to understand at its roots. Basically, the tech exists as a shared database filled with entries that must be confirmed by peer-to-peer networks and encrypted. It's helpful to envision it as a strongly encrypted and verified shared Google Document, in which each entry in the sheet depends on a logical relationship to all its predecessors, and is agreed upon by everyone in the network. But blockchain technology has many more potential use cases beyond other than just serving as the fuel behind Bitcoin.

FEATURES OF BLOCKCHAIN TECHNOLOGY

From the technical point of view, blockchain technology has four features: decentralization, traceability, immutability, and currency properties.

1. Decentralization refers to the processes of data verification, storage, maintenance, and transmission on blockchain which are based on a distributed system structure. In his structure, the trust between distributed nodes is built through mathematical methods rather than the centralized organizations.
2. Traceability means that all transactions on blockchain are arranged in chronological order, and a block is connected with two adjacent blocks by the cryptographic hash function. Therefore, every transaction is track able by examining the block information linked by hash keys.
3. Immutability, there are two reasons that blockchain technology is immutable. On the one hand, all transactions are stored in blocks with one hash key linking from the previous block and one hash key pointing to the next block. Tampering with any transaction would result in different hash values and would thus be detected by all the other nodes running precisely the same validation algorithm. On the other hand, blockchain is a shareable public ledger stored on thousands of node, and all ledgers continue to sync in real time. Successful tampering would need to change over 51% of the ledgers stored in the network (Tschorsch and Scheuermann 2016).
4. Currency properties meaning Blockchain technology and crypto currency are inseparable that is to say; any blockchain network has a form crypto currency

property. The essence of blockchain technology is point-to-point transactions; no third party is involved, which means that all transactions do not require the participation of third parties. Circulation of digital currency based on blockchain technology is fixed. Specifically, in Bitcoin, the currency base is set at 21 million caps, so the generation of digital currency is created by using a specific mining algorithm and is bounded by a pre-defined formula. Thus there won't be the problem of inflation, collapse and so on. In Blockchain 2.0 and 3.0 applications, the combination of other activities such as government activities, educational activities, and financial activities can make these non-financial activities have the property of currency.

FUNCTIONING OF BLOCKCHAIN

Think of a blockchain as a historical record of transactions. Each block is "chained" to the previous block in a sequence, and is immutably recorded across a peer-to-peer network. Cryptographic trust and assurance technology applies a unique identifier—or digital fingerprint—to each transaction. Trust, accountability, transparency, and security are forged into the chain. This enables many types of organizations and trading partners to access and share data, a phenomenon known as third-party, consensus-based trust.

All participants maintain an encrypted record of every transaction within a decentralized, highly scalable, and resilient recording mechanism that cannot be repudiated. Blockchain does not require any additional overhead or intermediaries. Having a decentralized, single source of truth reduces the cost of executing trusted business interactions among parties that may not fully trust each other. In a permissioned blockchain, used by most enterprises, participants are authorized to participate in the network, and each participant maintains an encrypted record of every transaction.

Any company or group of companies that needs a secure, real-time, shareable record of transactions can benefit from this unique technology. There is no single location where everything is stored, leading to better security and availability, with no central point of vulnerability.

BENEFITS OF BLOCKCHAIN: THE VALUE PROPOSITION

The use of blockchain technology is expected to significantly increase over the next few years. This game-changing technology is considered both innovative and disruptive because blockchain will change existing business processes with streamlined efficiency, reliability, and security. Blockchain technology delivers specific benefits that help in the following ways:

- Establishes trust among parties doing business together by offering reliable, shared data.
- Eliminates siloed data by integrating data into one system through a distributed ledger shared within a network that permissioned parties can access.
- Offers a high level of security for data.
- Reduces the need for third-party intermediaries.
- Creates real-time, tamper-evident records that can be shared among all participants.
- Allows participants to ensure the authenticity and integrity of products placed into the stream of commerce.
- Enables seamless tracking and tracing of goods and services across the value chain.

Thus, blockchain technology is a digital innovation that has the potential to significantly impact trusted computing activities and provide a basis for trusted computing on top of which various applications can be built.

BLOCKCHAIN IN HIGHER EDUCATION

Just like the other new technologies emerging quickly, such as artificial intelligence and extended reality, blockchain technology in the education sector has brought new waves of change and introduced solutions formulated from different industries that go beyond its initial financial and crypto currency focus. Accessing credentials and academic records and the validation of transcripts were done by following a vague process in the traditional educational model that was posing challenges in its expansion and growth (Baporikar, 2022; 2021). These issues could be easily solved by blockchain-based software. The main advantages blockchain brings are decentralized storage, the immutability of stored information, traceability, and transparency. The improvements that blockchain technology is making to education could provide opportunities for people from all backgrounds and nations. The features are undoubtedly are innovative because they have so many potential applications in the field of education. Many public educational institutions are now thinking about implementing blockchain-based tools.

UTILITY AND APPLICATION OF BLOCKCHAIN IN HIGHER EDUCATION

Blockchains have the ability to create distinctive digital assets that validate the legitimacy of academic qualifications and certifications. There are other applications of blockchain in the education industry and employment sectors in addition to just credential verification. Figure 1 gives the utility and application of Blockchain in higher education.

Figure 1. Utility and application of blockchain in higher education
Source: Self-Developed

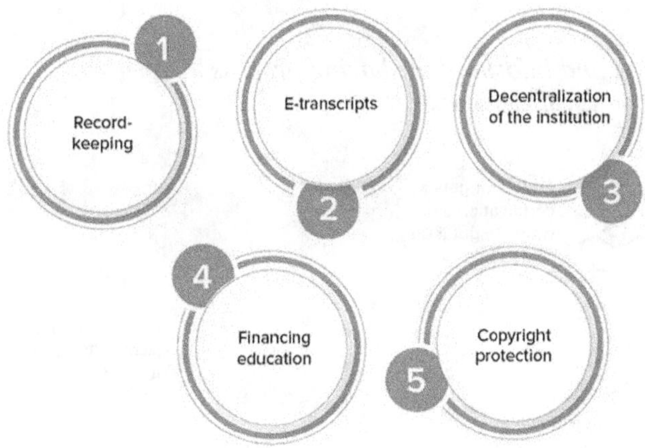

1. **Record-keeping:** Blockchain technology holds the promise of long-overdue changes to record-keeping practices, which have traditionally been primarily unreliable. A diverse set of educational documents, like diplomas, certificates, or credentials, that presently require validators can be verified and kept on file automatically by blockchain. Once the predefined parameters are satisfied, smart contracts powered by blockchain can handle all the work with instant, self-triggered approval of documents. It enables students and learners to quickly access their records and securely share them with prospective employers. Smart Contracts are basically self-executing contracts which are programmed in a way to ensure that the terms of agreements are met/unmet and then take a resulting action. A Smart Contract running on the blockchain network is essentially a computer protocol that simulates a real contract (such as economic transactions, employment, etc.) (Kosba et al. 2016). It can facilitate contract negotiation, simplify contract terms, implement contract execution, and verify

contract fulfillment state. It marks the unique and precise identity of parties in a transaction (contract subjects) through a digital way and stipulates the rights and obligations of both sides (contract terms) by code. The smart contract not only reduces "third party costs" in traditional transactions but also dramatically guarantees the transaction security and reliability. The smart contract greatly improves executive power and fairness than the traditional one. Therefore, if teachers and students carry out instructing and learning activities based on a smart contract, some of the educational issues would be solved. Additionally, it lessens the strain on employers because they no longer need to do laborious background checks to authenticate the applicant's accomplishments. The good thing about it is that it stays intact regardless of external problems. The process of storing and sharing information is given in Figure 2.

Figure 2. Storing and information sharing process
Source: Adapted from appinventiv.com/blog

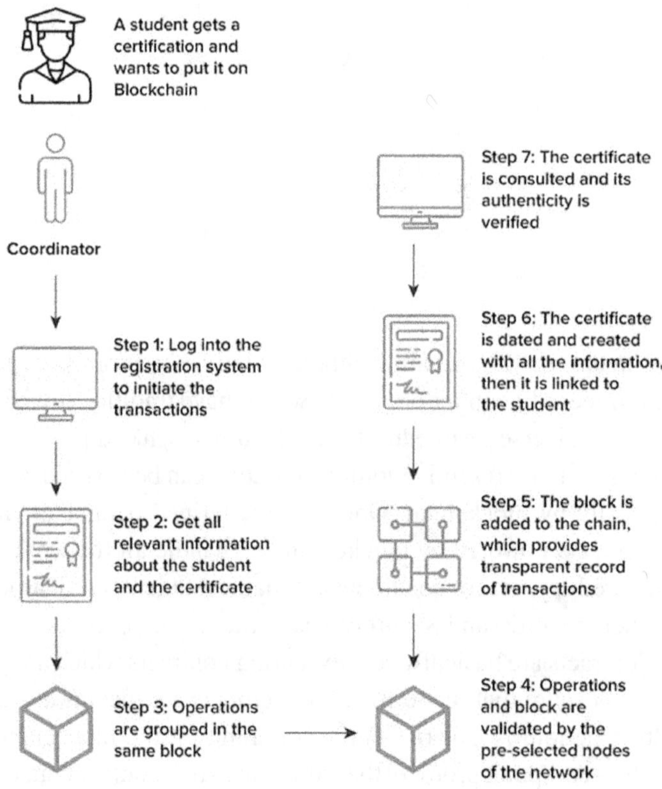

2. **E-transcripts:** Along with the simplicity of verification comes the amazing potential of E-transcripts. Producing transcripts is the academic institution's most time-consuming and labor-intensive task all over the world (Baporikar, 2020). To ensure correctness, each entry in a transcript needs to be manually checked. It requires case-by-case inspection and a mountain of paper records from high school to university (Baporikar, 2017a). Even in 2023, the majority of institutions still sends and receives transcripts using old techniques like mail. These processes might be readily made more efficient by distributed ledger technology and related solutions, which would also help reduce the number of fraudulent claims for unearned academic credits. Blockchains can undoubtedly work wonders for institutions by enabling tamper-resistant storage of sensitive data, such as a student's independent grades. Not only does it benefit educational institutions, but it also makes the vetting process simpler for recruiters and staffing firms. It also results in significant time and financial savings. Blockchain technology can formulate the whole transcript. In the formal learning context, this includes learning contents and outcomes as well as students' achievements and academic certificates. Subsequently, in the informal learning context, information about research experience, skills, online learning experience as well as individual interests are included. These data can be safely stored and accessed on a blockchain network in appropriate ways. Moreover, blockchain technology contributes to reducing degree fraud. In the past, there were numerous cases of degree fraud. However, it can be avoided by employing blockchain in granting and managing student's degree now. The data matched with users' ID and stored in blockchain are checked, validated, and maintained by the miners from all over the world. Blockchain distributed ledger is immutable and trustworthy. Thus, the reliability and authority are both ensured, which will significantly reduce degree fraud.
3. **Decentralization of the institution:** Due to its vast potential, blockchain can create a new business model and serve as an entire infrastructure for universities rather than just a tool. By using smart contracts to support and automate agreements and payments between students and teachers, the platform introduces online courses. As a result, students enjoy affordable tuition and dependable service. On the other hand, automation has allowed educators to liberate themselves from various administrative responsibilities, secure faculty and student data from hacks with the help of blockchain cryptography, and cut administrative costs by doing away with middlemen. Figure 3, below depicts how the decentralization of institutions and enables the faculty and students and helps in resources optimization.

Figure 3. Institute decentralization for resources optimization
Source: Adapted from appinventiv.com/blog

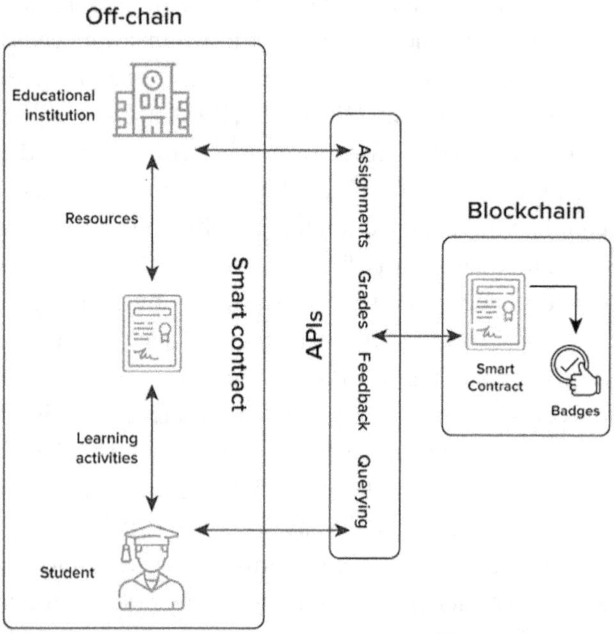

4. **Financing education:** In academic institutions, financial accounting plays a crucial role, and technology can be used in education in previously unheard-of ways (Baporikar, 2016a; 2016b; 2016c). Blockchain technology can be used to manage teacher wages and student scholarships, creating a transparent and equitable system for funding grants and projects.
5. **Copyright protection:** Plagiarism in the academic community is a severe issue (Baporikar, 2019a). When a research paper is copied or stolen, a lifetime's worth of labor can be lost. Low grades may stem from an assignment that was stolen (Baporikar, 2019a; 2019b). Blockchain-based solutions can be used to regulate how copyrighted content is distributed online. The technology's main purpose will be to securely store the data that has been recorded in a chain. Once it is stored, this data cannot be manually changed because it is protected by cutting-edge encryption. This makes it possible for students to access instructional materials safely (Baporikar, 2019c). The owner can simply manage access because the usage of the content is also tracked in the chain. Online usage tracking is possible and proving ownership is simple.

CHALLENGES OF ADOPTING BLOCKCHAIN TECHNOLOGY IN EDUCATION

One does face challenges in adopting blockchain despite its benefits. There is hesitation among educators and students in using a revolutionary technology that might have roots in the challenges that occur at implementation, including those with security and cost. Let us explore what these challenges are:

1. **Security issues:** Blockchain is known to be one of the most secure technologies. However, it is not impervious. Finance and education are two entirely different sectors; the security parameters also should be according to the specific sectors. The flexibility and vulnerability of blockchain currency might not fit into the security parameters of blockchain for edtech. The student's education credentials and reports are sensitive and should be stored in a manner that is in sync with state and federal data protection laws. Thus, it is important for institutions to be extra careful of the information and the way it is stored. Additional security measures like providing permissions and more robust data encryption should be implemented for better security.
2. **Scalability concerns:** The scope of student data and certification is ever-growing. Education institutions find it challenging to scale up the capabilities of blockchain with ever-growing needs. The simple logic is as the data increases, more blocks are added, which tends to slow down transactions on the blockchain platform. Additionally, peer to peer verification process makes the transaction process lengthier.
3. **Low adoption rate:** The benefit of blockchain is currently limited to a smaller group of students; majorly graduates, who can store their achievements and accolades in it. For organizations to use this feature of blockchain in education to ease their hiring process will need to adopt blockchain technology. The businesses will have to make additional investments for the same that might not be feasible or even beneficial for some organizations. This apprehension of additional costs might lead to low adoption rates.
4. **Cost:** Adoption of blockchain eventually saves costs in administrative activities. However, the scale at which this technology needs to be adopted and implemented is gigantic. This will, obviously, involve huge costs. While it might be difficult for some institutions to spend a huge amount of money, others might find it challenging as blockchain implementation will also require a huge change in existing infrastructure. Overall, the digital transformation of the education industry towards blockchain adoption will require humongous investment initially, which may refrain from education institutions from adopting blockchain technology.

ADVANTAGES OF BLOCKCHAIN TECHNOLOGY

Derived from the technical features, some advantages of their application using blockchain technology are as follows:

1. **Reliability:** The decentralized nature of a blockchain network changes the databases of the entire transaction records from closed and centralized ledgers maintained by only a few accredited institutions to open distributed ledgers maintained by tens of thousands of nodes. The failure of a single node does not affect the operation of the whole network. This avoids the single point of failure and ensures the high reliability of the applications which built on the blockchain technology.
2. **Trust:** Blockchain network makes the trust decentralized too. Unlike the centralized trust we take for granted, such as central governments issuing currencies and commercial banks, blockchain network acts as new trust bearers with decentralized ledgers. These ledgers are shared among a network of tamper-proofed nodes (Underwood 2016).
3. **Security:** Blockchain network uses the one-way hash function which is a mathematical function that takes a variable-length input string and converts it into a fixed-length binary sequence. The output bears no apparent relationship to the input. The process is hard to reverse because, given just the output, the input is impossible to determine (Yli-Huumo et al. 2016). Furthermore, the newly generated block is strictly following the linear sequence of time.
4. **Efficiency:** All data are automatically run through pre-set procedures. Therefore, blockchain technology can not only significantly reduce the cost of labor but also improve efficiency. For the digital currency of Blockchain 1.0, the automation of distributed ledger is mainly the automation of settlement. Blockchain technology could speed the clearing and settlement of certain financial transactions by reducing the number of intermediaries involved, and by making the reconciliation process faster and more efficient (Wang et al. 2016).

EXAMPLES OF BLOCKCHAIN APPLICATIONS IN EDUCATION

1. Nowadays, some universities and institutes have applied blockchain technology into education, and most of them use it to support academic degree management and summative evaluation for learning outcomes (Hoy 2017, Sharples and Domingue 2016, Skiba, 2017).

2. The University of Nicosia is the first school which uses blockchain technology to manage students' certificates received from MOOC platforms (Sharples and Domingue 2016).
3. Sony Global Education also used the blockchain technology to create a global assessment platform to provide services for storing and managing degree information (Hoy 2017).
4. Massachusetts Institute of Technology (MIT) and the Learning Machine Company cooperated to design a digital badge for online learning based on blockchain technology. Students who have attended the projects of MIT Media Lab and passed the assessment will receive a certification which will be stored on a blockchain network (Skiba 2017).
5. Holberton School is the first institute applying blockchain technology to store degrees and has claimed that they would share this information from 2017. The blockchain ledger can match all kinds of educational information with the user's unique ID. It includes learning behavior in class, micro academic project experience, and macro educational background, etc.

INNOVATIVE EDUCATIONAL APPLICATIONS USING BLOCKCHAIN

Blockchain technology can be applied to education in many innovative ways beyond just diploma management and achievements assessment. For both learners and teachers, blockchain technology has a great potential for broader application prospects on formative evaluation, learning activities design and implementation, and keep tracking the whole learning processes. Some innovative applications of using blockchain technology in the field of education are proposed as follows:

1. **Motivating slow and poor learners:** There are still some negative subjective or objective factors causing poor learning outcomes, such as the lack of motivation and financial pressure (Baporikar, 2020). Due to the trait of currency property, blockchain can be used to motivate students by implementing "learning is earning" (Sharples and Domingue 2016). The smart contract between teachers and students can be applied to the educational scenario. Real-time awards can be given to students through some simple clicks by the instructors. Students will get a certain number of digital currencies according to smart contract as rewards. This kind of money can be stored in the education wallet, used as tuition, even exchanged with real currencies.
2. **Student Evaluation:** A problematic issue in the education system though formative assessment has been advocated for a long time, and yet it is still

not ripe because it is not easy to track every detail of teaching and learning (Baporikar, 2014). Applying blockchain and smart contract can cope up with this challenge. Notably, the immutability, traceability, and reliability of blockchain mean that the data recorded on blockchain are more specific, authentic, and anti-theft. Take the "collaborative learning" for instance, which is regarded as an excellent way to carry out constructivism instruction and cultivate students' ability to work with others. However, it is often accompanied by the problem of free-riding hindering fair evaluation (Baporikar, 2018). Blockchain technology can mitigate this phenomenon. Each student submits his/her work to the learning platform through his/her unique account, the smart contract running on it will review student's performance, and the results will be recorded into blocks. All behaviors during collaboration will be saved into blocks as evidence for evaluation as well. Moreover, public blockchain has the trait of decentralization. It means that the distributed ledger ensures the consistency of most nodes. Thus, as nodes in blockchain network, students' opinions would be taken into consideration when assessing them. In this context, blockchain ensures the fairness of the evaluation.

3. **Faculty Evaluation:** From the perspective of faculty, the instruction is sophisticated and artistic hence, it is difficult to evaluate. The traditional method based on students' feedback tends to be one-sidedness, lacking subjectivity and is hardly helpful for teachers' improvement (Baporikar, 2015a). A new assessment system can be constructed based on blockchain network and smart contract. First, teachers need to submit preplanned instructional activities as a smart contract to the schools. During the teaching process, all teaching activities will be recorded in the blockchain network. The smart contract will verify the consistency of the teaching design and practice, which is going to be an important instruction evaluation indicator. What's more, a smart contract between teachers and schools, as well as the one between teachers and students can be verified and supplemented with each other. Teachers who meet the standards will get digital currency as a reward. It serves as both an appreciation and encouragement for teachers' teaching skills.
4. **Student Development:** For student development, supervisor or academic advisor is directly responsible for the supervision of the student's program. They have the responsibilities of assisting the student in planning study programs and staying informed of student's research activities and progress (Baporikar, 2014; 2015b). However, in practice, these issues are not checked and supervised, so it will be controversial to distinguish the responsibilities if something negative happens in the future. This situation will be changed if smart contract and blockchain technology is used in this area. All details should be monitored by smart contract platform and recorded into blockchain

ledger. Such as how many times has the supervisor discussed with students in the past semester? How many times has the supervisor reviewed the thesis both in draft and final form? Whether they provide appropriate guidance to the students in course selection and research design? Thanks to the traceability and immutability of blockchain technology, both students and supervisors' behaviors will be recorded in the blockchain ledger.

These innovative applications can protect the interests of both parties. Overall, blockchain can be used to construct a balance to measure learning process and outcomes. It is a reliable and an equal proof of value for everyone. Theoretically, blockchain can solve the problems of information asymmetry and trust among strangers because of its decentralization and immutability. It ensures the authenticity because the information and value are published and maintained collectively. It provides a trustworthy way for talent investment.

TEN MISCONCEPTIONS ABOUT BLOCKCHAIN

1. Blockchain is like the Internet – you need to build a network infrastructure around the country or in a state – so that everyone can use that infrastructure to do their e-governance and other applications.
2. Blockchain is secure.
3. Cryptography guarantees Blockchain data integrity.
4. Government must design a blockchain on its own and force every government organization to use its implementation of blockchain.
5. One has to have a government vetted closed source blockchain platform on which to develop e-governance solutions.
6. Blockchain cannot have data-privacy.
7. "Right to forget" in the data privacy law (being tabled in the parliament) is incompatible with blockchain usage.
8. Data localization is not guaranteed if we use off the shelf blockchain.
9. Government must regulate blockchain technology.
10. Blockchain is all about crypto-currency.

POTENTIAL ISSUES OF APPLYING BLOCKCHAIN IN EDUCATION

It is undeniable that there are potential drawbacks of applying blockchain technology in education. As a complex system, some learning behaviors and learning outcomes need to be reviewed by the instructors subjectively such as essays and classroom presentations. It is quite hard to evaluate this kind of learning activities by the pre-programmed smart contract without human intervention. If an educational blockchain system were put into use in schools, all students' educational data would be integrated into blockchain ledgers. The immutability feature of blockchain technology would act as a double-edged sword. It removes the possibility of modifying educational record for legitimate reasons for some students. Furthermore, many technical issues or barriers are not addressed for the blockchain to be used in education. For example, the classic Proof of Work consensus mechanism wastes energy and has a poor performance in terms of number of transactions per second (Vukolić 2015), which would cost an extra expense, and hinder its application in schools.

SOLUTIONS AND RECOMMENDATIONS

Education plays a vital role in human life. Cyber Security is all about who you trust.
So where is your trust anchor?

- Hardware to not leak your cryptographic keys?
- Operating system O/S to not peek into your computation memory?
- Hypervisor to not mess up your process memory?
- Applications to not be control hijacked or attack other applications?

What can go wrong?

- IoT sensor data may be intercepted by a middle man and changed before it reaches the server (data integrity)
- IoT sensors may be stopped and old readings may be replayed (replay attack)
- What the server gets purportedly from factory C, may be manufactured by supplier B (Authenticity)

What can be done?

- Use a message integrity proof (Hashing)
- Use digital signature of the individual IoT devices (Authenticity and non- repudiation); assuming the digital signatures cannot be forged and private keys are kept safe
- Use authentic time stamping with the IoT data before hashing for integrity (avoid replay attacks)

Other Solutions include:

- Having a trusted authority or a cloud provider to become a publish-subscribe service provider
- Every supplier sends their IoT data with message integrity, authentication code etc., to the cloud server where every consumer subscribes to the

events they are interested in on the cloud and every supplier becomes authenticated data generator on the cloud.

- Create a framework on which data is crowd sourced, validated by the crowd for the crowd
- Usability, scalability, platform and algorithm suitability must be taken into account to enhance the utility of Blockchain application in higher education.
- There is also a need to look into societal constraints, cost, privacy, and immutability for better application and adaptability of Blockchain in higher education.
- Compatible digital platforms to safely share and organize data, flexible smart contracts, affordable innovative projects, and privacy/learning issues to all the stakeholders involved in the administrative and learning processes in higher education must be assessed before making the shift from traditional ways to this new technology.
- Essential to find solutions for performance and security related issues, such as interoperability between distinct platforms/algorithms and secure access-control in the light of the potential adoption of smart contracts in higher education.

FUTURE AREAS FOR RESEARCH

Challenges identified by previous research on Blockchain, point out mainly its technical limits (Awaji, Solaiman, & Albshri, 2020) with focus mainly on the need to develop new algorithms and frameworks for implementing Blockchain in higher education. Moreover, Blockchain technology usability is a main limitation in higher education. The technology jargon is relatively new and lacks development. It is noteworthy that Blockchain includes very different specifications that can make it difficult for end users. Furthermore, users should deal with diverse issues that complicate security, such as primary keys and public keys (Palma, Vigil, Pereira, & Martina, 2019). Hence, Blockchain usability should be improved through new design interfaces that are more responsive to users, while training in its use should be delivered to professors, students, and staff (Hidrogo, Zambrano, Hernandez-de-Menendez, & Morales-Menendez, 2020), as the majority of the academic community is unaware of this technology (Bedi, Gole, Dhiman, & Gupta, 2020).

Therefore, further studies on Blockchain usability are required. These include, the need to develop an integrated model and ensuing value chain, from the moment students enter higher education to the moment they get their diplomas or n how to make the application more efficient in connecting platforms, methods and approaches to ensure decentralization and development of a prospective ecosystem among distinct software or universal standard file formats which will have the potential to evolve into a united, simplified and globally ubiquitous higher education credit and grading system through novel Blockchain platforms able to augment its ensuing scalability and usability.

Research to ward away societal constraints such as the lack of enthusiasm around Blockchain with regard to the ethical and secure use of data may constitute a substantial challenge that may hinder the adoption of Blockchain by HEIs. On the one hand, it is difficult to persuade education actors to implement Blockchain systems because of its novelty, which could be mitigated through appropriate research on how to train and the development of usable Blockchain-applications. Moreover, Blockchain reduces university administrative staff-related expenses and therefore, university administrations may resist its implementation. On the other hand, the extensive adoption of Blockchain systems requires political support amidst a context of indistinct legal status when it comes to deciding, for example, the Blockchain versions for governance decentralization. In so doing, both the will to adopt the platform and the legal mechanisms to support it play important roles in terms of its successful deployment. For example, some scholars posit that the wide use of Blockchain for IP commercialization purposes and the increasing number of conflicts related to the inclusion of IP objects in various registries require prompt progress on mitigating its legal risks. In this way, further studies in terms of legal frameworks on Blockchain transactions become crucial. Research is also needed in the delivering of a more user-friendly and efficient platform that effectively integrates into the existent credential verification ecosystem and optimizes on costs involved in Blockchain transactions, because dealing with large amounts of academic data on the platform may increase costs. It is also important to consider designing, implementing systems and platforms on how data can be securely accessed and used while maintaining privacy. Hence, further research should add greater emphasis on accurate mechanism of learning logs and ensuing privacy measures are needed to build standardized formats for permissions on the Blockchain.

CONCLUSION

This study aimed to understand the extent of Blockchain implications and utility in the higher education field. Blockchain is essentially a distributed ledger technology, which uses the cryptograph techniques and distributed consensus algorithms to create the features of decentralization, traceability, immutability, and currency properties. Its currency properties have the potential to trigger many innovative applications for education as discussed above. The discussion and the findings are used to sum up existing knowledge on Blockchain application in the distinct domain of higher education and summarize current thematic trends of academic work in this issue. The principal and emergent insights and challenges comprehend compatible digital platforms to safely share and organize data, flexible smart contracts, affordable innovative projects, and privacy/learning issues to all the stakeholders involved in the administrative and learning processes in higher education. Furthermore, researchers should adopt a holistic perspective of Blockchain deployment in order to build legally and culturally compliant ecosystems, because culture is central when it comes to develop customized and collaborative higher education solutions. To sum up, our contribution is a systematic review of the Blockchain implications and utility in higher education, together with its main challenges, opportunities and innovative applications in higher education. We hope these insights will assist researchers in understanding the main areas of research and identify further research paths.

To conclude, bringing a revolutionary change in is possible in HEIs by streamlining record keeping, enhancing transparency and security, supporting the hiring processes of the organizations, and providing the ownership of the academic records to the students. Blockchain is proving to be extremely beneficial in the education sector. It allows educational institutions to secure the data of their students. They are able to take ownership of their credentials, awards, certificates, and academic identity. It builds trust and transparency between educators, management, and learners.

Blockchain application in higher education no doubt, holds a great future **as** the technological advancements in the education sector will completely change the way courses are taken up and consumed by learners. Blockchain disruption in educational technology will automate the course progression and learning path of the learners with the help of smart contracts developed on blocks providing complete control to the learners. Being cognizant of the fact that blockchain in higher education, currently, is at an infancy stage, yet there is optimism that innovative solutions can help to fill the gaps that exist in the education sector in general and. higher education sector in particular.

REFERENCES

Awaji, B., Solaiman, E., & Albshri, A. (2020, July). Blockchain-based applications in higher education: A systematic mapping study. In *Proceedings of the 5th international conference on information and education innovations* (pp. 96-104). ACM. 10.1145/3411681.3411688

Baporikar, N. (2014). *Handbook of Research on Higher Education in the MENA Region: Policy and Practice*. IGI Global. doi:10.4018/978-1-4666-6198-1

Baporikar, N. (2015). Strategies for Promoting Research Culture to Support Knowledge Society. [IJICTHD]. *International Journal of Information Communication Technologies and Human Development*, *7*(4), 58–72. doi:10.4018/IJICTHD.2015100104

Baporikar, N. (2015a). Understanding Professional Development for Educators. [IJSEM]. *International Journal of Sustainable Economies Management*, *4*(4), 18–30. doi:10.4018/IJSEM.2015100102

Baporikar, N. (2016a). Academic Entrepreneurship for Scaling Innovation. [IJEEI]. *International Journal of E-Entrepreneurship and Innovation*, *6*(2), 21–39. doi:10.4018/IJEEI.2016070102

Baporikar, N. (2016b). Stakeholder Approach for Quality Higher Education. In W. Nuninger & J. Châtelet (Eds.), *Handbook of Research on Quality Assurance and Value Management in Higher Education* (pp. 1–26). Information Science Reference. doi:10.4018/978-1-5225-0024-7.ch001

Baporikar, N. (2016c). Technology Integration and Innovation during Reflective Teaching. [IJICTE]. *International Journal of Information and Communication Technology Education*, *12*(2), 14–22. doi:10.4018/IJICTE.2016040102

Baporikar, N. (2017a). Imperatives in Leading Institutions of Higher Learning: Focus B-School. [IJTEM]. *International Journal of Technology and Educational Marketing*, *7*(1), 38–51. doi:10.4018/IJTEM.2017010104

Baporikar, N. (2017b). Fundamentals of Higher Education - Fresh Vision (pp. 1-304). Himalaya Publishing House, Mumbai, India.

Baporikar, N. (2018). Improving Communication by Linking Student Centred Pedagogy and Management Curriculum Development. In N. P. Ololube (Ed.), *Encyclopaedia of Institutional Leadership, Policy and Management* (pp. 369–386). Pearl Publications.

Baporikar, N. (2019a). Preventing Academic Misconduct: Student-Centered Teaching Strategies. In D. Velliaris (Ed.), *Prevention and Detection of Academic Misconduct in Higher Education* (pp. 98–115). IGI Global. doi:10.4018/978-1-5225-7531-3.ch005

Baporikar, N. (2019b). Student Centered Strategies for Quality International Education. In B. Dutta & P. Chaudhuri (Eds.), Internationalization of Higher Education: Opportunities and Challenges (pp. 21-35). MTC Global: India.

Baporikar, N. (2019c). E-Learning Strategies for Emerging Economies in the Knowledge Era. In J. Pelet (Ed.), *Advanced Web Applications and Progressing E-Learning 2.0 Technologies in Higher Education* (pp. 150–171). IGI Global. doi:10.4018/978-1-5225-7435-4.ch008

Baporikar, N. (2020). Finer Student Engagement via Quality and Lifelong Learning for Sustainable Education. [IJPAE]. *International Journal of Political Activism and Engagement*, *7*(4), 38–55. doi:10.4018/IJPAE.2020100104

Baporikar, N. (2021). Relook at University Planning-Development for Sustainability in Higher Education. [IJESGT]. *International Journal of Environmental Sustainability and Green Technologies*, *12*(2), 13–28. doi:10.4018/IJESGT.2021070102

Baporikar, N. (2022). Entrepreneurial University Challenges and Critical Success Factors to Thrive. [IJAMTR]. *International Journal of Applied Management Theory and Research*, *4*(1), 1–15. doi:10.4018/IJAMTR.300347

Baporikar, N., & Sony, M. (2020). *Quality Management Principles and Policies in Higher Education*. IGI Global. doi:10.4018/978-1-7998-1017-9

Bedi, P., Gole, P., Dhiman, S., & Gupta, N. (2020). Smart contract based central sector scheme of scholarship for college and university students. *Procedia Computer Science*, *171*, 790–799. doi:10.1016/j.procs.2020.04.086

Hidrogo, I., Zambrano, D., Hernandez-de-Menendez, M., & Morales-Menendez, R. (2020). Mostla for engineering education: Part 1 initial results. [IJIDeM]. *International Journal on Interactive Design and Manufacturing*, *14*(4), 1429–1441. doi:10.100712008-020-00730-4

Hoy, M. B. (2017). An introduction to the blockchain and its implications for libraries and medicine. *Medical Reference Services Quarterly*, *36*(3), 273–279. doi:10.1080/02763869.2017.1332261 PMID:28714815

Kosba, A., Miller, A., Shi, E., Wen, Z., & Papamanthou, C. (2016). *Hawk: The Blockchain Model of Cryptography and*. IEEE Computer Society.

Palma, L. M., Vigil, M. A., Pereira, F. L., & Martina, J. E. (2019). Blockchain and smart contracts for higher education registry in Brazil. *International Journal of Network Management*, *29*(3), e2061. doi:10.1002/nem.2061

Sharples, M., & Domingue, J. (2016). The blockchain and kudos: A distributed system for educational record, reputation and reward. In Adaptive and Adaptable Learning: 11th European Conference on Technology Enhanced Learning. Springer.

Skiba, D. J. (2017). The potential of blockchain in education and health care. *Nursing Education Perspectives*, *38*(4), 220–221. doi:10.1097/01.NEP.0000000000000190 PMID:28622267

Tschorsch, F., & Scheuermann, B. (2016). Bitcoin and beyond: A technical survey on decentralized digital currencies. *IEEE Communications Surveys and Tutorials*, *18*(3), 2084–2123. doi:10.1109/COMST.2016.2535718

Underwood, S. (2016). Blockchain beyond bitcoin. *Communications of the ACM*, *59*(11), 15–17. doi:10.1145/2994581

Vukolić, M. (2016). The quest for scalable blockchain fabric: Proof-of-work vs. BFT replication. In *Open Problems in Network Security: IFIP WG 11.4 International Workshop, iNetSec 2015, Zurich, Switzerland, October 29, 2015, Revised Selected Papers* (pp. 112-125). Springer International Publishing.

Wang, H., Chen, K., & Xu, D. (2016). A maturity model for blockchain adoption. *Financial Innovation*, *2*(1), 1–5. doi:10.118640854-016-0031-z

Yli-Huumo, J., Ko, D., Choi, S., Park, S., & Smolander, K. (2016). Where is current research on blockchain technology?—A systematic review. *PLoS One*, *11*(10), e0163477. doi:10.1371/journal.pone.0163477 PMID:27695049

KEY TERMS AND DEFINITIONS

Accountability in Higher Education: The fact or condition of being accountable. It is an obligation to accept responsibility. A management, for example, needs to care about using public money to the best possible advantage for students who come to a university for an education. The management should also be accountable to students and teachers.

Database: A set of data structured to support the storage, retrieval, and analysis of information, often custom-designed for specific business applications. Databases are central to information processing since they allow new and more efficient ways of assembling records and organizing work for better decision-making.

Education: The process of formal knowledge giving process. The actions in process of imparting for acquiring general knowledge, developing the powers of reasoning and judgment, especially at schools, generally for preparing oneself or others for mature life.

E-Learning: Electronic learning (or e-Learning or eLearning) is a type of education where the medium of instruction is computer technology. In some instances, no in-person interaction takes place. It can be defined as a planned teaching/learning experience that uses a wide spectrum of technologies, mainly internet or computer-based, to reach learners.

Higher Education: The act or process of imparting and acquiring knowledge, developing the powers of reasoning and judgment, the act and practice of imparting knowledge, especially at college, or university, the theory of teaching and learning generally of preparing oneself or others intellectually for mature life.

Impact: To have effect on, effect of coming into contact with a thing or person; the force exerted by a new idea, concept, technology, or ideology, the impression made by an idea, cultural movement, social group, it is to drive or press (an object) firmly into (another object, thing, etc.) so as to have an impact or strong effect (on).

Information Technology (IT): The umbrella term that encompasses the entire field of computer-based information processing: computer equipment, applications, and services, telecommunication links and networks, digital databases, and the integrated technical specifications that enable these systems to function interactively. IT is study or use of systems (especially computers and telecommunications) for storing, retrieving, and sending information.

INTERNET: A global computer network providing a variety of information and communication facilities, consisting of interconnected networks using standardized communication protocols; it denotes a computer network connecting two or more smaller networks.

Learning Management Systems: "Learning Management" is the capacity to design pedagogic strategies that achieve learning outcomes in students, where the emphasis is placed on student learning rather than instructor preparation. A learning management system (LMS) is a software application or Web-based technology used to plan, implement, and assess a specific learning process.

Stakeholder: A person with an interest or concern in something, especially in an organization or institution. Stakeholder is a member of a type of organization or system in which as a member or participant seen as having an interest in its success.

Student: Pupil, a person formally engaged in learning, especially one enrolled in a school or college; any person who studies, investigates, or examines thoughtfully.

Teaching: To impart knowledge or skill; give instruction, inform, enlighten, discipline, drill, school, indoctrinate; coach to help to learn.

Technology: The branch of knowledge that deals with the creation and use of technical means and their interrelation with life, society, and the environment, drawing upon such subjects as industrial arts, engineering, applied science, and pure science; method for convening resources into goods and services.

Chapter 5
Blockchain Revolution in Education

Shankar Subramanian Subramanian
https://orcid.org/0000-0003-0598-9543
S.P. Jain School of Global Management, Dubai, UAE

Amritha Subhayan Krishnan
Westford University College, Sharjah, UAE

Arumugam Seetharaman
S.P. Jain School of Global Management, Singapore

ABSTRACT

Blockchain technology has the potential to revolutionize higher education by enabling the secure and efficient sharing of academic records, digital credentials, and other important information. This chapter explores the potential of blockchain technology to transform higher education by examining its key features, benefits, and challenges. It also discusses several use cases of blockchain in higher education, such as student records management, digital credentialing, enabling micro-credentials and digital badges, and learning analytics. The study concludes by highlighting the opportunities, limitations, and future directions of blockchain technology in higher education. The chapter will propose future trends and the way forward for the revolution to advent. The major stakeholders will be explored: Learners, teachers, government, top education management, UNDP, technocrats, and major corporates involvement and consensus. Expert opinion is consolidated to suggest the blockchain education framework.

DOI: 10.4018/979-8-3693-0405-1.ch005

INTRODUCTION

The Higher Education sector is currently experiencing a significant transformation due to advancements in technology. One such innovative technology that has the potential to revolutionize learning and credential verification is blockchain technology (Oke et al., 2020; Mohanta et al., 2019). Blockchain, being a decentralized and distributed ledger system, creates a secure and unalterable record of transactions. This record can be shared and verified by multiple parties without the need for intermediaries. The impact of blockchain technology has already been observed in various industries, and now it is set to make its mark on the Higher Education sector (Alammary et al., 2019).

The potential of blockchain in Higher Education is vast. It can provide secure and transparent records of academic achievements and credentials. Additionally, it enables the implementation of micro-credentials and digital badges, facilitates the creation of decentralized learning platforms, and promotes the sharing of educational resources. One significant issue that blockchain can address is credential fraud and the prevalence of fake degrees (Cheng et al., 2020).

However, there are challenges and limitations to implementing blockchain in education. Technical, social, and legal barriers need to be overcome to fully utilize the capabilities of blockchain technology (Alam et al., 2020). Several use cases of blockchain technology in Higher Educationalready exist. Platforms like Learning Machine, Sony Global Education's Higher Education Infrastructure, ODEM, the University of Bahrain's degree verification platform, and Parchment have successfully demonstrated how blockchain can provide learners with secure and tamper-proof methods of verifying their academic achievements (Alshahrani et al., 2021). Various successful use cases of blockchain technology in Higher Educationalready exist, showcasing its potential in revolutionizing the way academic achievements are verified.

Blockchain applications in Higher Education have shown varying levels of success, with some being widely adopted while others are still in the early stages of development. To fully harness the potential of blockchain in education, more research and development are needed to overcome technical, social, and legal challenges (Aisyah et al., 2022); (Alsobhi et al., 2023). However, the benefits of blockchain technology in Higher Education are vast. It provides a secure and transparent system for storing and sharing data, addressing security and privacy concerns. The use of encryption algorithms ensures data integrity and makes it difficult for unauthorized users to access or modify data (Carmichael et al., 2023); (Vaigandla et al., 2023) . The decentralized nature of blockchain eliminates the risk of cyberattacks on centralized databases (Steiu, 2020). Smart contracts automate verification processes and can be used to award degrees and certificates, reducing time and costs. Blockchain can securely store academic records, facilitate collaborative research, and track donations and funding (Mikroyannidis et al., 2020). Standardization and interoperability are crucial for seamless data sharing across different blockchain applications (Satybaldy et al., 2022). They enhance efficiency, transparency, and accessibility in higher education. Blockchain technology also plays a vital role in lifelong learning and continuous professional development. It enables individuals to store and share secure digital credentials, including micro-credentials, and facilitates personalized learning experiences. Implementing blockchain in Higher Education comes with challenges such as technical infrastructure requirements, integration with existing systems, governance, and regulatory issues, and ensuring adoption and trust. Institutions need to carefully consider these challenges and develop strategies to successfully implement blockchain technology in their operations (Prewett et al., 2020).

Implementing blockchain in higher education can bring numerous benefits, such as enhanced data security, improved credential verification, and increased transparency. However, there are a few reasons why its widespread adoption has not happened yet. Blockchain technology is complex and requires technical expertise to implement and maintain. Many educational institutions lack the necessary resources and expertise to develop and manage blockchain solutions. Implementing blockchain requires a significant shift in the existing systems and processes. Resistance to change, bureaucracy, and institutional inertia can hinder the adoption of new technologies, including blockchain. Higher education institutions operate independently, and implementing blockchain on a large scale would require collaboration and standardization across institutions. Achieving interoperability among different systems and platforms is a significant challenge (Grech et al., 2021). The legal framework around blockchain and data privacy needs to be addressed before widespread adoption can occur. Institutions must ensure compliance with relevant laws and regulations to protect student data and privacy. Implementing blockchain systems can be costly, requiring investment in infrastructure, resources, and training. Limited budgets and competing priorities may hinder the adoption of blockchain technology in higher education. Despite these challenges, some institutions are exploring the potential of blockchain in higher education. Initiatives are underway to develop blockchain-based student credentials, secure student data, and streamline administrative processes. As technology evolves and awareness increases, the adoption of blockchain in higher education is likely to grow (Kosasi et al., 2022).

Several strategies have been attempted to implement blockchain in higher education, but they have faced challenges and limitations. Some institutions have explored the use of blockchain to issue and verify digital credentials, such as degrees and certifications. However, the adoption has been slow due to the need for standardization and interoperability across institutions. Additionally, the lack of awareness and trust in blockchain technology has hindered its widespread use. Blockchain can provide a secure and decentralized platform for managing student data. However, implementing this strategy requires a significant investment in infrastructure and integration with existing systems. The complexity and cost associated with transitioning to blockchain-based data management have been barriers to its implementation. Blockchain has the potential to streamline the verification of academic records, making the process more efficient and reliable. However, the challenge lies in ensuring that all institutions adopt and maintain compatible blockchain systems (Mecozzi et al., 2022). The lack of standardization and collaboration among educational institutions has hindered the successful implementation of this strategy. Blockchain can provide a platform for issuing, storing, and verifying micro-credentials, which can support lifelong learning and skill development. However, the fragmented nature of the higher education ecosystem and the lack of a unified framework for recognizing and accepting micro-credentials have limited the adoption of this strategy. The failure of these strategies can be attributed to various factors, including the complexity of blockchain technology, resistance to change within institutions, interoperability challenges, legal and regulatory concerns, and limited resources and expertise. Overcoming these barriers requires collaboration, standardization, awareness, and investment in infrastructure and training. It is important to note that while some strategies may have faced challenges, there are ongoing efforts to address these issues and explore new avenues for implementing blockchain in higher education. As technology matures and the benefits become more apparent, further progress in the adoption of blockchain in the education sector can be expected (Xi et al., 2022).

RESEARCH SCOPE

The research will investigate the potential of blockchain technology to revolutionize the Higher Education system. The study will focus on the various applications of blockchain technology in higher education, such as personalized curriculums, accreditation approval, delivery of education, assessment of skills, teacher course materials, and instruction language. The research will also explore the challenges that blockchain technology faces in the Higher Education sector and the strategies that can be adopted to overcome these challenges.

RESEARCH QUESTIONS

1. What are the potential applications and benefits of blockchain technology in the Higher Education system?

2. What are the challenges that blockchain technology faces in the Higher Education sector?
3. What strategies can be adopted to effectively implement blockchain technology in education?

RESEARCH OBJECTIVES

1. To assess the potential applications and benefits of blockchain technology in education.
2. To analyze the challenges that blockchain technology faces in the Higher Education sector.
3. To develop strategies to effectively implement blockchain technology in Higher Education

LITERATURE SURVEY

The Interface between the Higher Education model, the Higher Education stakeholders and the Blockchain technology features has been portrayed well in the figure below (Iyer, 2022). The figure summarizes the various aspects of the Blockchain technology in education. Higher education is facing turmoil due to the various disruptions like COVID, digital transformations, lack of employment opportunities, recession, and lack of trust in the education system. The USA and European markets are seen students and parents opting for the shorter courses due to lack of funds, lack of employment opportunities and market conditions. The recent McKinsey report quotes 33% on an average shift from the normal University course to short courses. The need for having a framework to have student portfolios with registering the micro credentials is the need of the hour (Iyer, 2020).

Blockchain technology has the potential to revolutionize Higher Education by providing improved security, authentication, trust, decentralized ledgers, transparency, and archiving. It offers robust security features, protecting sensitive student data from unauthorized access and tampering. Blockchain can verify the identity of students, faculty, and stakeholders securely. It builds trust through a decentralized ledger, reducing the risk of data breaches and ensuring data accuracy. This can help reduce the risk of data breaches and ensure that data is available to all parties in a transparent and secure manner (Yaqoob et al., 2021). By leveraging these features, educational institutions can improve the security and integrity of their data, build trust with stakeholders, and provide a more transparent and efficient Higher Education system (Ayub Khan et al., 2021). Blockchain enables transparency in accessing

Figure 1. Research Framework showing the Interface between Blockchain Technology, New Education Model, and Stakeholders
Borrowed from Iyer, 2022.

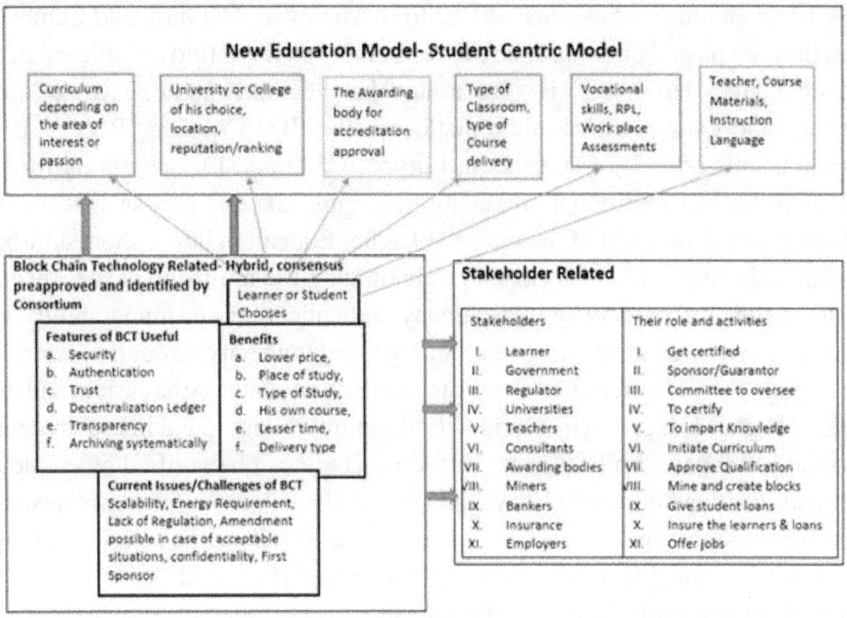

academic records and credentials, preventing fraud, and maintaining accurate records for accreditation (Merlec et al., 2022). It addresses various Higher Education needs, including personalized curriculums, accreditation approval, Higher Education delivery, skills assessment, and short courses (Cahyadi et al., 2021). It can also handle short courses by issuing and verifying certificates, facilitating payments, and creating decentralized learning platforms (Tsai et al., 2022). Collaboration among stakeholders is necessary to leverage blockchain's benefits fully.

The Stakeholders Theory portrays a framework for considering the interests of all parties involved and ensuring fairness and equity in implementation. Blockchain technology aligns with the future shift toward short skill-based professional courses, offering security, transparency, and longevity of data storage. It facilitates verifiable certifications and credentials, enhancing employment prospects and further education. The Stakeholders Theory guides decision-making and ensures the consideration of all stakeholders in the implementation process (Tan et al., 2023). Stakeholder Theory is appropriate to apply for this implementation initiative of the BCT in higher education. The stakeholder needs to have secure data portfolio can pressure the regulators and governments to adopt this technology as the future seems to shift towards short courses and micro credentials and which need to be recorded and produced securely and authentically (Han et al., 2023).

The study aims to address the challenges posed by the dilution of brand names of well-known universities, such as Stanford, Michigan, Harvard, and Cambridge, when they are placed on a common platform. It proposes to find a viable solution to these challenges. However, it is worth noting that these universities have also started offering short courses on common platforms like IBM Coursera. Recent surveys indicate a shift of 18% of students in Europe, USA, and Europe opting for short courses instead of traditional university programs. Experts predict that this shift will surpass 60% by 2030. If the future of Higher Education lies in short skill-based professional courses, then Blockchain technology is the most suitable option due to its inherent features of security, transparency, authentication, and immutability. It also offers tokenization, tamper-proof data storage, and longevity through decentralized folders and smart contracts. Blockchain technology can cater to the current and future needs of Higher Education by storing certifications, badges, and micro-credentials in a secure manner within student portfolios. These can be verified by employers, administrators, and educationists to enhance students' employment prospects and further education. The process is cost-effective, efficient, and secure, allowing authorized personnel to verify certifications (Hoyos et al., 2023).

The Research study identified the gaps as recommended by earlier researchers to arrive at conceptual model using the Stakeholders theory and formulating the Hypotheses. The gap variables identified and forming the basis of the conceptual model need to be understood and their significance on the implementation of BCT in Higher education explored further.

The student-centric shift in Higher Education emphasizes placing students at the center of their learning experience. Blockchain technology can support this shift by providing a decentralized and transparent platform that allows students to have more control over their educational records and achievements. With blockchain, students can securely store and manage their academic credentials, certifications, and achievements, ensuring that they have ownership and control over their educational data. Customized curriculum and delivery refer to tailoring educational content and learning experiences to meet the unique needs and preferences of individual students. Blockchain can enable a more personalized and adaptive learning environment by securely tracking and recording individual learning paths, preferences, and progress (Kabashi et al., 2023). This information can be used to create personalized learning plans and recommendations, enhancing the overall educational experience. Preferred awards/certificates and student portfolios are important elements in showcasing a student's achievements and skills. Blockchain provides a tamper-proof and verifiable record of these accomplishments, eliminating the need for traditional paper-based certificates. By using blockchain, educational institutions can issue digital certificates and awards that are securely stored on the blockchain, making it easier for employers, universities, and other institutions to validate and verify a student's qualifications and skills. Overall, the student factors mentioned can greatly benefit from blockchain implementation in education. Blockchain technology provides a secure, transparent, and decentralized platform that empowers students to have greater control over their educational journey, personalizes their learning experiences, and ensures the integrity of their achievements and credentials (Eliwa et al., 2023).

Educators play a significant role in shaping the brand image of educational institutions. By embracing blockchain, institutions can showcase their commitment to innovation and technology adoption, thereby enhancing their brand image. Student payments are another crucial factor. Blockchain can streamline and secure payment processes, making transactions more efficient and transparent. By implementing blockchain-based payment systems, institutions can provide students with a seamless payment experience, thereby improving overall satisfaction. Standardized courses are essential for maintaining quality and consistency across educational institutions. Blockchain technology can facilitate the creation and sharing of standardized course materials, ensuring that students receive the same level of education regardless of the institution they attend. This promotes fairness and equal opportunities for all students. Student employability is a key consideration for higher education institutions (Jackson et al., 2023). Blockchain can help establish a reliable and tamper-proof record of students' academic achievements, certifications, and skills. This verified and immutable record can enhance students' employability by providing potential employers with a trustworthy verification of their qualifications. Authentication and data security are crucial aspects of implementing blockchain in higher education. Blockchain's decentralized and cryptographically secure nature ensures that student records and sensitive data are protected from unauthorized access and tampering. This strengthens the overall security and integrity of educational systems. Data privacy is another significant concern. Blockchain technology allows for selective data sharing, where students have control over who can access their personal information. This empowers students to maintain their privacy while still benefiting from the advantages of a decentralized and transparent system. By embracing blockchain technology, educational institutions can enhance their reputation, improve payment processes, ensure standardized education, boost student employability, strengthen data security, and respect student privacy (Guustaaf et al., 2021).

Employers play a crucial role in shaping the implementation of blockchain technology in higher education. Employers often face challenges when it comes to verifying the authenticity of student records and qualifications. By implementing blockchain, educational institutions can provide a tamper-proof and transparent record of students' academic achievements. This makes the verification process easier and more reliable for employers, saving them time and effort. Blockchain technology enables the creation of secure and verifiable digital certificates. Employers can rely on these certificates, as they are stored on a decentralized and immutable ledger, ensuring their validity. This enhances trust between employers and educational institutions, making the hiring process more efficient and reliable. Employers are interested in hiring candidates with the necessary skills and competencies. Blockchain can facilitate the recording and verification of students' competencies, such as project work, internships, and extracurricular activities (Chatterjee et al., 2023). This allows employers to assess candidates' abilities more accurately and match them with suitable job roles. Blockchain implementation in higher education can attract students who are interested in emerging technologies. This, in turn, creates a pool of talent that employers can tap into for their specific needs. By offering blockchain-related courses and programs, educational institutions can help meet the demand for skilled professionals in this field. Traditional recruitment processes can be time-consuming and expensive for employers. Blockchain can streamline and automate certain aspects of recruitment, such as verifying credentials and conducting background checks. This reduces costs for employers, making the hiring process more affordable and efficient. Time is a valuable resource for employers, and they often seek ways to expedite the recruitment process. Blockchain-based systems can accelerate the verification and validation of student records, certifications, and competencies. This helps employers make faster and more informed hiring decisions, reducing the time required to fill job positions. The cost of recruitment can be a significant factor for employers, especially for large organizations. Implementing blockchain technology can reduce costs associated with manual record-keeping, verification processes, and third-party background checks. This cost-effectiveness makes blockchain implementation an attractive proposition for employers. By leveraging blockchain technology, educational institutions can address employers' needs for reliable and efficient verification processes, access to skilled talent, and cost-effective recruitment practices (Vhatkar et al., 2023).

Government policies play a crucial role in shaping the implementation of blockchain in higher education. Governments can provide regulatory frameworks that support the use of blockchain technology, ensuring data privacy and security. Additionally, government funding and initiatives can encourage educational institutions to adopt blockchain for various purposes, such as issuing digital credentials or improving administrative processes. Community needs also impact the implementation of blockchain in higher education. If the community demands more transparency, accountability, and trust in educational institutions, blockchain can serve as a technology solution. Blockchain can enable secure and tamper-proof records of academic achievements, facilitate efficient transfer of credits, and enhance the verification of qualifications (Sangiuliano Intra et al., 2023). The United Nations Development Programme (UNDP) goals can also influence the adoption of blockchain in higher education. UNDP promotes sustainable development and aims to leverage technology for social progress. If blockchain aligns with UNDP's agenda by enhancing transparency, reducing fraud, and improving access to education, it can gain support and momentum in implementation. Parent keenness on their children's education can drive the adoption of blockchain in higher education. Parents increasingly value transparency and accountability in educational institutions. Blockchain can provide a decentralized and immutable record of their child's academic achievements, ensuring trust and facilitating the transfer of credentials between institutions. Financial indebtedness can also influence the implementation of blockchain in higher education (Guustaaf et al., 2021). As educational institutions face financial challenges, they may seek cost-effective solutions to streamline administrative processes. Blockchain can help reduce bureaucracy, lower costs, and enhance efficiency, making it an attractive option for adoption. Furthermore, insurance companies can play a role in the implementation of blockchain in higher education. They may see the potential benefits of blockchain in verifying and validating educational credentials, reducing the risk of fraudulent claims. By supporting the adoption of blockchain, insurance companies can enhance the reliability and accuracy of their underwriting processes. In summary, government policies, community needs, UNDP goals, parent keenness on children's education, financial indebtedness, and insurance companies all contribute to the influence on the implementation of blockchain in higher education. These factors collectively shape the environment and incentives for educational institutions to adopt blockchain technology (Haque et al., 2023).

H1: There is a significant relationship between Student Factors and the Blockchain implementation in Higher Education.

H2: There is a significant relationship between Educator Factors and the Blockchain implementation in Higher Education.

H3: The Employer Factors significantly influences the Blockchain implementation in Higher Education

H4: The Blockchain Implementation in Higher Education is significantly influenced by the Other Stakeholders Factors.

METHODOLOGY

In order to understand how blockchain technology can address the needs of the Higher Education sector, a mixed research methodology will be employed. Expert opinions from Higher Education and technology experts will be gathered to provide

Figure 2. Conceptual model
Conceptual model developed by the authors

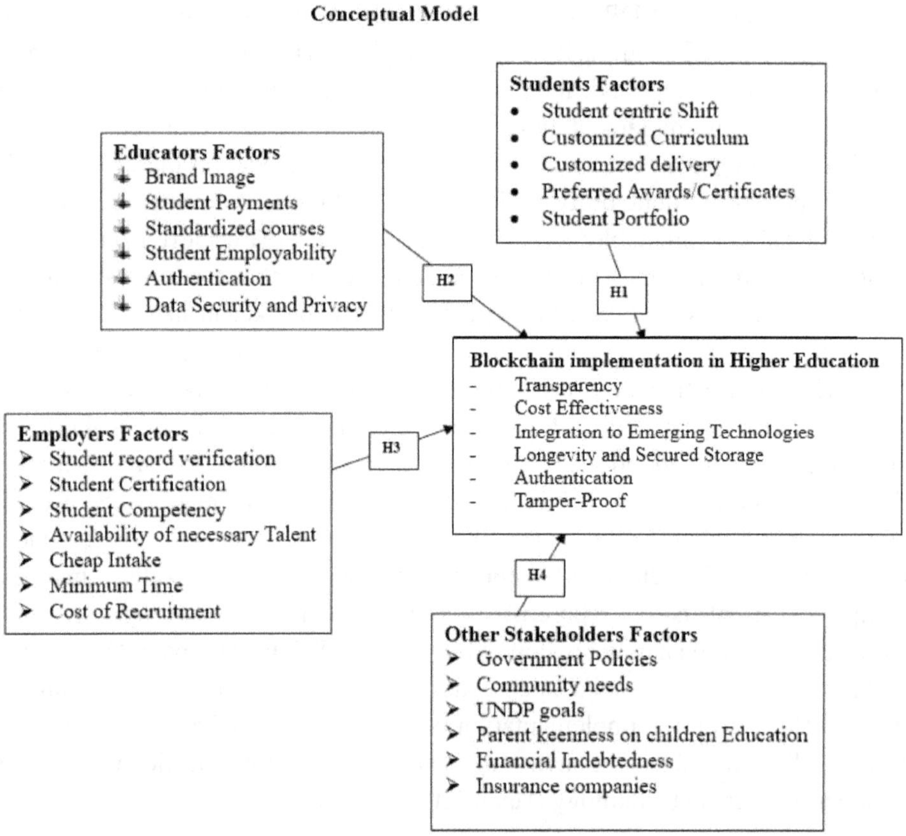

insights into the implementation of blockchain in education. Additionally, the perspectives of stakeholders will be collected through a questionnaire survey to gather their expectations regarding the use of blockchain in Higher Education and how it can benefit all parties involved. Thus, a quantitative survey will be developed through the creation of a questionnaire to collect data on stakeholders' expectations of blockchain in education (Iyer et al., 2021).

DATA COLLECTION

The researchers used a questionnaire to gather primary data from the participants. The questionnaire had closed-ended and open-ended questions that enabled the participants to provide detailed responses. The questionnaire was clear and easy to understand. The researchers also used secondary data from various sources, books, online databases, and research papers, relevant to the topic of research. The secondary data helped them to comprehend the research topic better, identify gaps in the literature, and create a research framework. The combination of primary and secondary data methods enhanced the reliability, validity, and credibility of the research. It also helped them to achieve the research objectives by verifying the primary data collected. The paragraph concludes by stating the use of both secondary and primary data methods to comprehend the research topic and the concepts related to it (Mehralian, 2022).

DATA ANALYSIS

The researcher applied descriptive and inferential statistics to the data from the questionnaire/survey. Descriptive statistics, such as median, mean, mode, and standard deviation, helped to display the data and to comprehend the responses. Inferential statistics, using regression analysis and correlation, helped to explore the relationships among various variables and to evaluate the outcomes significance. The researcher could organize and analyse a large amount of data using the quantitative research technique. However, this technique had some limitations, such as not being able to explain the participants selection of answer options. The research used open-ended questions to enable participants to give more detailed explanations and feedback to overcome any limitations. The paragraph ends by stating that the usefulness of statistical analysis and quantitative research technique to provide a comprehensive data analysis and to make valid inferences from the study results (Iyer, 2020).

SAMPLE SIZE

The researchers collected data from 407 participants from different countries to ensure a diverse and representative sample size. They used a well-designed questionnaire that covered all the relevant aspects of the research topic, with clear and concise questions. They used both qualitative and quantitative research techniques to gain a holistic research topic understanding, with qualitative data providing detailed insights and quantitative data providing statistical analysis. The paragraph concludes by stating that the researchers used an appropriate and effective methodology to achieve the research objectives and obtain valid and reliable results (as shown in Annexure 1) and (as shown in Annexure 2) (Timans et al., 2021).

The stakeholders of higher education Higher education students, teachers, policy makers, parents, employers were involved in the survey as they have the knowledge of the higher education needs and future expectations and the BCT features can satisfy them. The interview sample size has been worked using the same statistical calculator indication more than 15 sample size as expert interviewees. The survey Participants were from India, Malaysia, UAE, Singapore, and other parts of the World like Australia, to get the cross sectional prospective as Blockchain knowledge and implementation knowhow is less. The Interviews of the experts was done using Zoom, Microsoft teams, transcript the recordings and suing thematic analysis to tabulate the findings. The survey sample demographics is given in the statistical report showing the fields, the location, and the knowledge levels of the participants.

Figure 3.

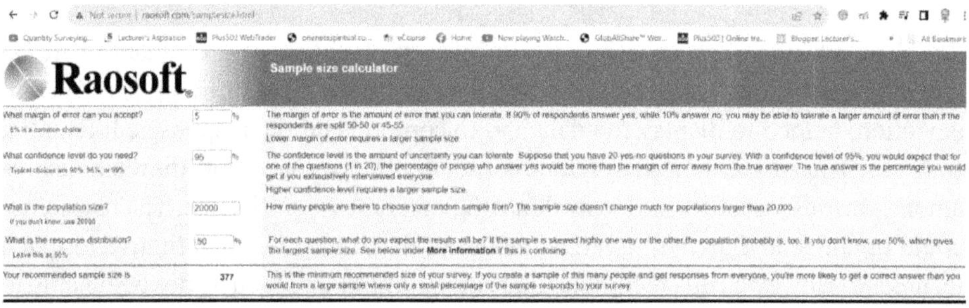

The sample size is calculated statistically using the sample size calculator which indicated > 377.

DATA COLLECTION

The researcher used purposive sampling to collect qualitative data from experts who knew about environmental digital transformation challenges (Marlina et al., 2022). The researcher applied the Fuzzy Delphi Method to ensure the analysis was accurate and impartial. The researcher conducted semi-structured interviews with 16 key informants over two months to learn about current issues in Blockchain implementation in Higher Education(Iyer et al., 2020). The data was valid and reliable because of the purposive sampling, and credible because of the Fuzzy Delphi Method. The researcher considered job specification and gender diversity to get a range of opinions and guaranteed anonymity and privacy to encourage honest responses. The methodology was effective in getting relevant and insightful data from the experts (Yıldırım, 2022); (Hakizimana et al., 2022).

DATA ANALYSIS

The researcher applied thematic analysis to the data from the interviews to discover and examine the main themes and patterns. The researcher transcribed the paper information and replayed the responses to ensure the accuracy of the data. The researcher presented the interview findings using thematic analysis in Table 1 in an effective way. It provided a clear and concise summary of the main themes and sub-themes found in the study. The paragraph ends by stating that the researcher used thematic analysis appropriately and effectively to discover and examine the main patterns and themes in the data from the interviews (Varma et al., 2022).

Table 1. Interview summary

Interviewee Serial no, (Experience in years), Location Designation,	Main Comments on Blockchain Revolution in Higher Education(Other Interviewees in agreement to the comments)
1. (14) Vice President Emerging Technologies, Dubai	- Transparent and Secure Student Records - all student data, including academic achievements, certifications, and transcripts, can be securely stored in a decentralized and immutable manner - BCT ensures that students have complete ownership and control over their records, eliminating the need for intermediaries like traditional transcript providers. - Educators and Employers can easily verify the authenticity of their credentials, reducing fraud and fake qualifications - (Interviewee 5, 9, 14) (Prawiyogi et al., 2021)
2. (12) CEO, Private University London, UK	- Secured Portable Digital Identity is established for individual student - Credentialing and Micro-credentials. - blockchain technology can provide a decentralized platform for issuing and verifying these micro-credentials on short courses - This ensures that student's achievements are recognized and transferable across institutions and allows for a more personalized and flexible learning experience. (Interviewee 4, 7, 11), (Alsobhi et al., 2023).
3. (16), Senior Vice President, Higher Education sector, Singapore	- Smart Contracts for Student Services - Blockchain-based smart contracts can streamline and automate various student services, such as enrollment, financial aid, and course registration. - These smart contracts can be programmed to automatically execute predefined conditions, ensuring efficient and accurate service delivery - Individualized Learning Paths (Interviewee 3, 8, 12) (Khan et al., 2021); (Ayub Khan et al., 2021)
4. (15) CEO, Logistics Company, Fujairah	- Level of customization allows students to have a more tailored educational experience, enhancing their engagement and overall satisfaction. - Competency-Based Education - Blockchain-Verified Credentials - Students can then share their blockchain-verified credentials with potential employers or other educational institutions - Collaboration and Feedback (Interviewee 1, 7, 13) (Alamri et al., 2020).

continued on following page

Table 1. Continued

Interviewee Serial no, (Experience in years), Location Designation,	Main Comments on Blockchain Revolution in Higher Education(Other Interviewees in agreement to the comments)
5. (10) HR Manager Technology sector, Dubai	- Lifelong Learning and Skill Upgrading - Blockchain can support lifelong learning and skill upgrading initiatives. - Blockchain provides a transparent and tamper-proof platform for recording and verifying educational data, credentials, and achievements. - Blockchain transparency builds trust among stakeholders, including students, parents, employers, and the larger community - This enhances the university's brand image as a reputable and trustworthy institution (Interviewee 6, 8, 10), (Chukowry et al., 2021); (Schlesinger et al., 2020).
6. (12) Public sector Administration Manager Singapore	- With blockchain-based credentialing systems, universities can issue digital certificates, degrees, and badges that are stored on the blockchain. - This secure credentialing system enhances the brand image of the university - Universities are centers of knowledge creation and research. Blockchain can help protect the intellectual property generated by faculty and students. - Blockchain can facilitate collaboration and partnerships between universities and other institutions or organizations. (Interviewee 3, 8, 12, 15) (Elsayed, 2023).
7. (6) General Manager Cargo Services Malaysia	- By utilizing blockchain-based platforms, universities can securely share and exchange data, research findings, or educational resources with partners. - This fosters a positive brand image for the university, showcasing its commitment to collaboration, innovation, and knowledge sharing. - By utilizing blockchain-based platforms, universities can maintain a lifelong record of alumni achievements, contributions, and ongoing learning. - This engagement with alumni and the ability to showcase their success. (Interviewee 6, 9,14) (Malik et al., 2023)
8. (8) Head of University IT Operations, Dubai	- Blockchain technology can securely facilitate the payment process for students without the need for intermediaries like banks. - Reduced transaction costs, increased payment transparency, and ensure that students receive their funds promptly. - smart contracts on the blockchain can automate payment releases based on predefined conditions, such as completion of specific milestones or courses. - Blockchain can provide a secure and verifiable way for students to showcase their skills, qualifications, and achievements. This enhances student employability by reducing the risk of counterfeit credentials. (Interviewee 3, 5, 10, 13), (Halkiopoulos et al., 2023)
9. (7) International Consultant, Abu Dhabi	- Implementing blockchain in Higher Education can enable the creation of standardized and interoperable course frameworks. - This ensures consistency and quality across multiple institutions and allows for seamless transfer of credits between different programs or universities. - Awareness is created by Societal pressures, leading to increased focus and investment to gain Competitive advantage. - Students can have greater confidence in the recognition and transferability of their completed courses or degrees. (Interviewee 2, 9, 13) (Perisic et al., 2023)

continued on following page

Table 1. Continued

Interviewee Serial no, (Experience in years), Location Designation,	Main Comments on Blockchain Revolution in Higher Education(Other Interviewees in agreement to the comments)
10. (8) Commercial Manager Airport ITC Services, India	- Higher Education blockchain ensures that student records are stored in a tamper-proof manner. Once data is recorded on the blockchain, it cannot be altered or deleted, providing a trustworthy source of information. - With Higher Education blockchain, students have control over their own data. They can grant access to institutions, employers, or any other relevant parties. - Blockchain technology allows for secure sharing of student data reducing the risk of data breaches. - Higher Education blockchain reduces the risk of data leaks or unauthorized access, promoting privacy, confidentiality, and Fraud Prevention. (Interviewee 2, 7, 9, 11), (Awerika et al., 2023).
11. (6) Vice President, Higher Education Agency, Dubai	- Talent Pool Visibility is enabled by Higher Education blockchain - With the Higher Education blockchain, the recruitment process can be streamlined and made more efficient. - By leveraging the Higher Education blockchain, recruitment costs can be minimized by avoiding intermediaries. - Higher Education blockchain enables the validation and verification of student qualifications in real-time. - Blockchain technology transcends geographical boundaries, allowing employers to reduce Counterfeit Credentials (Interviewee 1, 4, 8, 10, 13), (Dewangan et al., 2023); (Datta et al., 2022).
12. (13) Senior President, Corporate Operations Sharjah	- Higher Education blockchain can provide governments with accurate and reliable data on student enrollment, performance, and qualifications. - This data can help policymakers make informed decisions and develop effective Higher Education policies. - All transactions and changes made to the data are visible to all participants in the network, ensuring transparency and accountability. - Higher Education blockchain eliminates the need for intermediaries, reduces administrative costs and streamlines processes, making Higher Education more cost-effective. (Interviewee 1, 5, 8, 13), (Shakan et al., 2021); (Wylde et al., 2022).
13. (3) Senior Maintenance Director, Singapore	- Higher Education blockchain can enable communities to identify their specific educational needs and gaps. - tailor educational programs to meet the specific needs of a community. This ensures that Higher Education is relevant and responsive to the requirements of the local economy and society. - Higher Education blockchain can easily integrate with other emerging technologies such as artificial intelligence (AI), machine learning (ML), and the Internet of Things (IoT). - Blockchain technology ensures the longevity and permanence of educational records. (Interviewee 2, 7, 10, 14), (Mishra et al., 2022)
14. (4) General Manager Healthcare Group, Malaysia	- The United Nations Development Programme (UNDP) aims to achieve inclusive and quality Higher Education for all. - Higher Education blockchain can facilitate the verification of educational qualifications for insurance purposes. Insurance companies often require proof of Higher Education or certification for certain policies or claims. - Higher Education blockchain uses cryptographic algorithms to secure data and prevent unauthorized access or tampering. - 1000 times scalability possible and unlimited ROI, 10% of Higher Education and that too can be financed, and the Industry is totally involved. (Interviewee 1, 5, 11, 13) (O'Sullivan et al., 2021); (Grima et al., 2020); (Vlk, 2023).

continued on following page

Table 1. Continued

Interviewee Serial no, (Experience in years), Location Designation,	Main Comments on Blockchain Revolution in Higher Education(Other Interviewees in agreement to the comments)
15. (7) Entrepreneur - Sustainability Startup Venture, Delhi, India	- Higher Education blockchain can address the issue of financial indebtedness in Higher Education by promoting transparency and accountability in student loan programs. Blockchain can provide a secure and immutable record of loan disbursements, repayments, and interest rates, reducing the risk of fraud and ensuring fair lending practices. - Tamperproof nature of blockchain ensures the integrity and authenticity of educational records, preventing fraud or manipulation. - Blockchain can help individuals from marginalized communities or disadvantaged backgrounds access educational opportunities and certifications. - Common goal- students to be graduated, same level of all participants is possible, all other sectors can be rallied around this Higher Education activity and in common Blockchain, employment opportunity, Investor, sponsor, (Interviewee 2, 7,11, 15), (Nehru et al., 2023); (Kshetri et al., 2023); (Son-Turan, 2022)
16. (11) Mall ITC Manager, Muscat, Oman	- Higher Education blockchain can increase parents' confidence in the Higher Education system by providing a secure and transparent record of their children's educational journey. Parents can have real-time access to their children's grades, attendance, and achievements, fostering greater involvement and engagement in their education. - Blockchain can also enable parents to easily verify the authenticity of educational institutions and programs, ensuring that their children receive quality education. - Blockchain is the only answer to meet Higher Education needs- Common platform, tokenization to ensure valuation, cheap, cost, indebtedness, future are short courses, and it is shifting and BCT is the only answer, and all other domains can be part of this BCT later (Interviewee 4, 5, 8, 9, 12), (Rahardja et al., 2021)

Source: Developed by the Author

It is interesting to know how blockchain technology can transform Higher Education and why it is important for the Higher Education sector to keep up with technological innovations. The key driver is the Technology involved in creating unique business opportunities, services, and products. The Higher Education sector needs to stay updated on the latest technological developments and actively try out recent technologies to discover their potential benefits. Moreover, the Higher Education sector needs to be aware of the ethical issues related to the use of technology in their activities, ensuring that their use of technology matches their core values. While technology offers great possibilities for education, its use should be done carefully, considering the potential risks and impacts it may have (Chan, 2023).

Questionnaire Survey Demographic Profile

Table 1 shows the demographics of participants of the online survey. A total of 1078 survey questionnaires were distributed to students, parents, policy makers,

Table 2. Demographics of respondents

Demographic Variable	Category	Percentage
Age Group	18-24	13.25
	25-34	23.55
	35-44	27.74
	45-59	27.29
	60+	8.17
Gender	Male	52.47
	Female	47.53

Demographic Variable	Category	Percentage	Demographic Variable	Category	Percentage
Education	Highschool	2.43	Region	India	26.97
	Undergraduate	19.54		UAE	37.60
	Postgraduate	59.34		Malaysia & Singapore	17.28
	Doctoral	18.69		Rest of the World	18.15

Demographic Variable	Category	Percentage	Demographic Variable	Category	Percentage
Knowledge of the Blockchain Implementation in Higher Education?	Extremely familiar- Expert in the field	22.12	Association with Blockchain Technology?	Researcher	22,45
				Student/Learner	17.98
				Working IT Professional	11.24
				Business Owner	9.87
				Project Manager	5.78
				Consultant	8.73
				Government Official	5.05
	Very Familiar working on the Blockchain Implementation in Higher Education	29.34		Regulator	2.24
				Public	5.45
	Somewhat Familiar- only researching and yet to work on BCT in Higher Education	48.54		Trader	3.53
				Miner	3.23
				Others	4.45

IT professional, education professionals and working professionals in UAE, India, Singapore, Malaysia, and several other countries clubbed under the 'rest of the world.' A total of 407 respondents participated in this research survey. (see table 1)

OUTPUT OF ADANCO

Measurement Model Analysis

The study used the values of AVE and the Dijkstra-Henseler's rho coefficient (ρA), as well as discriminant validity analysis, to check the distinctiveness of the constructs. The discriminant validity analysis revealed the correlations within each construct were higher than those between different constructs, confirming excellent discriminant validity. The research uses structural equation modeling (SEM) to test hypotheses and establish the relationships among the constructs (Iyer et al., 2020).

The study used indicator variables and their outer loading values to measure construct validity in PLS path modeling. This is a common and accepted approach. A measure is considered good if its standardized outer loading value is 0.70 or higher. This means that the indicator variable reflects the construct well. The study showed the outer loading values for each indicator variable in Table 3. This made it easy to see and understand the outer loading values. It helped to evaluate construct validity effectively. The paragraph concludes by stating that the study used indicator variables and their outer loading values appropriately and fruitfully. The results revealed that the indicator variables measured their constructs well, as their outer loading values were above 0.7 (Sarstedt et al., 2022).

Table 3. Measurement model analysis

Latent Variables	Convergent Validity		Construct reliability	
	AVE >0.50	ρA reliability >0.70	Pc reliability >0.70	Cronbach's alpha(α) >0.70
Students Factors	0.5654	0.8489	0.8832	0.8839
Educators Factors	0.5340	0.8755	0.8712	0.8759
Employers Factors	0.5623	0.8638	0.8625	0.8653
Other Stakeholders Factors	0.5287	0.8723	0.8694	0.8668
Blockchain implementation in Higher Education Factors	0.5567	0.8647	0.8625	0.8612

Source: ADANCO result, 2023

Table 4. The Discriminant validity (heterotrait-monotrait ratio)

Construct	Students Factors	Educators Factors	Employers Factors	Other Stakeholders Factors	Blockchain implementation in Higher Education Factors
Students Factors					
Educators Factors	0.8645				
Employers Factors	0.7135	0.8426			
Other Stakeholders Factors	0.6568	0.7875	0.8135		
Blockchain implementation in Higher Education Factors	0.6147	0.6919	0.7923	0.8654	

Source: ADANCO results, 2023

Since the tabulated p-values are well below 0.05 meaning it supports the relationship validity. The results output table authenticates all the hypotheses suggested (Hair et al., 2021).

The Fornell-Larcker criterion is used in the study and cross-loadings to measure discriminant validity, which shows how much a variable is related to other variables in the structural model. The study presented the results in table 5, using Adanco 2.3 output. The diagonal bold numbers are the highest in each row and column, indicating that the discriminant validity is confirmed. (Sarstedt et al., 2022).

Table 7 illustrates the cross loadings to study the impact of the variables on each other. The (R^2) determination coefficient explains the relationship between constructs in the study. The earlier studies indicated that the minimum R^2 is 0.25, indicating the relevance and significance of the construct (Magno et al., 2022). Based on the result table, R^2 value of Blockchain Implementation was 0.7613, which means that the construct was relevant and significant, and able to explain research variables.

The PLS-SEM Validation thrown by the ADANCO 2.3 software is confirmed in Fig 4.

The study developed and tested a research framework using PLS-SEM and obtained a consensus of 407 respondents- stakeholders of the Blockchain Higher Education application. This is a useful contribution of this research paper. The study also addressed the lack of relevant data for future researchers and suggested further research based on this model or similar models. The study acknowledged the importance of the theories cited in specific situations with stable economies, equal Higher Education opportunities, and infrastructure availability. The study also

Table 5. Direct effect interference

Direct Effect	Original coefficient β	Standard bootstrap results				
		Mean value	Standard error	t-value	p-value (2-sided)	Hypotheses Supported
Students Factors -> Blockchain implementation in Higher Education Factors	0.2816	0.2229	0.0874	5.9313	0.0041	Yes
Educators Factors -> Blockchain implementation in Higher Education Factors	0.1894	0.1248	0.0904	6.9844	0.0033	yes
Employers Factors -> Blockchain implementation in Higher Education Factors	0.8341	0.8021	0.0413	19.2163	0.0000	Yes
Other Stakeholders Factors -> Blockchain implementation in Higher Education Factors	0.8084	0.8768	0.0253	35.3483	0.0000	Yes
Employers Factors -> Educators Factors	0.8217	0.8003	0.0832	10.7568	0.0000	yes
Other Stakeholders Factors -> Students Factors	0.2905	0.1752	0.1672	3.5347	0.0029	yes
Employers Factors -> Students Factors	0.4390	0.3959	0.2077	3.1131	0.0034	yes
Employers Factors -> Other Stakeholders Factors	0.3330	0.3071	0.1502	2.8174	0.0040	yes
Students Factors -> Educators Factors	0.6341	0.5875	0.1346	2.9750	0.0000	Yes
Other Stakeholders Factors -> Educators Factors	0.5217	0.4903	0.0802	11.4568	0.0000	yes

Source: ADANCO results, 2023

Table 6. Discriminant validity

Construct	Students Factors	Educators Factors	Employers Factors	Other Stakeholders Factors	Blockchain implementation in Higher Education Factors
Students Factors	**0.5819**				
Educators Factors	0.5768	**0.6557**			
Employers Factors	0.5356	0.6353	**0.7843**		
Other Stakeholders Factors	0.5245	0.6213	0.6539	**0.8178**	
Blockchain implementation in Higher Education Factors	0.4345	0.5224	0.6341	0.7431	**0.8869**

developed a concrete and sound research-based framework to contribute to further work (Iyer et al.,2020).

The next level relationships can be ignored as the β value will be well below the 0.01 levels which is not relevant (Sarstedt et al., 2022).

Table 10 shows the Outcomes similarity, ascertained by Quantitative and Qualitative methodologies.

Table 7. Loadings of indicator loadings

Indicator	Students Factors	Educators Factors	Employers Factors	Other Stakeholders Factors	Blockchain implementation in Higher Education Factors
(STF1)	0.7445				
(STF2)	0.6643				
(STF3)	0.8215				
(STF4)	0.7791				
(STF5)	0.7348				
(EDF1)		0.7568			
(EDF2)		0.7253			
(EDF3)		0.6903			
(EDF4)		0.7385			
(EDF5)		0.7823			
(EDF6)		0.8226			
(EMPF1)			0.7604		
(EMPF2)			0.7550		
(EMPF3)			0.6505		
(EMPF4)			0.6916		
(EMPF5)			0.7561		
(EMPF6)			0.7117		
(EMPF7)			0.7211		
(EMPF8)			0.7100		
(OSF1)				0.7828	
(OSF2)				0.6610	
(OSF3)				0.7660	
(OSF4)				0.8754	
(OSF5)				0.6834	
(OSF6)				0.7261	
(BIEF1)					0.6845
(BIEF2)					0.7632
(BIEF3)					0.7545
(BIEF4)					0.7385
(BIEF5)					0.7834
(BIEF6)					0.7514

Table 8. R^2

Construct	Coefficient of determination (R^2)	Adjusted R^2
Students Factors	0.4653	0.4315
Educators Factors	0.3853	0.3356
Employers Factors	0.5613	0.5385
Other Stakeholders Factors	0.6643	0.6132
Blockchain implementation in Higher Education Factors	0.7613	0.7293

Figure 4. PLS-SEM validation

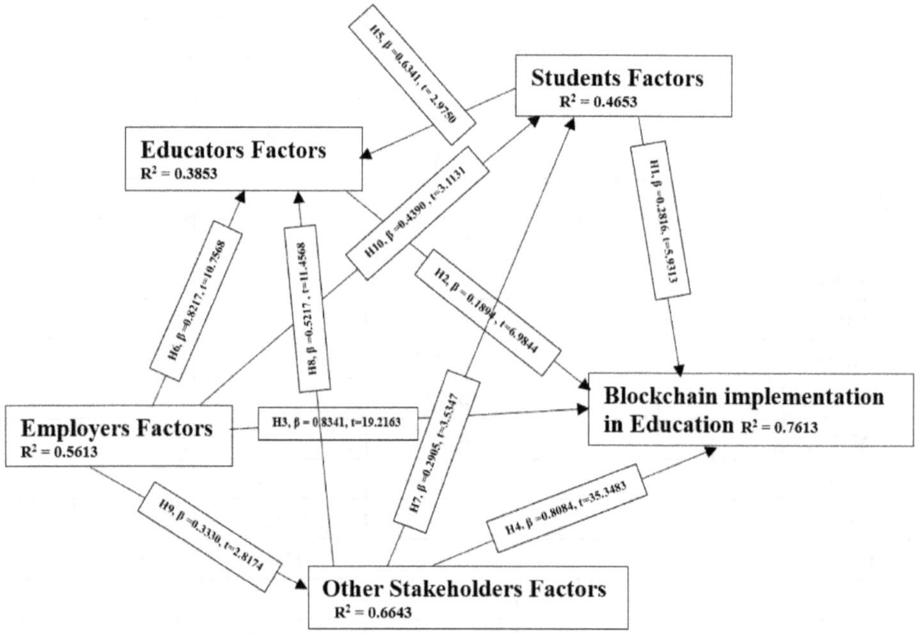

Outcomes Differences

The outcomes differences observed from either of the methodologies is minimal and irrelevant (Mikalef et al., 2019).

From the expert interviews conducted, the Strategies to effectively implement blockchain technology in Higher Education to ensure a successful implementation of blockchain technology in higher education, improving data security, administrative efficiency, and academic credential verification can be summarized in figure 3 below.

Table 9. Showing the direct relationships

Hypotheses no	Construe Description	β- value	t-value	Significance t ≥2.59 1.96 ≤ t ≤2.59	Hypotheses Supported or not supported
H1	Students Factors -> Blockchain implementation in Higher Education Factors	0.2816	5.9313	Strong	Yes
H2	Educators Factors -> Blockchain implementation in Higher Education Factors	0.1894	6.9844	Strong	Yes
H3	Employers Factors -> Blockchain implementation in Higher Education Factors	0.8341	19.2163	Strong	yes
H4	Other Stakeholders Factors -> Blockchain implementation in Higher Education Factors	0.8084	35.3483	Strong	yes

Table 10. Indirect relationships

Hypotheses No	Construe Description	β- value	t-value	Significance t ≥1.96	Hypotheses Supported or not supported
H52	Student Factors -> Blockchain implementation in Higher Education Factors through Educators Factors	0.1201	6.3332	Strong	Yes
H62	Employers Factors -> Blockchain implementation in Higher Education Factors through Educators Factors	0.1556	7.1791	Strong	Yes
H71	Other Stakeholders Factors -> Blockchain implementation in Higher Education Factors through Students Factors	0.0816	6.4463	Strong	Yes
H82	Other Stakeholders Factors -> Blockchain implementation in Higher Education Factors through Educators Factors	0.0989	6.7451	Strong	Yes
H94	Employers Factors-> Blockchain implementation in Higher Education Factors through Other Stakeholders Factors	0.2691	5.8742	Strong	Yes
H101	Employers Factors-> Blockchain implementation in Higher Education Factors through Students Factors	0.1236	9.8543	Strong	Yes

Table 11. Outcomes similarity

Qualitative Outcomes	Quantitative Outcomes
The Students Factors, Educators Factors, Employers Factors, Other Stakeholders Factors, will enhance the Blockchain implementation in Education.	H1, H2, H3, H4, H52, H62, H71, H82, H94 & H101 has a strong relationship and is well supported as suggested by the Conceptual model and Hypotheses is formulated.
Both the methodologies match and hence it is validated, and the reliability tested to large extent (Stentoft et al., 2018)	

Figure 5. Strategies to effectively implement blockchain technology in higher education
Figure developed by authors

CONCLUSION AND RECOMMENDATION

Implications of This Research

Practical Implications: The research study "Blockchain Revolution in Higher Education" has practical implications that can positively impact the Higher Education sector. By leveraging blockchain technology, various aspects of Higher Education can be transformed. Blockchain ensures the secure and tamper-proof storage and verification of educational credentials, minimizing the risk of fraud. It can streamline administrative processes, reducing bureaucracy and enhancing efficiency. With blockchain, students have ownership and control over their educational records, allowing for easy sharing with employers and educational institutions. Blockchain also enables the creation and recognition of micro-credentials, facilitating personalized learning pathways and continuous upskilling. Additionally, it provides a secure platform for collaboration among students, educators, and researchers, fostering innovation and knowledge exchange (Pirkkalainen et al., 2023).

Social implications: The research study on "Blockchain Revolution in Higher Education" has significant social implications. Blockchain technology fosters trust and transparency in the Higher Education sector, increasing trust between educational institutions, students, employers, and stakeholders. It empowers learners by giving them ownership and control over their educational records, enabling them to share verified credentials globally and access educational opportunities. Blockchain recognizes and validates informal learning experiences, promoting inclusivity and bridging educational inequalities. It also enhances data privacy, allowing individuals to have control over their personal data and address concerns related to data breaches. Furthermore, blockchain facilitates secure collaboration and knowledge sharing among students, educators, researchers, and institutions globally, fostering a global learning community for collective growth and innovation. (Savelyeva et al., 2022).

Managerial implications: The research study "Blockchain Revolution in Higher Education" has managerial implications for educational institutions. Managers need to strategically plan for integrating blockchain technology, understanding its benefits and challenges, and aligning initiatives with institutional goals. Collaboration with technology providers and stakeholders is crucial for developing interoperable systems and standards. Adequate infrastructure and resources must be allocated, including training staff with technical expertise. Establishing governance structures and policies, such as data privacy and security protocols, is essential. Managers must also address organizational change by implementing change management strategies and monitoring the impact of blockchain implementation through evaluation and adjustments (Jain et al., 2021).

Limitations and Future Research

The study "Blockchain Revolution in Higher Education" highlights managerial implications for educational institutions. Managers should plan strategically to integrate blockchain technology, considering its advantages and challenges, and aligning it with institutional goals. Collaboration with technology providers and stakeholders is important for developing interoperable systems and standards. Adequate resources and infrastructure, as well as training for staff, are necessary. Establishing governance structures and policies, including data privacy and security protocols, is crucial. Managers must address organizational change by implementing change management strategies and evaluating the impact of blockchain implementation for necessary adjustments.

THE CONTRIBUTION AND ORIGINALITY

Value of the Research

This study's main contribution is the conceptual model based on the Stakeholders theory. The study discusses the challenges and issues that the stakeholders face in Higher Education BCT implementation and assimilates the industry expert's consensus in various domains using primary research. The study is validated, and the conceptual model tested for reliability by using PLS-SEM 2.3 ADANCO in statistical quantitative methodology. The study collects data from different Emirates, which is relevant to the Higher Education sector as most of the Universities are located in the United Arab Emirates. This was possible because of the various domain experts who collaborated with the working PhD students from domains, countries, and authors, which is another major study contribution. The study objectives lead to using a conceptual model that integrates two theories: Technology theory and Stakeholders theory, resulting in a new model for future studies. The study has given a Higher Education Block chain framework and served the purpose of exploring the potential applications and impacts of blockchain technology in the field of higher education and got the consensus of major stakeholders on its usefulness. The interviews conducted with experts across the various countries and the survey respondents across the various countries addressed the sample reliability (Iyer et al., 2021).

CONCLUSION

The Stakeholders theory offers a holistic framework for studying the factors that drive BCT in the Higher Education sector and its benefits. Review of Literature has found many key factors that can encourage BCT implementation, such as leadership, organizational culture, collaboration, and resources. However, we also acknowledge that BCT implementation is a complex phenomenon that depends on various individual, organizational, and environmental factors. Future research should aim to empirical hypotheses testing derived from the review of literature and investigate the impact of specific organizational practices and policies on Higher Education BCT implementation. Moreover, future research should consider the potential negative outcomes of promoting BCT, such as resistance to change or increased risk-taking. By continuing to improve and broaden our understanding of the factors that drive Higher Education BCT implementation, enabling organizations to prepare themselves to succeed in today's dynamic external environment.

REFERENCES

Aisyah, E. S. N., Haryani, H., Budiarto, M., Prihastiwi, W. Y., Santoso, N. P. L., & Hayadi, B. H. (2022). Blockchain ilearning platform in education. In *2022 International Conference on Science and Technology (ICOSTECH)* (pp. 01-08). IEEE. 10.1109/ICOSTECH54296.2022.9829160

Alam, A. (2022). Platform utilising blockchain technology for eLearning and online Higher Educationfor open sharing of academic proficiency and progress records. In *Smart Data Intelligence: Proceedings of ICSMDI 2022* (pp. 307-320). Singapore: Springer Nature Singapore. 10.1007/978-981-19-3311-0_26

Alam, T., & Benaida, M. (2020). Blockchain and internet of things in higher education. *Universal Journal of Educational Research, 8*, 2164-2174., doi:10.13189/ujer.2020.080556

Alammary, A., Alhazmi, S., Almasri, M., & Gillani, S. (2019). Blockchain-based applications in education: A systematic review. *Applied Sciences (Basel, Switzerland), 9*(12), 2400. doi:10.3390/app9122400

Alamri, H., Lowell, V., Watson, W., & Watson, S. L. (2020). Using personalized learning as an instructional approach to motivate learners in online higher education: Learner self-determination and intrinsic motivation. *Journal of Research on Technology in Education, 52*(3), 322–352. doi:10.1080/15391523.2020.1728449

Alshahrani, M., Beloff, N., & White, M. (2021). *Towards a blockchain-based smart certification system for higher education: an empirical study*. International Journal Of Computing and Digital System. doi:10.12785/ijcds/110145

Alsobhi, H. A., Alakhtar, R. A., Ubaid, A., Hussain, O. K., & Hussain, F. K. (2023). Blockchain-based micro-credentialing system in higher Higher Educationinstitutions: Systematic literature review. *Knowledge-Based Systems, 110238*, 110238. doi:10.1016/j.knosys.2022.110238

Awerika, C. K., Amerila, Z. M. A., Ameria, S., Ameriya, T., & Atsumi, M. (2023). Exploring Integration in Higher Educationthrough Blockchain Technology. *Blockchain Frontier Technology, 3*(1), 119–127. doi:10.34306/bfront.v3i1.359

Ayub Khan, A., Laghari, A. A., Shaikh, A. A., Bourouis, S., Mamlouk, A. M., & Alshazly, H. (2021). Educational blockchain: A secure degree attestation and verification traceability architecture for higher Higher Educationcommission. *Applied Sciences (Basel, Switzerland), 11*(22), 10917. doi:10.3390/app112210917

Cahyadi, D., Faturahman, A., Haryani, H., Dolan, E., & Millah, S. (2021). Bcs: Blockchain smart curriculum system for verification student accreditation. *International Journal of Cyber and IT Service Management*, *1*(1), 65–83. doi:10.34306/ijcitsm.v1i1.20

Carmichael, J. J., & Eaton, S. E. (2023). Security risks, fake degrees, and other fraud: A topic modelling approach. In *Fake Degrees and Fraudulent Credentials in Higher Higher Education* (pp. 227–250). Springer International Publishing. doi:10.1007/978-3-031-21796-8_11

Chan, C. K. Y. (2023). A comprehensive AI policy Higher Educationframework for university teaching and learning. *International Journal of Educational Technology in Higher Education*, *20*(1), 1–25. doi:10.118641239-023-00408-3

ChatterjeeP.DasD.RawatD. (2023). Securing Financial Transactions: Exploring the Role of Federated Learning and Blockchain in Credit Card Fraud Detection. TechRxiv. doi:10.36227/techrxiv.22683403.v1

Cheng, H., Lu, J., Xiang, Z., & Song, B. (2020). A Permissioned Blockchain-Based Platform for Higher EducationCertificate Verification. In Z. Zheng, H. N. Dai, X. Fu, & B. Chen (Eds.), *Blockchain and Trustworthy Systems. BlockSys 2020. Communications in Computer and Information Science* (Vol. 1267). Springer. doi:10.1007/978-981-15-9213-3_36

Chukowry, V., Nanuck, G., & Sungkur, R. K. (2021). The future of continuous learning–Digital badge and microcredential system using blockchain. *Global Transitions Proceedings*, *2*(2), 355–361. doi:10.1016/j.gltp.2021.08.026

Datta, P. K., & Mitra, S. (2022). 7 Application of. *The Data-Driven Blockchain Ecosystem: Fundamentals, Applications, and Emerging Technologies*, *103*. doi:10.1201/9781003269281

Dewangan, S., Verma, S. K., Parganiha, B., & Dewangan, S. (2023). Applications and Implementations of Blockchain Technology Across the Various Sectors. In Building Secure Business Models Through Blockchain Technology: Tactics, Methods, Limitations, and Performance (pp. 1-19). IGI Global. doi:10.4018/978-1-6684-7808-0.ch001

Eliwa, E., & Hameed, H. A. (2023). The Effectiveness of Using Blockchain Technology in Building High-Quality Educational Content Based on A Participatory Learning Environment and Its Impact on Increasing Student Achievement. *International Journal of Intelligent Systems and Applications in Engineering*, *11*(1), 50–62. https://www.ijisae.org/index.php/IJISAE/article/view/2443

ElsayedA. N. (2023). The Use of Blockchain Technology in Education: A Comprehensive Review and Future Prospects. SSRN 4523322. doi:10.2139/ssrn.4523322

Grech, A., Sood, I., & Ariño, L. (2021). Blockchain, self-sovereign identity and digital credentials: Promise versus praxis in education. *Frontiers in Blockchain*, *4*, 616779. https://www.frontiersin.org/articles/10.3389/fbloc.2021.616779/full. doi:10.3389/fbloc.2021.616779

Grima, S., Spiteri, J., & Romānova, I. (2020). A STEEP framework analysis of the key factors impacting the use of blockchain technology in the insurance industry. *The Geneva Papers on Risk and Insurance. Issues and Practice*, *45*(3), 398–425. doi:10.105741288-020-00162-x

Guustaaf, E., Rahardja, U., Aini, Q., Maharani, H. W., & Santoso, N. A. (2021). Blockchain-based Higher Educationproject. *Aptisi Transactions on Management (ATM), 5*(1), 46-61. https://ijc.ilearning.co/index.php/ATM/article/view/1433

Hair, J. F. Jr, Hult, G. T. M., Ringle, C. M., Sarstedt, M., Danks, N. P., & Ray, S. (2021). *Partial least squares structural equation modeling (PLS-SEM) using R: A workbook.* Springer Nature. doi:10.1007/978-3-030-80519-7

Hakizimana, D., Ntizimira, C., Mbituyumuremyi, A., Hakizimana, E., Mahmoud, H., Birindabagabo, P., Musanabaganwa, C., & Gashumba, D. (2022). The impact of Covid-19 on malaria services in three high endemic districts in Rwanda: A mixed-method study. *Malaria Journal*, *21*(1), 48. doi:10.118612936-022-04071-3 PMID:35164781

Halkiopoulos, C., Antonopoulou, H., & Kostopoulos, N. (2023). *Utilizing Blockchain Technology in Various Applications to Secure Data Flows. A Comprehensive Analysis.* Technium. doi:10.47577/technium.v11i.9132

Han, H., Shiwakoti, R. K., Jarvis, R., Mordi, C., & Botchie, D. (2023). Accounting and auditing with blockchain technology and artificial Intelligence: A literature review. *International Journal of Accounting Information Systems*, *48*, 100598. doi:10.1016/j.accinf.2022.100598

Haque, M. A., Haque, S., Zeba, S., Kumar, K., Ahmad, S., Rahman, M., & Ahmed, L. (2023). Sustainable and efficient E-learning internet of things system through blockchain technology. *E-Learning and Digital Media, 20427530231156711.* doi:10.1177/20427530231156711

Hoyos, C. A., & Kloos, C. D. (2023). Experiences with Micro-Credentials at UC3M: Academic and Technological Aspects. In 2023 IEEE World Engineering Higher EducationConference (EDUNINE) (pp. 1-6). IEEE. doi:10.1109/EDUNINE57531.2023.10102848

Iyer, S. S. (2022). Adopting a Student Centric Higher EducationBlockchain System. *International Journal of Information and Communication Sciences*, *7*(3), 48–65. Retrieved June 25, 2023, from https://www.researchgate.net/publication/369551569_Adopting_a_Student_Centric_Education_Blockchain_System. doi:10.11648/j.ijics.20220703.11

Iyer, S. S., Seetharaman, A., & Maddulety, K. (2020). Higher EducationTransformation Using Block Chain Technology-A Student Centric Model. In *Re-imagining Diffusion and Adoption of Information Technology and Systems: A Continuing Conversation: IFIP WG 8.6 International Conference on Transfer and Diffusion of IT,* (pp. 201-217). Springer International Publishing.

Iyer, S. S., Seetharaman, A., & Ranjan, B. (2021). Researching Blockchain Technology and its Usefulness in Higher Education. *Machine Learning, IOT and Blockchain Technologies & Trends*, 27-48. AIRCC. doi:10.5121/csit.2021.111203

Jackson, D., Michelson, G., & Munir, R. (2023). Developing accountants for the future: New technology, skills, and the role of stakeholders. *Accounting Education*, *32*(2), 150–177. doi:10.1080/09639284.2022.2057195

Jain, G., Sharma, N., & Shrivastava, A. (2021). Enhancing training effectiveness for organizations through blockchain-enabled training effectiveness measurement (BETEM). *Journal of Organizational Change Management*, *34*(2), 439–461. doi:10.1108/JOCM-10-2020-0303

Kabashi, F., Neziri, V., Snopce, H., Luma, A., Aliu, A., & Shkurti, L. (2023). The possibility of blockchain application in Higher Education. In *2023 12th Mediterranean Conference on Embedded Computing (MECO)* (pp. 1-5). IEEE. 10.1109/MECO58584.2023.10154919

Khan, M., & Naz, T. (2021). Smart contracts based on blockchain for decentralized learning management system. *SN Computer Science*, *2*(4), 260. doi:10.100742979-021-00661-1

Kosasi, S., Rahardja, U., Lutfiani, N., Harahap, E. P., & Sari, S. N. (2022). Blockchain technology-emerging research themes opportunities in higher education. In *2022 International Conference on Science and Technology (ICOSTECH)* (pp. 1-8). IEEE. 10.1109/ICOSTECH54296.2022.9829053

Kshetri, N., Miller, K., Banerjee, G., & Upreti, B. R. (2023). International Journal of Emerging and Disruptive Innovation in Education: *Visionarium*. *1*(1). https://digitalcommons.lindenwood.edu/ijedie/vol1/iss1/4/

Magno, F., Cassia, F., & Ringle, C. M. (2022). A brief review of partial least squares structural equation modeling (PLS-SEM) use in quality management studies. *The TQM Journal*. doi:10.1108/TQM-06-2022-0197

Malik, V., Mittal, R., Mavaluru, D., Narapureddy, B. R., Goyal, S. B., Martin, R. J., & Mittal, A. (2023). *Building a Secure Platform for Digital Governance Interoperability and Data Exchange using Blockchain and Deep Learning-based frameworks*. IEEE. doi:10.1109/ACCESS.2023.3293529

Marlina, E., Hidayanto, A. N., & Purwandari, B. (2022). Towards a model of research data management readiness in Indonesian context: An investigation of factors and indicators through the fuzzy delphi method. *Library & Information Science Research*, *44*(1), 101141. doi:10.1016/j.lisr.2022.101141

Mecozzi, R., Perrone, G., Anelli, D., Saitto, N., Paggi, E., & Mancini, D. (2022). Blockchain-related identity and access management challenges:(de) centralized digital identities regulation. In *2022 IEEE International Conference on Blockchain (Blockchain)* (pp. 443-448). IEEE. 10.1109/Blockchain55522.2022.00068

Merlec, M. M., Islam, M. M., Lee, Y. K., & In, H. P. (2022). A consortium blockchain-based secure and trusted electronic portfolio management scheme. *Sensors (Basel)*, *22*(3), 1271. doi:10.339022031271 PMID:35162016

Mikalef, P., Boura, M., Lekakos, G., & Krogstie, J. (2019). Big data analytics and firm performance: Findings from a mixed-method approach. *Journal of Business Research*, *98*, 261–276. doi:10.1016/j.jbusres.2019.01.044

Mikroyannidis, A., Third, A., & Domingue, J. (2020). A case study on the decentralisation of lifelong learning using blockchain technology. *Journal of Interactive Media in Education*, *2020*(1), 1–10. doi:10.5334/jime.591

Mishra, S., & Tyagi, A. K. (2022). The role of machine learning techniques in internet of things-based cloud applications. *Artificial intelligence-based internet of things systems*, 105-135. doi:10.1007/978-3-030-87059-1_4

Mohanta, B. K., Jena, D., Panda, S. S., & Sobhanayak, S. (2019). Blockchain technology: A survey on applications and security privacy challenges. *Internet of Things : Engineering Cyber Physical Human Systems*, *8*, 100107. doi:10.1016/j.iot.2019.100107

Nehru, R. S. S., Cuong, T. Q., Prakash, A. R., & Huong, B. T. T. (2023). Higher Education: AI Applications for Blockchain-Based IoT Technology and Networks. In *AI Models for Blockchain-Based Intelligent Networks in IoT Systems: Concepts, Methodologies, Tools, and Applications* (pp. 261–283). Springer International Publishing. doi:10.1007/978-3-031-31952-5_12

O'Sullivan, K., Clark, S., Marshall, K., & MacLachlan, M. (2021). A Just Digital framework to ensure equitable achievement of the Sustainable Development Goals. *Nature Communications*, *12*(1), 6345. doi:10.103841467-021-26217-8 PMID:34732699

Oke, A., & Fernandes, F. A. P. (2020). Innovations in teaching and learning: Exploring the perceptions of the Higher Educationsector on the 4th industrial revolution (4IR). *Journal of Open Innovation*, *6*(2), 31. doi:10.3390/joitmc6020031

Perisic, A., Perisic, I., Lazic, M., & Perisic, B. (2023). The foundation for future education, teaching, training, learning, and performing infrastructure-The open interoperability conceptual framework approach. *Heliyon*, *9*(6), e16836. doi:10.1016/j.heliyon.2023.e16836 PMID:37484382

Pirkkalainen, H., Sood, I., Padron Napoles, C., Kukkonen, A., & Camilleri, A. (2023). How might micro-credentials influence institutions and empower learners in higher education? *Educational Research*, *65*(1), 40–63. doi:10.1080/00131881.2022.2157302

Prawiyogi, A. G., Aini, Q., Santoso, N. P. L., Lutfiani, N., & Juniar, H. L. J. (2021). Blockchain Higher Educationconcept 4.0: Student-centered ilearning blockchain framework. *JTP-Jurnal Teknologi Pendidikan*, *23*(2), 129–145. doi:10.21009/jtp.v23i2.20978

Prewett, K. W., Prescott, G. L., & Phillips, K. (2020). Blockchain adoption is inevitable—Barriers and risks remain. *Journal of Corporate Accounting & Finance*, *31*(2), 21–28. doi:10.1002/jcaf.22415

Rahardja, U., Aini, Q., Oganda, F. P., & Devana, V. T. (2021). Secure framework based on blockchain for e-learning during covid-19. In *2021 9th International Conference on Cyber and IT Service Management (CITSM)* (pp. 1-7). IEEE. 10.1109/CITSM52892.2021.9588854

Sangiuliano Intra, F., Nasti, C., Massaro, R., Perretta, A. J., Di Girolamo, A., Brighi, A., & Biroli, P. (2023). Flexible Learning Environments for a Sustainable Lifelong Learning Process for Teachers in the School Context. *Sustainability (Basel)*, *15*(14), 11237. doi:10.3390u151411237

Sarstedt, M., Radomir, L., Moisescu, O. I., & Ringle, C. M. (2022). Latent class analysis in PLS-SEM: A review and recommendations for future applications. *Journal of Business Research, 138*, 398–407. doi:10.1016/j.jbusres.2021.08.051

Satybaldy, A., Subedi, A., & Nowostawski, M. (2022). A Framework for Online Document Verification Using Self-Sovereign Identity Technology. *Sensors (Basel), 22*(21), 8408. doi:10.339022218408 PMID:36366105

Savelyeva, T., & Park, J. (2022). Blockchain technology for sustainable education. *British Journal of Educational Technology, 53*(6), 1591–1604. doi:10.1111/bjet.13273

Schlesinger, W., Cervera-Taulet, A., & Wymer, W. (2023). The influence of university brand image, satisfaction, and university identification on alumni WOM intentions. *Journal of Marketing for Higher Education, 33*(1), 1–19. doi:10.1080/08841241.2021.1874588

Shakan, Y., Kumalakov, B., Mutanov, G., Mamykova, Z., & Kistaubayev, Y. (2021). Verification of University student and graduate data using blockchain technology. *International Journal OF Computers Communications & Control, 16*(5). https://univagora.ro/jour/index.php/ijccc/article/view/4266

Son-Turan, S. (2022). Fostering equality in education: The blockchain business model for higher Higher Education(BBM-HE). *Sustainability (Basel), 14*(5), 2955. doi:10.3390u14052955

Steiu, M. F. (2020). Blockchain in education: Opportunities, applications, and challenges. *First Monday*. doi:10.5210/fm.v25i9.10654

Tan, E., Lerouge, E., Du Caju, J., & Du Seuil, D. (2023). Verification of Higher EducationCredentials on European Blockchain Services Infrastructure (EBSI): Action Research in a Cross-Border Use Case between Belgium and Italy. *Big Data and Cognitive Computing, 7*(2), 79. doi:10.3390/bdcc7020079

Thomason, J., & Ivwurie, E. (Eds.). (2023). *Advancements in the New World of Web 3: A Look Toward the Decentralized Future: A Look Toward the Decentralized Future*. IGI Global. doi:10.4018/978-1-6684-6658-2

Tsai, C. T., & Wu, J. L. (2022). A Blockchain-Based Fair and Transparent Homework Grading System for Online Education. In *Principles and Practice of Blockchains* (pp. 303–326). Springer International Publishing. doi:10.1007/978-3-031-10507-4_13

Vaigandla, K. K., Karne, R., Siluveru, M., & Kesoju, M. (2023). Review on Blockchain Technology: Architecture, Characteristics, Benefits, Algorithms, Challenges and Applications. *Mesopotamian Journal of CyberSecurity, 2023*, 73–85. doi:10.58496/MJCS/2023/012

Varma, P., Nijjer, S., Sood, K., Grima, S., & Rupeika-Apoga, R. (2022). Thematic Analysis of Financial Technology (Fintech) Influence on the Banking Industry. *Risks*, *10*(10), 186. doi:10.3390/risks10100186

Vhatkar, H. V., Singh, H. G., Sonavane, A. S., Singh, S., & Pulgam, N. (2023). Crowdfunding using Blockchain. In *2023 11th International Conference on Emerging Trends in Engineering & Technology-Signal and Information Processing (ICETET-SIP)* (pp. 1-6). IEEE. 10.1109/ICETET-SIP58143.2023.10151618

Vlk, A. (2023). The role of industry in higher Higher Educationtransformation. Research Handbook on the Transformation of Higher Education: 0, 192.

Wylde, V., Rawindaran, N., Lawrence, J., Balasubramanian, R., Prakash, E., Jayal, A., & Platts, J. (2022). Cybersecurity, data privacy and blockchain: A review. *SN Computer Science*, *3*(2), 127. doi:10.100742979-022-01020-4 PMID:35036930

Xi, P., Zhang, X., Wang, L., Liu, W., & Peng, S. (2022). A review of Blockchain-based secure sharing of healthcare data. *Applied Sciences (Basel, Switzerland)*, *12*(15), 7912. doi:10.3390/app12157912

Yaqoob, I., Salah, K., Jayaraman, R., & Al-Hammadi, Y. (2021). Blockchain for healthcare data management: Opportunities, challenges, and future recommendations. *Neural Computing & Applications*, 1–16. doi:10.100700521-020-05519-w

Yıldırım, H. (2022). Psychosocial status of older adults aged 65 years and over during lockdown in Turkey and their perspectives on the outbreak. *Health & Social Care in the Community*, *30*(3), 899–907. doi:10.1111/hsc.13542 PMID:34390281

Chapter 6
Blockchain Revolution in Education and Lifelong Learning

Charu Banga
https://orcid.org/0000-0002-6288-1419
De Montfort University, Dubai, UAE

Farhan Ujager
https://orcid.org/0000-0002-7080-5141
De Montfort University, Dubai, UAE

ABSTRACT

The current chapter presents an overview on the importance of blockchain technology in the field of education and lifelong learning. It discusses the existing blockchain models applicable to the education sector such as decentralized student records and credentials verification systems, secure and transparent transaction platforms for micro-credentials, and blockchain-based student identity management systems. Sustainable blockchain-led strategies and framework for responsible blockchain for empowering the stakeholders involved, enhancing educational innovation and infrastructure, and reducing the inequalities are discussed. Moreover, the chapter throws light on the innovative practices to revolutionize traditional education systems, credentialing, and payment methods, offering several significant benefits to the world of higher education.

DOI: 10.4018/979-8-3693-0405-1.ch006

INTRODUCTION

Blockchain technology has significant potential in the education sector and lifelong learning. The peer-to-peer distributed ledger technology is revolutionizing the management and transactions of data. It securely stores transactions and student records, eliminates manual processes, reduces cost, decentralizes data, and promotes integration between the network users (Bucea-Manea-Ţoniş et al., 2021). The technology is implemented within educational institutions based on the blocks created to validate each record. Since the records are permanent and cannot be revoked, technology provides the potential for securing transparency in micro-credentials, student identity management system, verification of transcripts, and provides easy access to shared resources (Arenas & Fernandez, 2018) (Meria et al., 2021). Despite numerous benefits and incredible applications across the education sector, the technology faces certain challenges in its implementation due to the cost involved, scalability, security, and interoperability. Regardless of these implementation challenges, there exist strategies and framework that promote responsible and ethical use of blockchain in the education sector. These strategies provide solutions to overcome the challenges around scalability, interoperability, integration, and common framework and regulations using smart contracts and private blockchain systems (Anwar et al., 2022). Further, it is crucial to transform blockchain-led education into a sustainable model to foster equality within the education sector and empower the stakeholders. Cooperation between the network users, diversity between the interacting agents, access to shared resources, and educational logistics are a few strategies that facilitate transparent and accountable systems for tracking and managing sustainability initiatives within academic institutions (Son-Turan, 2022).

This chapter contributes to the existing literature in the following ways: First, it provides insights into the IT infrastructure and computing solutions to transform a traditional higher education system where there exists an informal exchange of resources to more formal and secure shared resources using a centralized ledger framework. Secondly, it provides how innovative and revolutionary technology benefits and empowers the education stakeholders such as the instructors, administration, management, and learners. Thirdly, the chapter discusses strategies for sustainable blockchain in the education sector that actively contribute towards the UN SDG -4 Quality Education, SDG – 9 of 'Industry, Innovation, Infrastructure', and SDG - 10 of 'Reduces Inequalities.' Establishing a quality network cooperation and enhancing interoperability assists in resolving interaction and engagement within the larger community and accomplishing quality education (SDG -4). Last but not least, despite the challenges of implementing blockchain in the education sector, the chapter proposes strategies such as scalability, interoperability, a common legal framework to promote standardization, and integration for free and homogenous data exchange for responsible and ethical blockchain-led education and lifelong learning.

The remaining chapter is structured as follows: Section 2 presents the background of blockchain and higher education; Section 3 discusses the advantages of blockchain technology in the education sector and the existing models involved. Sector 4 illustrates the types of blockchain. While Section 5 provides insights into the framework for responsible blockchain in the education sector and lifelong learning, Section 6 offers strategies for responsible blockchain. Section 7 discusses the three real-world case studies and provides critical insights that underscore the significance of blockchain in higher education. Section 8 presents a critical analysis and future direction of work.

BACKGROUND OF THE STUDY: BLOCKCHAIN AND HIGHER EDUCATION

In this section, we will explore the fundamental components of blockchain and their role in the higher education sector. We'll explore blockchain implementation within the context of higher education and illustrate how these foundational elements contribute to delivering exceptional services in this domain. Additionally, we will introduce various blockchain models with the potential for application in higher education, highlighting their transformative capabilities.

FUNDAMENTAL COMPONENTS

Introducing readers to these concepts is crucial because they form the foundation of blockchain technology (Puthal et al., 2018), which has far-reaching implications across various industries.

1. **BLOCKCHAIN:** A blockchain is like a digital ledger or record book. It's made up of a chain of blocks, where each block contains a list of transactions. This chain of blocks is constantly growing, forming a chronological and unchangeable history of transactions. It operates on a decentralized network of computers, ensuring that no single entity has control over the entire ledger.
2. **BLOCK:** A block is a collection of data, like a page in a ledger. It contains a group of transactions that have been verified through a consensus process. Each block also includes a reference to the previous block, creating a sequential chain. This linkage enhances security as altering one block would require changing all subsequent blocks, which is computationally infeasible.

3. **TRANSACTIONS:** Transactions are like entries in the ledger, representing actions within the blockchain network. They record a wide range of activities, from financial transfers in cryptocurrencies like Bitcoin to any digital interactions. These transactions are grouped into blocks and can include sender and receiver addresses, timestamps, and digital signatures for security.
4. **NODES:** Nodes are like computers or participants in the network. They store copies of the entire blockchain, making it decentralized and resistant to data loss or manipulation. Nodes come in various types, including full nodes that maintain the complete blockchain and lightweight nodes that rely on full nodes for validation. Nodes play a critical role in reaching consensus and maintaining the network's integrity.
5. **CONSENSUS MECHANISM:** The consensus mechanism is like the rule or process that everyone in the network follows to agree on which transactions are valid and which should be added to the blockchain. In addition to Proof of Work (PoW), there are other mechanisms like Proof of Stake (PoS) and Delegated Proof of Stake (DPoS). These mechanisms ensure that the majority of nodes agree on the state of the blockchain, preventing double-spending and fraudulent activities.
6. **DECENTRALIZATION:** Blockchain is often decentralized, meaning there's no central authority or intermediary like a bank or government agency. Instead, transactions are verified by nodes distributed across the network. This decentralization fosters trust among network participants, reduces the risk of single points of failure, and enhances security by eliminating the need for a central controlling entity.
7. **CRYPTOGRAPHIC HASH:** A cryptographic hash is like a unique fingerprint for each block. It's generated through a cryptographic algorithm and is a fixed-length string of characters. Even a tiny change in the data within a block will result in a significantly different hash. This property ensures the integrity of the data in the block, making it practically impossible to alter past transactions without detection. Cryptographic hashes are a fundamental security feature of blockchain technology.
8. **SMART CONTRACTS:** Smart contracts are self-executing, programmable contracts that automate and enforce the terms of an agreement or transaction within a blockchain network. Think of them as digital contracts with built-in rules and logic. Smart contracts operate on the blockchain and execute automatically when predefined conditions are met. They eliminate the need for intermediaries, such as lawyers or notaries, and ensure trust and transparency in transactions.

ADVANTAGES OF BLOCKCHAIN TECHNOLOGY IN HIGHER EDUCATION

We're here to discuss how blockchain has the potential to transform higher education in the near future (Raimundo & Rosário, 2021). In this section, we'll describe how blockchain services benefit students, learners, schools, and employers, showcasing the incredible capabilities of blockchain technology. This exploration will probe into the conceptual foundations of blockchain, the practical applications within higher education, and the advantages it offers to individuals and institutions alike.

A Foundation of Trust

Blockchain technology can be served as the foundation of trust in higher education (Lizcano et al., 2020). It operates much like a digital ledger, continuously expanding to chronicle a history of academic transactions and activities. In this educational context, a blockchain can assume the role of a digital transcript ledger, capturing a student's entire academic journey from the moment of enrollment to the triumphant graduation day.

Imagine each blockchain as a virtual repository of academic accomplishments. Within this digital ledger, each block takes on the role of a page in a student's academic record, and within those pages are meticulously recorded and verified transactions. These transactions mirror real-world academic actions, ranging from the pivotal step of course enrollment to the diligent submission of assignments and the victorious completion of exams.

These transactions are organized and consolidated into blocks to create a comprehensive and unalterable record of a student's educational voyage. Through this blockchain-based system, higher education institutions can ensure transparency, security, and accuracy in managing student records, enhancing the overall academic experience and the lifelong value of educational achievements.

Empowering Lifelong Learning

In an era where lifelong learning is gaining greater significance, blockchain technology can be emerged as a pivotal tool for safeguarding the credibility and accessibility of educational accomplishments (Kuleto et al., 2022). Within this paradigm, universities, colleges, and lifelong learning platforms take on the role of nodes within a blockchain network. They not only store copies of academic records but also play a crucial role in verifying transactions related to these records.

The consensus mechanism adds reliability to the system, which guarantees the accuracy and integrity of academic records. In this educational context, a Proof of Stake (PoS) mechanism prevails, ensuring that most educational institutions reach a consensus on the validity of these academic transactions.

One of the most significant advantages of this decentralized approach is that it places control over a student's academic records outside the dominion of any single institution. Instead, it disperses this control across a network of educational entities. This decentralization not only enhances the security and immutability of records but also fosters a sense of trust among students, institutions, and prospective employers. With blockchain, the lifelong learning journey becomes not only credible but also transparent.

Smart Contracts Streamlining Administrative Processes

Smart contracts can serve as the technological backbone for the automation of administrative tasks within the realm of higher education (Arndt & Guercio, 2020). Think of them as digital academic advisors, quietly working behind the scenes, ready to step in when certain conditions are met. These conditions might include a student successfully completing all course requirements or achieving a certain grade point average.

For instance, when a student fulfills all the necessary criteria for their degree, a smart contract steps in and instantaneously issues that well-deserved diploma. This streamlined automation not only expedites the process but also ensures accuracy and transparency, reducing the administrative burden on educational institutions while bolstering trust in the system.

Benefits to the Students

Traditionally upon graduation, students typically get physical certificates or diplomas, which are vulnerable to theft, tampering, and destruction. Blockchain technology, coupled with smart contracts, offers a multitude of advantages for students and lifelong learners in the realm of education. One of the benefits is security. Academic records, which hold immense value for students, are rendered exceptionally secure and tamper-proof through the implementation of cryptographic hashes within the blockchain (Raimundo & Rosário, 2021). It means that once a student's achievements and records are entered into the blockchain, they become impermeable to manipulation or falsification. This feature infuses confidence in the authenticity and integrity of academic accomplishments.

Furthermore, blockchain technology introduces a layer of transparency into the educational landscape. Transparent blockchain records are readily accessible to students, providing them with a window into their educational journey. They can effortlessly monitor their progress, track completed courses, and verify their achievements. This newfound transparency empowers students to take control of their academic endeavors, fostering a sense of ownership and accountability.

Moreover, the transparent nature of blockchain records extends beyond the individual. Students can easily share their verified achievements with potential employers, institutions, or other stakeholders. It simplifies the often-cumbersome process of credential verification and validation, streamlining career opportunities and educational pathways.

In essence, blockchain and smart contracts not only fortify the security and integrity of academic records but also usher in a new era of transparency and empowerment for students and lifelong learners, ultimately enhancing their educational experiences and prospects.

Universities and Colleges Benefit Significantly From Blockchain Technology

Most educational institutions currently manage administrative processes manually with physical paperwork, without many checkpoints, thus impacting their operational efficiency. Universities and colleges can find substantial advantages in embracing blockchain technology. One of the primary benefits lies in enhanced efficiency. By integrating blockchain into their systems, administrative processes undergo a significant transformation, leading to the reduction of cumbersome paperwork and the need for manual verification (Arndt & Guercio, 2020). This streamlined approach not only saves time and resources but also minimizes the likelihood of errors, ensuring that academic records are accurate and easily accessible.

Moreover, the global recognition of blockchain-based credentials is vital for educational institutions. These credentials carry a universal acceptance, transcending geographical borders. Whether a student graduates from a local college or a university, their academic achievements are recorded securely on the blockchain, accessible and verifiable anywhere in the world. It simplifies the often complex and time-consuming process of validating academic accomplishments, fostering trust, and facilitating seamless transitions for students pursuing further education or entering the workforce. Blockchain technology empowers universities and colleges to offer efficient, globally recognized academic services, ultimately benefiting both institutions and the students they serve.

Benefits for Employers and Organizations

Employers and organizations hiring graduates stand to gain significant benefits from the integration of blockchain technology into the verification of academic credentials

(Garg, 2021). One of the most notable advantages is its operational efficiency in the verification process. Traditionally, confirming the authenticity of a candidate's degree involves a time-consuming and often labor-intensive procedure. However, with blockchain, this task becomes quick and straightforward. By accessing the blockchain ledger, employers can verify a candidate's educational background swiftly, eliminating the need for time-consuming back-and-forths with universities or other educational institutions.

Moreover, blockchain instills a high degree of confidence in the credentials presented by job applicants. Employers can rely on the immutability and transparency of blockchain records, knowing that academic records have not been tampered with or falsified. This benefit heightened trust in the validity of academic qualifications and reduced the risk of hiring unqualified candidates, ultimately leading to more informed hiring decisions and improved workforce quality.

In this blockchain-enabled future of higher education, the seamless flow of verified academic data empowers students, institutions, and employers alike. It fosters a lifelong learning culture where educational achievements are secure, transparent, and globally recognized. Blockchain and smart contracts have revolutionized how we learn and validate credentials, ensuring trust and efficiency at every stage of the educational journey.

BLOCKCHAIN TYPES

In this section, we look at the three types of blockchain systems – the public blockchain, the private blockchain, and the permissioned blockchain.

Public Blockchain

A public blockchain is an open, transparent, decentralized digital ledger or database that is kept up to date by a distributed network of participating nodes or computers. It allows anybody to observe, access, and interact with the network without having authorization because the data is publicly available. The term "permissionless" is frequently applied to public blockchains because they function without the need for a central authority or reliable intermediary to verify or log transactions. Usually, they are connected to cryptocurrencies like Ethereum and Bitcoin, which record and validate transactions using public blockchain (Zheng Z., 2017).

With the help of public blockchain, educational records like transcripts, diplomas, and certificates can't be easily falsified because they provide an unchangeable and transparent ledger. As a result, there is less chance of fraud, and academic credentials are more secure and reliable. By offering a safe and unchangeable record of academic accomplishments, public blockchain can dramatically lower the occurrence of bogus diplomas and certificates. Furthermore, it provides ease of institution transfer. It is difficult for learners to have their credits recognized when they transfer between universities. Public blockchain can streamline this process by enabling students to provide their new university with safe, authenticated records of their courses and accomplishments (Sharples, 2016).

To sum up, public blockchain has a lot of benefits for higher education, especially when it comes to cost reduction, security, and openness. It, however, also presents some limitations with accessibility, regulation, and scalability. In the increasingly globalized realm of higher education, technology can revolutionize the management and exchange of academic credentials, ultimately helping both institutions and learners as it develops and solves these problems.

Private Blockchain

A private blockchain is a decentralized ledger with controlled access and shares some features with a public blockchain. In contrast to public blockchains that are accessible to all users, a specific set of people within the educational institution usually maintain private blockchain. Private blockchain usually provides confidentiality and privacy of data. There is increased confidence among authorized users that their data won't be made public, which is crucial in situations that involve sensitive data (Smith, 2018).

In comparison to the public blockchain, the private blockchain offers a higher degree of data privacy and secrecy. This technology can be a significant advantage in higher education, where student records and research data are sensitive. Furthermore, private blockchain are not subject to the same network congestion or processing demands as public blockchain; they usually are faster and more effective. As a result, administrative procedures such as sharing of resources and record-keeping can be streamlined. Moreover, private blockchain allow educational institutions to maintain compliance with regulatory requirements and data protection laws, as they have greater control over who can access and manage data on the blockchain (Sharples, 2016).

To sum up, private blockchain has varied benefits in improved compliance, efficiency, customization, and data protection. However, they also bring up issues such as interoperability, limited transparency, and centralization.

Permissioned Blockchain

A permissioned blockchain is a kind of decentralized ledger technology in which data access, transaction validation, and network membership are restricted to authorized users and institutions. In contrast to public blockchains, which are accessible to all users of information, the permissioned blockchain retains a certain degree of control and restrictions (Zheng Z., 2017).

The exchange of data and research is vital in the academic sector. Secure and effective data sharing between educational institutions, researchers, and collaborators can be made possible by permissioned blockchain. It is especially helpful for group research projects where data integrity, trust, and restricted access to sensitive data are necessary. Furthermore, credential verification is one of the most promising applications of permissioned blockchain in education. On a permissioned blockchain, educational institutions can issue and store digital credentials like transcripts, diplomas, and certificates. Employers, other organizations, and learners themselves can then safely and effectively verify these credentials. It streamlines the verification procedure and lowers the possibility of bogus credentials (Pelletier, 2018).

Thus, permissioned blockchain has the power to completely change how education data is shared, learner records are updated, and educational credentials are validated. Its increased efficiency, security, and privacy make it an invaluable resource for higher education and lifelong learning. It does, however, also offer challenges with interoperability, limited transparency, and centralization.

Hence, in this section, we looked into the three types of blockchain. While privacy and control are given priority on a private blockchain, openness is a hallmark of the public blockchain. To fulfill the unique needs of consortiums and educational institutions, the permissioned blockchain provides a medium ground by balancing these factors. Finally, the choice of use of blockchain type should ultimately be made in light of the particular goals and challenges of the higher education institution.

SUSTAINABILITY OF BLOCKCHAIN IN THE EDUCATION SECTOR

The higher education sector is witnessing technology-driven knowledge transformation involving blockchain, big data, robotics, and artificial intelligence integration. This evolving change has led to technology-led teaching and learning, assessment and evaluation practices, administration, and financing transformation. This technology potential must be capitalized and aligned with sustainable and equitable knowledge transformation. It must be people-centered, socially responsive, and inclusive. Sustainable blockchain in education should empower the stakeholders – educators, administrators, and learners, by prioritizing education quality, equity, and sustainable development.

For sustainable use of blockchain in higher education and lifelong learning, this section focuses on four strategies – network cooperation, diversity of interacting agents, shared resources, and educational logistics, as shown in Figure 1 (Savelyeva & Fang, 2022). These strategies for sustainable blockchain in the education sector actively contribute to UN SDG -4 Quality Education, SDG – 9 of 'Industry, Innovation, Infrastructure', and SDG - 10 of 'Reduces Inequalities.'

Figure 1. Sustainable use of blockchain in education sector

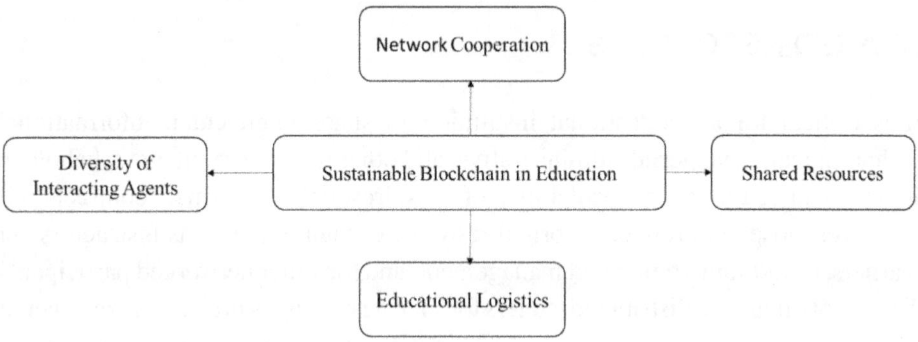

NETWORK COOPERATION

Establishing a quality network cooperation using blockchain is highly instrumental in addressing the teaching and learning capabilities and requirements while trustfully sharing resources amongst the network users (Cummings, 2008). The network cooperation framework should be clearly defined with a comprehensive project outcome. It should empower the institutional stakeholders with voluntary affiliation to the network, autonomy to participate or not, independence of all cooperating partners, equal access to all networking partners for knowledge resources, and autonomy in adding and creating new educational resources and opportunities. It shall enhance the interoperability of voluminous data exchanged between educational institutions by restricting who can access, enter, participate, and append new blocks. Thus, network cooperation can strengthen the sustainable use of blockchain within the education sector.

DIVERSITY OF INTERACTING AGENTS

Interacting agents in an educational setting include educational institutions, management associations, not-for-profit public or private institutions or training centers, educators or instructors, and other volunteers. To materialize the sustainable blockchain-led education setting, it is imperative to create an innovative learning environment where participants safely share, access, and evaluate knowledge-related materials and resources. The setting must empower the interacting agents to have collaborative diversity in their communications and actions to address the needs of the community and create quality education (SDG -4) in the short-run as well as in the long-run.

SHARED RESOURCES

It is critical for an educational institution to share intellectual, informational, technological, managerial, administrative, and other resources with its stakeholders in an organized manner. Availability of these resources via smart contracts will empower those who rely on informal resource exchanges, such as instructors and learners, the administration and management, and the other networked participants. The use of organized distributed ledgers for sharing resources in an organized manner will replace the existing informal exchange prevalent within education institutions and support inter-professional collaborations (Maloney et al., 2013).

EDUCATIONAL LOGISTICS

The typical hierarchical structure of the education sector involves a team at the top controlling the quality of the education system, the flow of education resources, and other processes and operations. A sustainable centralized distributed ledger system involves self-managing 'proof of work' verification performed by participating blockchain miners at all levels, digital teaching and learning infrastructure, instructional materials, and methodological support to the participants or stakeholders.

To conclude this section, blockchain technology is playing a pivotal role in educational innovation and infrastructure by empowering the stakeholders involved and reducing inequalities. The above-discussed four strategies will provide grounds for sustainable blockchain application in higher education and lifelong learning.

STRATEGIES FOR RESPONSIBLE BLOCKCHAIN

The fourth generation blockchain technology contributes to data security, reliability, and transparency in the education sector and lifelong learning. Though at a nascent stage, the technology is being efficiently implemented to satisfy all stakeholders at different levels of the education system – the students, instructors, and the educational institutions. This section discusses the strategies for the responsible use of blockchain technology for a better future in education and lifelong learning. The strategies are mainly divided into scalability, interoperability, common framework and regulations, and integration, as shown in Figure 2.

Figure 2. Future strategies for responsible blockchain

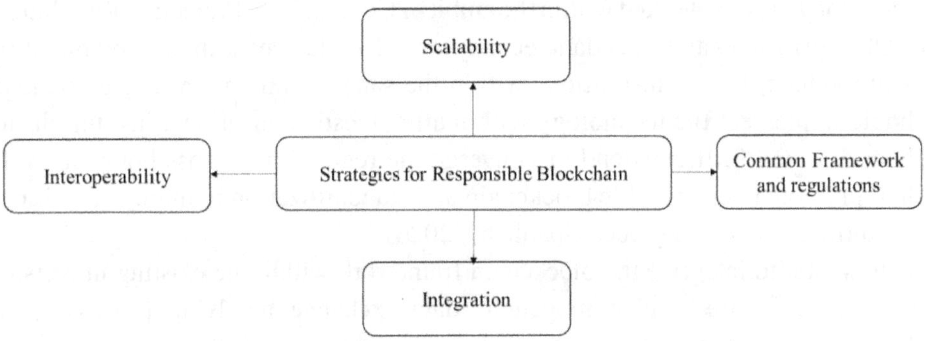

Scalability is the ability of the technology to continuously respond and operate as the input size increases (Santos & Duffy, 2019). Since blockchain is still in its early development stages, many universities and schools worldwide have piloted the projects at a small scale. However, future use of blockchain will involve *scalability and inter-operationality*. Each educational institution has an enormous volume of student data and hence needs processing time and power to increase the number of blocks and peer-to-peer verification of transactions in the blockchain, especially public blockchains (Steiu, 2020). Also, proofing of records shall take longer and require immense electrical energy that may be challenging for an educational institution to manage. With high electricity usage, the technology poses climate risks and involves a more significant carbon footprint (Tett, 2021). At present, it is a general hindrance to implementing the technology for the entire educational institution. To enhance scalability and consistency, it will be crucial to execute phased projects within the institutions. Further, the educational institution can make appropriate use of private and public blockchains, providing restrictions on who can access, enter, participate, and append new blocks. Public blockchains are not constrained in terms of access and appending new blocks. In contrast, private blockchains can be implemented with more restrictions on managing transactions, thus improving scalability in a trusted environment.

Different education institutions are under different legal and regulatory ambit. They follow different standards that can make it challenging to integrate blockchain technology. Uniformity among blockchain protocols, for instance, mass acceptance and consistency in standards, is critical. Limited standardization and interoperability reduce the capacity of the systems to properly collaborate, exchange, and share data that can be accessed and used by the interoperating systems (Zhong, Xie, Zou, & Chui, 2018). Therefore, it is essential for institutions to come forward and discuss *common standards* that shall enable the multiple blockchain networks to communicate with one another. However, these common standards for using technology must be worked within the ambit of General Data Protection Regulation (GDPR) principles and other data security laws. To enhance the inter-operationality of blockchain, firstly, institutions within the same common law, say a country, should implement the technology within all domestic educational institutions to share data and further extend or converge the regulations across boundaries. It shall promote inter-operable blockchain and standardization in more educational institutions across the globe (Upadhyay, 2020).

It is vital to integrate the blockchain framework within the existing university institutions for free and homogenous data exchange involving processes, IT structures, and restructuring systems. It is crucial to use a fully integrated model not only for intra-institution consistency, i.e., allowing a learner to move from one course to another with an educational institution, but also allowing for comparing curricula from different courses and degrees and assisting learners to move from one educational institution to another (Ceke D., 2020). Blockchain deployment must ensure compatibility within different academic institutions while protecting transaction data of sensitive academic information from the moment a learner enters the educational institution until the learner completes their diploma/degree (Shen H., 2018). Blockchain deployment in the education sector has also raised societal constraints, challenging its ethical and secure usage of data. Also, adopting a blockchain framework will reduce the administrative staff's expenses and will require to train the administrative staff appropriately. This may cause resistance to its implementation (Sharma, 2020). However, relying on third-party agencies can resolve the issue of accessing the required skills and expertise for implementing the technology within the education systems. This may raise alarming concerns relating to security. Data leakages and protection of private keys can pose a threat to educational institutions and raise trust concerns over the technology.

To conclude, the above-discussed strategies and framework are critical for the responsible use of blockchain technology in educational institutions. It is important to emphasize that the technology's usage and acceptability will increase with enhanced stakeholder acceptance. The stakeholders include academics, government, and industries, who need a broader understanding of different business models of blockchain, features, and the necessary governance structures. The government is a crucial stakeholder having the most significant impact on adopting blockchain across the education industry. The collaboration between government and educational institutions can help technology developers and innovators to produce credible solutions and enable successful and long-term integration of blockchain technology in higher education and lifelong learning.

CASE STUDIES AND CRITICAL INSIGHTS

Blockchain technology has emerged as a transformative force across various industries, and its potential impact on higher education is evident through innovative initiatives by institutions like Southern New Hampshire University (SNHU), the University of Dubai, and the University of Nicosia. These institutions have recognized the power of blockchain to revolutionize traditional education systems, credentialing, and payment methods, offering several significant benefits to the world of higher education.

Blockchain's inherent security features, including cryptographic encryption and decentralization, provide robust protection for sensitive academic and financial data. This ensures the integrity and confidentiality of records, safeguarding them from tampering or unauthorized access. Moreover, the transparency and tamper-resistant nature of blockchain builds trust within the educational ecosystem, reducing the risk of credential fraud. Blockchain also enhances global accessibility, simplifying access to academic records and tuition payments for international students, thereby streamlining administrative tasks, reducing costs, and fostering data ownership. Lastly, the innovation and competitiveness associated with blockchain adoption position institutions as forward-thinking and tech-savvy, attracting students and faculty while creating a more efficient and secure learning environment.

In this section, we will delve into three case studies that underscore the significance of blockchain in higher education. Real-world examples play a pivotal role in helping readers grasp the technology's maturity and practical relevance.

SOUTHERN NEW HAMPSHIRE UNIVERSITY

Southern New Hampshire University (SNHU) has taken a pioneering step in the realm of higher education by implementing a revolutionary application of blockchain technology known as the "Stackable Credentials" program (Lerman et al., 2020). This forward-thinking initiative is designed to elevate the teaching and learning experience by providing students with a secure and efficient means of showcasing their academic accomplishments and skills to potential employers, ultimately fostering a stronger connection between education and employment. At the heart of this innovative program lies the utilization of blockchain technology to securely store and manage academic credentials. Blockchain, a decentralized and tamper-resistant digital ledger, underpins the credibility and authenticity of these credentials. By leveraging blockchain's inherent features, SNHU ensures that the achievements and competencies earned by students remain trustworthy and verifiable (Dede & Richards, 2020).

In practice, SNHU bestows digital badges upon students upon successful completion of specific courses, projects, or skills assessments (Chivu et al., 2022). Each badge serves as a digital representation of a particular competency or accomplishment, offering a more granular and informative insight into a student's capabilities beyond traditional transcripts. These digital badges are recorded on the blockchain, functioning as a transparent and immutable ledger that enables swift and dependable verification of badge authenticity. This verification process can be conducted by a wide range of parties, including prospective employers and other educational institutions, with complete confidence in the accuracy of the information.

What sets this initiative apart is the ease with which students can share their digital badges. They can simply provide a link or QR code, simplifying the process of showcasing their skills and achievements on various platforms, such as resumes and LinkedIn profiles. As students continue their educational journey, they have the opportunity to accumulate multiple badges over time. This accumulation enables them to build a comprehensive portfolio of skills and achievements that align closely with their career aspirations, offering potential employers a more holistic representation of their capabilities. By seamlessly incorporating blockchain technology into the "Stackable Credentials" program, SNHU has not only transformed the way students document their educational achievements but also provided employers with a highly reliable method for credential verification. This pioneering application of blockchain in higher education stands as a testament to the transformative potential of technology in redefining the documentation and sharing of educational accomplishments, bridging the gap between academia and the workforce, and creating a more robust and dynamic ecosystem for education and employment.

SNHU's "Stackable Credentials" program harnesses blockchain technology to offer students a secure and transparent means of showcasing their academic achievements and skills to prospective employers. Digital badges representing specific competencies are stored on the blockchain, facilitating easy and verifiable verification by a wide range of stakeholders. This innovative initiative exemplifies the transformative potential of blockchain in higher education, bridging the gap between academia and employment and revolutionizing credential documentation and verification.

UNIVERSITY OF DUBAI

The University of Dubai introduced a cutting-edge student credential verification system powered by blockchain technology. It is an ambitious project to pioneer a cutting-edge digital certificate system, harnessing the potential of blockchain technology. This endeavor represents a significant step forward in higher education, offering numerous advantages to both the university and its students (Emirates News Agency, 2023).

The central of this innovative certificate platform revolves around enhancing the security and reliability of digital certificates. By employing blockchain technology, the university has established a robust and tamper-proof system that reinforces the trustworthiness of its academic credentials. The primary aim of this platform is to revolutionize how academic achievements are recorded, verified, and shared. At its essence, this initiative, named "Shahada," seamlessly aligns with the UAE Blockchain Strategy introduced in April 2018. This strategy aims to propel the UAE into the digital era by leveraging the transformative capabilities of blockchain across various sectors, including education (Jun, 2018).

One of the primary advantages of this blockchain-based solution is its ability to empower the university to create, generate, and distribute academic credentials efficiently. This streamlined process leads to significant time and resource savings for the institution. Furthermore, it fosters a more adaptable and responsive educational environment, enabling certificates to be issued promptly upon meeting the necessary requirements.

In practice, university students can now export their certificates in various formats to suit their specific needs. These certificates can be easily shared through multiple communication channels, such as email, SMS, WhatsApp, and other messaging platforms. This flexibility in sharing academic achievements simplifies the process for students, allowing them to provide proof of their qualifications quickly and conveniently. Importantly, the blockchain technology at the core of this system ensures robust privacy and security. Only authorized individuals can access and interact with the certificates, ensuring the confidentiality of sensitive academic records. This aspect is crucial for maintaining the integrity and privacy of students' credentials, preventing unauthorized tampering or access.

The University of Dubai's forward-thinking in implementing blockchain technology for academic credentialing marks a significant advancement in higher education. This initiative not only aligns with the UAE's strategic vision for blockchain adoption but also offers tangible benefits to both the university and its students. Through improved security, efficiency, and privacy, this blockchain-powered certificate platform is poised to reshape how academic achievements are acknowledged and shared in the digital age.

THE UNIVERSITY OF NICOSIA

The University of Nicosia (UNIC) in Cyprus has made a groundbreaking move in higher education by embracing blockchain technology, particularly by becoming among the first universities to accept Bitcoin as a legitimate method for paying tuition fees (Themistocleous et al., 2020). This forward-looking decision not only demonstrates the institution's progressive mindset but also highlights the profound impact of blockchain technology on reshaping the landscape of higher education (Kamišalić et al., 2019).

This adoption of Bitcoin for tuition fees is a significant milestone in integrating blockchain technology into the academic sector. Several key factors contribute to the importance of this initiative.

Firstly, UNIC recognizes the disruptive potential of blockchain technology. The university acknowledges that blockchain has the capacity to revolutionize traditional financial transactions and various aspects of academia. By offering Bitcoin as a payment option, UNIC caters to the diverse demographics of its student body. Many international students, a significant portion of the university's community, often face challenges with cross-border payments. Cryptocurrency payments offer a seamless and borderless solution, enhancing accessibility and simplifying international financial transactions.

Secondly, UNIC's commitment to safeguarding financial data and promoting transparency aligns perfectly with the foundational principles of blockchain. The immutable and tamper-resistant nature of blockchain ensures the security and traceability of all transactions, thereby enhancing trust in financial operations. Beyond security and accessibility, the adoption of Bitcoin streamlines the payment process, eliminating the bureaucratic delays often associated with traditional banking systems. This newfound efficiency benefits both the university and its students.

The University of Nicosia's pioneering adoption of Bitcoin for tuition fees serves as a prime example of blockchain technology's transformative potential in higher education. This bold move underscores the institution's dedication to global accessibility, security, efficiency, and innovation. Furthermore, UNIC's involvement in blockchain-related educational programs and research underscores its commitment to shaping the future of academia and finance. As blockchain continues to evolve, its role in higher education is poised to expand, offering fresh opportunities and solutions for students, institutions, and the broader educational landscape. as a whole.

CRITICAL ANALYSIS AND FUTURE DIRECTION

In the context of higher education, blockchain technology has gained significant attention due to its transformative potential. Several universities, including Southern

New Hampshire University (SNHU), the University of Dubai, and the University of Nicosia, have embraced blockchain to varying degrees, introducing innovative initiatives. These initiatives aim to address critical challenges within the education sector, such as credential verification, data security, and accessibility.

The adoption of blockchain in higher education is driven by several compelling factors. Firstly, blockchain's security features, including cryptographic encryption and decentralization, enhance the protection of academic and financial data. This ensures the integrity and confidentiality of records, effectively safeguarding them from tampering with or unauthorized access. This aspect alone addresses a significant concern in higher education, where data security and integrity are paramount.

Furthermore, blockchain's transparency and tamper-resistant nature instill trust within the educational ecosystem, reducing the risk of credential fraud. This transparency is particularly important for educational institutions and potential employers, as it provides a reliable means of verifying academic achievements. Blockchain also promotes global accessibility, simplifying access to academic records and tuition payments for international students. This streamlines administrative tasks, reduces costs, and fosters data ownership, thereby improving the overall experience for students and institutions alike.

Additionally, the adoption of blockchain in higher education positions institutions as forward-thinking and tech-savvy. It reflects an innovative approach to addressing age-old challenges within the education sector. This, in turn, can attract students and faculty members who are drawn to institutions that leverage cutting-edge technology to enhance the learning environment.

However, despite these benefits, it is essential to critically analyze the case studies presented. While they showcase the potential of blockchain, certain limitations and challenges remain unexplored in the text. These include:

1. **Cost and Technical Expertise:** Implementing blockchain systems can be costly and requires technical expertise. The text does not delve into the financial implications of adopting blockchain or the need for specialized personnel to manage and maintain these systems.
2. **Data Privacy and Security Concerns:** Blockchain technology is not immune to data privacy and security concerns. While the text highlights blockchain's security features, it does not address potential vulnerabilities or measures taken to mitigate risks.
3. **Interoperability and Standardization:** The text does not discuss the interoperability of various blockchain platforms and the need for standardization across institutions. Ensuring that academic credentials are universally recognized and compatible is crucial.

4. **Regulatory and Legal Frameworks:** Regulatory and legal frameworks surrounding the use of blockchain and cryptocurrencies in education vary across countries and regions. This lack of uniformity can create complexities for universities operating internationally, a point not explored in the text.
5. **Adoption Challenges:** The text does not mention potential resistance to change within academic institutions, which can hinder the adoption of blockchain technology.

In terms of future directions, there are several key considerations. Firstly, the efforts should focus on finding ways to seamlessly integrate blockchain with existing educational infrastructure. Hybrid models that combine blockchain with traditional record-keeping systems may serve as a transitional solution. Developing standardized protocols and increasing interoperability between different blockchain platforms will be crucial for achieving a unified and efficient ecosystem for academic credentials and payments.

CONCLUSION

This chapter provides the extent of blockchain application in higher education and lifelong learning. We present the fundamental components of blockchain and their role in the higher education sector. The foundational elements such as blocks, nodes, transactions, consensus mechanisms, decentralization, cryptographic hash, and smart contracts contribute to blockchain implementation and deliver exceptional services in this domain. Additionally, various blockchain models with potential for application in higher education highlight their transformative capabilities and empower the educational stakeholders. Blockchain technology serves as a foundation of trust and enhances the digital transcript ledger, capturing a learner's academic journey. Consensus mechanism and Proof of work (POW) guarantee the accuracy and integrity of educational records and play a critical role in higher education and lifelong learning. Smart contract automates and enforces the agreement terms within a blockchain network and eliminates the intermediaries from the system, thus acting as the technological backbone. Blockchain and smart contracts have revolutionized the way we learn and validate credentials, ensuring trust and efficiency at every stage of the educational journey. Establishing a network cooperation framework between universities, catering to diverse educational stakeholders setting, sharing resources within an institution in an organized and formal manner, and verifying the educational logistics can provide a ground for sustainable blockchain application in higher education and lifelong learning.

Moreover, the chapter explores three universities' real-world experiences to better understand the relationship between the practical applicability and maturity of the technology. SHNU students receive digital badges on successful completion of courses, projects, or skills tests. Every badge serves as a digital depiction of a specific skill or achievement, providing a more detailed and insightful view of a student's talents than conventional transcripts via blockchain technology. The University of Dubai has implemented a state-of-the-art student credential verification system, demonstrating the revolutionary potential of blockchain technology. Further, by embracing blockchain technology, the University of Nicosia (UNIC) in Cyprus has achieved a revolutionary move in higher education by recognizing Bitcoin as a valid form of payment for tuition fees.

It has policy implications for varied stakeholders in the higher education sector, such as the government, educational institutions, management, administration, educators, and learners. Even though blockchain technology is still in its infancy, it is being effectively applied to satisfy all stakeholders involved in the education system. It is crucial to stress that greater stakeholder acceptance will lead to an increase in the technology's usage and acceptability. Educators, the government, and the education industry are among the stakeholders who require a deeper comprehension of the many blockchain business models, features, and required governance frameworks. The government is a significant stakeholder that will have the most influence on blockchain adoption in the education sector. The successful and long-term integration of blockchain technology in higher education and lifelong learning can be made possible through the cooperation of government agencies and educational institutions with technology developers and innovators to generate solutions that are credible. Despite several benefits of blockchain technology, there are some challenges to the technology, such as data privacy, security concerns, cost, technical expertise, standardization, interoperability, and legal and regulatory standards. As we advance, it will be necessary to concentrate on figuring out how to combine blockchain technology with the current educational framework. Achieving a cohesive and effective ecosystem for academic credentials and payments will require standardized protocols and enhanced interoperability across various blockchain platforms.

REFERENCES

Arenas, R., & Fernandez, P. (2018). CredenceLedger: a permissioned blockchain for verifiable academic credentials. Paper presented at the *2018 IEEE International Conference on Engineering, Technology and Innovation (ICE/ITMC),* (pp. 1-6). IEEE. 10.1109/ICE.2018.8436324

Arndt, T., & Guercio, A. (2020). Blockchain-based transcripts for mobile higher-education. *International Journal of Information and Education Technology (IJIET), 10*(2), 84–89. doi:10.18178/ijiet.2020.10.2.1344

Bucea-Manea-Ţoniş, R., Martins, O. M., Bucea-Manea-Ţoniş, R., Gheorghiţă, C., Kuleto, V., Ilić, M. P., & Simion, V. (2021). Blockchain technology enhances sustainable higher education. *Sustainability (Basel), 13*(22), 12347. doi:10.3390u132212347

Ceke, D., & Kunosic, S. (2020) *Smart contracts as a diploma anti-forgery system in higher education—A pilot project.* Proceedings of the 2020 43rd International Convention on Information, Communication and Electronic Technology, Opatija, Croatia.

Chivu, R., Popa, I., Orzan, M., Marinescu, C., Florescu, M. S., & Orzan, A. (2022). The role of blockchain technologies in the sustainable development of students' learning process. *Sustainability, 14*(3), 1406. doi:10.3390u14031406

Cummings, T. G. (2008). *Handbook of organization development.* Sage.

Dede, C. J., & Richards, J. (2020). *The 60-year curriculum New models for lifelong learning in the digital economy*. Routledge. doi:10.4324/9781003013617

Emirates News Agency. (2023, 19 July). *University of Dubai successfully publish e-Credentials of graduates on blockchain platform* WAM. https//wam.ae/en/details/1395302866361

Garg, R. (2021). *Blockchain Ecosystem for Education and Employment Verification.* Paper presented at the 13th International Conference on Network & Communication Security, Toronto Canada.

Jun, M. (2018). Blockchain government-a next form of infrastructure for the twenty-first century. Journal of Open Innovation, 4(1), 7.

Kamišalić, A., Turkanović, M., Mrdović, S., & Heričko, M. (2019). *A preliminary review of blockchain-based solutions in higher education.* Paper presented at the Learning Technology for Education Challenges 8th International Workshop, LTEC 2019, Zamora, Spain.

Kuleto, V., Bucea-Manea-Ţoniş, R., Bucea-Manea-Ţoniş, R., Ilić, M. P., Martins, O. M., Ranković, M., & Coelho, A. S. (2022). The potential of blockchain technology in higher education as perceived by students in Serbia, Romania, and Portugal. *Sustainability (Basel), 14*(2), 749. doi:10.3390u14020749

Lerman, R. I., Loprest, P. J., & Kuehn, D. (2020). *Training for jobs of the future Improving access, certifying skills, and expanding apprenticeship.*

Lizcano, DLara, J. AWhite, BAljawarneh, S. (2020). Blockchain-based approach to create a model of trust in open and ubiquitous higher education. Journal of Computing in Higher Education, 32, 109–134.

Maloney, S., Moss, A., Keating, J., Kotsanas, G., & Morgan, P. (2013). Sharing teaching and learning resources perceptions of a university's faculty members. *Medical Education*, *47*(8), 811–819. doi:10.1111/medu.12225 PMID:23837427

Meria, L., Aini, Q., Santoso, N. P. L., Raharja, U., & Millah, S. (2021). Management of Access Control for Decentralized Online Educations using Blockchain Technology. Paper presented at the *2021 Sixth International Conference on Informatics and Computing (ICIC),* (pp. 1-6). IEEE. 10.1109/ICIC54025.2021.9632999

Pelletier, S. (2018). Blockchain in higher education. *The Chronicle of Higher Education.*

Puthal, D., Malik, N., Mohanty, S. P., Kougianos, E., & Das, G. (2018). Everything you wanted to know about the blockchain Its promise, components, processes, and problems. *IEEE Consumer Electronics Magazine*, *7*(4), 6–14. doi:10.1109/MCE.2018.2816299

Raimundo, R., & Rosário, A. (2021). Blockchain system in the higher education. *European Journal of Investigation in Health, Psychology and Education*, *11*(1), 276–293. doi:10.3390/ejihpe11010021 PMID:34542464

Santos, J., & Duffy, K. H. (2019). *A Decentralized Approach to Blockcerts Certificate Revocation*. Github. https://github.com/WebOfTrustInfo/rwot5-boston/tree/master/final-documents

Savelyeva, T., & Fang, G. (2022). *Sustainable tertiary education in Asia Policies, practices, and developments*. Springer Nature. doi:10.1007/978-981-19-5104-6

Sharma, S., & Batth, R. S. (2020). *Blockchain technology for higher education system: A mirror review*. Proceedings of the International Conference on Intelligent Engineering and Management, London, UK.

Sharples, M., & Domingue, J. (2016). The blockchain and kudos: A distributed system for educational record, reputation, and reward. *Adaptive and Adaptable Learning*, 490-496.

Shen, H., & Xiao, Y. (2018). *Research on online quiz scheme based on double-layer consortium blockchain*. Proceedings of the 9th International Conference on Information Technology in Medicine and Education, ITME; Hangzhou, China. 10.1109/ITME.2018.00213

Smith, S. (2018). Blockchain augmented audit – Benefits and challenges for accounting professionals. *The Journal of Theoretical Accounting Research*, *14*(1), 117–137.

Son-Turan, S. (2022). Fostering equality in education: The blockchain business model for higher education (BBM-HE). *Sustainability (Basel), 14*(5), 2955. doi:10.3390u14052955

Steiu, M. F. (2020). Blockchain in education: Opportunities, applications, and challenges. *First Monday, 25*(9). doi:10.5210/fm.v25i9.10654

Tett, G. (2021). A contest to control crypto is under way. *Financial Times.*

Themistocleous, M., Christodoulou, K., Iosif, E., Louca, S., & Tseas, D. (2020). Blockchain in Academia Where do we stand and where do we go? Paper presented at the *Hicss,* (pp. 1-10). IEEE. 10.24251/HICSS.2020.656

Upadhyay, N. (2020). Demystifying blockchain: A critical analysis of challenges, applications and opportunities. *International Journal of Information Management, 54*, 1–26. doi:10.1016/j.ijinfomgt.2020.102120

Zheng, Z., Xie, S., Dai, H., Chen, X., & Wang, H. (2017). An overview of blockchain technology: Architecture, consensus, and future trends. *Proceedings of 6th IEEE international Congress on Big Data* (pp. 557-564). IEEE.

Zhong, J., Xie, H., Zou, D., & Chui, D. K. (2018). *A blockchain model for word-learning systems.* In Proceedings of the 2018 5th International Conference on Behavioral, Economic, and Socio-Cultural Computing (BESC), Kaohsiung, Taiwan. 10.1109/BESC.2018.8697299

KEY TERMS AND DEFINITIONS

Blockchain: A blockchain is like a digital ledger or record book. It's made up of a chain of blocks, where each block contains a list of transactions.

Cryptographic Hash: It is like a unique fingerprint for each block. It's generated through a cryptographic algorithm and is a fixed-length string of characters.

Interoperability: Interoperability in blockchain refers to capability of networks to communicate with other blockchain networks.

Scalability: Scalability is the ability of the technology to continuously respond and operate as the input size increases

Smart Contract: Smart contracts are self-executing, programmable contracts that automate and enforce the terms of an agreement or transaction within a blockchain network.

Chapter 7
Geospatial Blockchain Applications for Land Administration in Pakistan

Munir Ahmad
https://orcid.org/0000-0003-4836-6151
Survey of Pakistan, Islamabad, Pakistan

ABSTRACT

In an era characterized by rapid technological progress, the persistent challenges of land administration are on the verge of a groundbreaking transformation through the adoption of blockchain technology. Originating with the advent of Bitcoin in 2008, blockchain has emerged as a beacon of hope, promising transparency, trust, immutability, and security in recording transactions. This innovative technology holds immense potential to revolutionize the landscape of land administration in Pakistan, a nation burdened by antiquated paper-based systems, corruption, land disputes, and inefficiencies. Embracing blockchain can offer Pakistan the prospect of an era marked by improved governance, diminished fraud, streamlined record-keeping, and equitable access to vital land information. Nonetheless, the path forward is strewn with challenges, necessitating the establishment of robust legal frameworks, capacity-building initiatives, and the resolution of privacy concerns.

INTRODUCTION

Land Administration (LA) refers to the procedure of ascertaining, documenting, and distributing data concerning land ownership, valuation, and utilization, as delineated by the United Nations Economic Commission for Europe (UNECE) (UNECE, 1996).

DOI: 10.4018/979-8-3693-0405-1.ch007

Land administration assumes a pivotal role in fostering economic development, ensuring social stability, and preserving the environment. It can establish the essential infrastructure for transparent land transactions, mitigate land-related conflicts, and promote responsible land utilization and governance.

The realm of land administration systems has undergone a surge of pioneering technologies with the overarching goal of revolutionizing the systematic and legal documentation of various aspects related to real estate and land ownership. Among these transformative developments, a particularly noteworthy revolution has emerged in the form of transitioning towards a blockchain-based approach to land administration. Blockchain can serve as a collaborative and unalterable ledger employed for the registration of transactions and asset monitoring within a network. This technology can store information in blocks, which are then interlinked in a sequential manner, forming a chain. Blockchain is a decentralized ledger system where each block represents a collection of data. Its applications extend beyond cryptocurrencies; it can also serve as a repository for land-related information.

Land administration in Pakistan grapples with a multitude of challenges, encompassing an antiquated and inefficient registration system that contributes to delays and impediments in economic development. Furthermore, complex and undocumented land tenure systems fuel disputes, while insufficient digitalization hinders transparency. Issues related to unauthorized land occupation and encroachments persist, and urbanization pressures strain the management of urban land. Corruption within land agencies remains pervasive, access to justice for land disputes is limited, and land fragmentation is prevalent. Resistance to policy and institutional reforms is also observed, emphasizing the necessity for more inclusive stakeholder engagement. To effectively address these issues, a holistic approach is required, involving comprehensive legal, technological, and governance reforms. These reforms aim to establish secure property rights, reduce disputes, and promote equitable land management, ultimately facilitating sustained economic growth.

Against this backdrop, the main objective of this chapter is to explore how blockchain technology can offer potential solutions to the challenges encountered in land administration in Pakistan. To achieve this objective, the chapter is structured as follows: The second section will illustrate the background knowledge of blockchain technology and land administration. The third section will delve into the specific challenges faced by the land administration in Pakistan. The subsequent section will explore how blockchain technology can be applied to address the challenges faced by the land administration in Pakistan. The final section will provide a concluding overview of the chapter's findings and insights.

BACKGROUND

Within this section, foundational insights pertaining to the dynamic intersection of blockchain technology and the domain of land administration are presented.

Blockchain Technology

The inception of Blockchain technology can be traced back to 2008, credited to an anonymous entity or group operating under the pseudonym "Satoshi Nakamoto" (Nakamoto, 2008). Its primary objective was to serve as the foundational infrastructure for the decentralized digital currency known as Bitcoin. Bitcoin employs a distributed ledger system to facilitate direct peer-to-peer transactions among users. This groundbreaking technology saw its first transaction in January 2009 and has since garnered considerable attention and widespread adoption, paving the way for the creation and integration of numerous other cryptocurrencies.

Blockchain technology has emerged as a prominent buzzword in the tech industry, thanks to its potential to revolutionize a wide range of businesses and processes. In essence, a blockchain serves as a digital ledger that offers a secure and transparent method of recording transactions. It leverages cryptographic techniques to ensure security and enables the establishment of transparent and decentralized networks. Essentially, it operates as a decentralized database, distributing data across a network of interconnected computers. Each of the individual blocks within the blockchain comprises records documenting multiple transactions, and once a block is added to the chain, it becomes immutable (Beck et al., 2018). The integrity and security of the blockchain are upheld by a consensus mechanism, which mandates agreement among all nodes within the network. Blockchain technology represents a versatile innovation with a multitude of potential applications spanning diverse industries and domains. Below, we explore some of the most significant use cases for blockchain technology, all of which hold great promise in enhancing existing systems and processes:

In the realm of supply chain management, blockchain technology brings about improved efficiency and a reduction in fraudulent activities. Kshetri, (2018) underscored how blockchain enhances transparency and efficiency by maintaining a secure and tamper-proof record of goods movement. In the healthcare sector, blockchain technology holds the promise of creating a secure and decentralized system for the storage and sharing of medical records, leading to heightened patient privacy and data security. Adere, (2022) and Kamruzzaman et al., (2022) accentuated the potential of blockchain technology in establishing a decentralized and secure medical records system. Y. Liu et al., (2020) described how blockchain technology can be harnessed to establish a secure and decentralized identity management system, empowering individuals to take charge of their own identity information. By leveraging distributed ledgers, blockchain technology can enhance the objectivity, validity, and control of information in education, reducing the influence of socioeconomic instabilities, as highlighted by (Alammary et al., 2019; Park, 2021). Blockchain technology improves basic disaster recovery processes by increasing transparency and preventing potential fraud. It fosters increased resilience, rapid response, transparent communication, and the integration of new contributors like the Internet of Things (Demir et al., 2020).

Some of the potential benefits of blockchain technology include:

- **Transparency and Trust:** Blockchain can offer an incorruptible and transparent ledger (Haleem et al., 2021), thus can support to significantly lowering the potential for corruption and fraudulent activities. This enhancement in transparency can build trust among participants and ensure the accuracy and security of records. For instance, in a supply chain scenario, every participant in the chain can trace the journey of a product from its origin to the end consumer through the transparent and unchangeable ledger, thereby ensuring the authenticity and quality of the product.
- **Immutable Records:** Once data is registered on a blockchain, it becomes impervious to alteration or deletion without unanimous agreement from all participants (Tiwari, 2020). This unwavering integrity can enhance the security of records and significantly reduce the possibility of unauthorized modifications. In the context of land administration, once property ownership is recorded on a blockchain, it can remain immutable, providing property owners with confidence in the permanence of their ownership rights.
- **Security:** Blockchain harnesses cutting-edge cryptographic methods to fortify data security (Gong & Zhao, 2020). Record owners can trust that their record entries are shielded, thereby reducing the likelihood of disputes and conflicts. For example, in the healthcare sector, patient records stored on a blockchain are protected by encryption, ensuring the privacy and integrity of sensitive medical data.
- **Decentralization:** By operating on a decentralized network, blockchain technology can mitigate the risk of manipulation or bias by centralized authorities (Anderson, 2019). This decentralization can foster a more equitable and impartial environment for transactions and data management. In financial services, decentralized blockchain networks can enable peer-to-peer transactions without the need for intermediaries, reducing the influence of central banks and financial institutions.

Types of Blockchain

There are four primary classifications of blockchain technology:

- Public blockchains are characterized by their openness and permissionless nature. In this type of blockchain, anyone can become a participant in the network, engaging in transaction validation and accessing the ledger. Prominent examples of public blockchains include Bitcoin and Ethereum.
- Private blockchains, in contrast, are exclusive and limited to a select group of authorized participants who possess the privilege to access and validate transactions. These blockchains are commonly employed by organizations for internal purposes, such as supply chain management or record-keeping.
- Consortium blockchains operate in a semi-decentralized manner and are overseen by a consortium or group of organizations, rather than being under the control of a single entity. These collaborating organizations collectively validate transactions, making consortium blockchains well-suited for industries where multiple stakeholders require blockchain access, such as healthcare or finance.
- Hybrid blockchains offer a fusion of characteristics from both public and private blockchains. They provide flexibility by permitting certain data to be publicly accessible while keeping other data private. This type of blockchain is often favored in scenarios where a balance between transparency and privacy is crucial.

These diverse classifications of blockchains are tailored to meet a wide array of use cases, ranging from fully open and decentralized systems to more tightly controlled and permissioned environments. The selection of the most appropriate blockchain type hinges on the precise requirements of a given project or application.

Geospatial Blockchain

Geospatial blockchain signifies the fusion of blockchain technology with geospatial data and Geographic Information Systems (GIS). This amalgamation entails the merging of geospatial data, encompassing location information, with the capabilities of blockchain technology, yielding an array of applications and advantages, notably enriched data accuracy and heightened security. These geospatial blockchains find utility across a broad spectrum of use cases, encompassing secure data sharing, supply chain tracking, and the management of land registries, harnessing the unchanging nature of blockchain to safeguard the integrity of location-centric information. Furthermore, they not only record location data but also subject it to validation through associated proofs of location, thereby ensuring the trustworthiness and precision of geospatial data. The blockchain's tamper-resistant ledger bolsters the security of this data, effectively thwarting unauthorized alterations and fraudulent activities within location-related records. As an exemplar, the XYO Network stands out as a blockchain geospatial network, employing cryptographic methods to anonymously gather and validate geospatial data (Anusuya, 2022). In the forthcoming section, it will be referred to simply as "blockchain" for clarity in its connection to land administration.

Land Administration

Land, as one of the fundamental components of production, plays a pivotal role in the economic development of any nation. Land administration serves as a vital tool for governments in their efforts to combat poverty, safeguard human rights, and ensure food security. To provide a comprehensive understanding, land can be defined as the physical space encompassing the Earth's surface, along with all its associated elements both above and below, including seawater (Dale & McLaughlin, 1999).

In the context of economic development, the production of goods and services serves as a catalyst, and land constitutes one of the essential factors of production, alongside labor, capital, and entrepreneurship (O'Sullivan & Sheffrin, 2007). The land possesses substantial revenue-generating potential, thus earning its status as a "key economic resource, intricately interlinked with access to, utilization of, and control over other economic and productive resources" (FAO, 2019). Access to land, the security of land tenure, and effective land management are of paramount importance for fostering economic growth within a country (Robin McLaren, 2013).

Furthermore, effective land administration plays a pivotal role in promoting good governance within governments. This, in turn, has a ripple effect, stimulating revenue generation, poverty alleviation, protection of human rights, and the assurance of food security. The interconnectedness of these factors underscores the critical role that land administration plays in shaping the trajectory of a nation's development.

Land Administration Systems (LASs) serve as comprehensive repositories, encompassing not only information pertinent to land tenure and ownership but also crucial data regarding land value and land use (Bandeira et al., 2010; Williamson, 2001). These systems function as the primary source for documenting the intricate web of rights, restrictions, and responsibilities associated with individuals, policies, and geographical locations (A. Ali & Imran, 2021).

It is important to note that land-related data is inherently spatial data, and the significance of such data cannot be overstated. It has been estimated that a staggering 80% of all human decisions are intrinsically linked to geographical factors (Worrall,

1991). This underscores the pivotal role of land data in informing and influencing various facets of human activity and decision-making processes. The concept of a National Spatial Data Infrastructure (NSDI) encompasses a comprehensive framework that encompasses aspects such as policy, technology, standards, human resources, and geospatial data (Rajabifard, A., Feeney, M. E. F., & Williamson, 2003). According to insights from (Masser, 1999), the primary mission of the majority of NSDIs revolves around three core objectives: advancing socio-economic development, enhancing government efficiency, and fostering environmental sustainability. Although Spatial Data Infrastructures encompass a wide array of functions beyond the scope of land administration, it's worth noting that land administration can be seen as a pivotal catalyst influencing the evolution of SDIs (Williamson & Feeney, 2001). Even blockchain has the potential to support SDI (Ahmad, 2023).

Regrettably, a sobering reality prevails: only a limited number of countries, numbering between 30 to 50, have established comprehensive land registration systems. Moreover, in many nations, operational land administration systems remain conspicuously absent. This void in proper land administration poses a significant threat to the public, exposing them to the risks of land conquest and insecure tenancy arrangements (Robin McLaren, 2013). Addressing this deficiency and establishing robust land administration systems are imperative steps toward ensuring the protection and welfare of citizens in such countries.

MAIN FOCUS OF THE CHAPTER

The main focus of this chapter is to explore the challenges facing land administration in Pakistan and to examine the potential benefits and implications of implementing blockchain technology as a solution. The chapter discusses the existing conventional paper-based land administration system in Pakistan and the various challenges it faces, including inefficient land registration systems, land tenure complexity, lack of digitalization, land grabbing and encroachments, urbanization pressures, corruption, limited access to justice, fragmented land ownership, and resistance to policy and institutional reforms. It emphasizes the need for comprehensive modernization initiatives.

The chapter also delves into international experiences of using blockchain technology in land administration, citing examples from countries like Ghana, Sweden, UAE, Honduras, Ukraine, India, Bangladesh, and many more. It highlights the advantages of blockchain, such as transparency, trust, mitigation of land title fraud, efficient record-keeping, land ownership dispute resolution, improved accessibility, corruption mitigation, data security, and more.

Furthermore, the chapter discusses the specific implications of adopting blockchain technology in Pakistan's land administration, including the development of a legal framework, data privacy and security policies, interoperability standards, recognition of smart contracts, user access and training, dispute resolution mechanisms, regulatory oversight, public awareness, and the importance of pilot programs for testing and refining the technology.

DISCUSSIONS

This section offers a detailed examination of land administration in Pakistan, highlighting its complex challenges. It also explores the global adoption of blockchain technology in land records management, showcasing international examples. Additionally, it delves into the specific implications of introducing blockchain in Pakistan's land administration system.

Land Administration in Pakistan and Its Challenges

The prevailing land administration system of Pakistan heavily relies on conventional paper-based formats, employing land registers and cadastral maps to record vital information such as land ownership and property boundaries (Z. Ali & Nasir, 2010). The Board of Revenue (BOR) assumes a pivotal role as the chief executive overseeing land administration matters within provinces, while also providing advisory support to Provincial Governments regarding land-related policies (UN-Habitat, 2012). The primary focus of the land administration system predominantly revolves around the assessment of land revenue and the collection of taxes for fiscal purposes, underscoring its pronounced financial orientation. Notably, despite the ever-evolving technological landscape, the available data suggests limited headway in modernization endeavors, as the system persists in its dependence on traditional methodologies and paper-based documentation, indicating a potential imperative for more extensive modernization initiatives.

Land administration in Pakistan grapples with a multitude of formidable challenges, each with significant ramifications for property rights, land management, and economic development. Some of the principal challenges are described below and summarized in Figure 1.

- **Inefficient Land Registration Systems:** The antiquated and convoluted land registration processes in Pakistan represent a significant roadblock to efficient land management and economic progress (Z. Ali & Nasir, 2010; IIPS, 2023). These cumbersome procedures often lead to exasperating delays

Figure 1. Challenges of land administration in Pakistan

to discourage much-needed investments and can impede overall economic growth. For instance, a budding entrepreneur who wishes to acquire land for a new business venture. The labyrinthine registration system and its associated delays could cause this entrepreneur to miss crucial opportunities and incur additional costs, hindering the timely establishment of their business.

- **Land Tenure Complexity:** Pakistan's land tenure landscape is characterized by a complex interplay of formal and informal ownership structures, often compounded by inadequate documentation (Z. Ali & Nasir, 2010). This intricate web of land tenure systems frequently gives rise to disputes and conflicts, creating barriers to the establishment of clear property rights and hindering land transactions. For instance, imagine a scenario in which multiple parties claim ownership of the same piece of land due to historical disputes and informal agreements. Resolving such disputes within the existing framework can be a protracted and costly endeavor, deterring potential investors and stalling land development projects.
- **Lack of Digitalization:** A substantial portion of land records in Pakistan still rely on traditional paper-based documentation, leaving them susceptible to loss, tampering, and corruption (Qurat ul Ain, 2019). The sluggish pace of digitization within land administration can impede transparency and efficient land management. As an example, envision a situation where a critical land record is inadvertently damaged or destroyed due to a natural disaster or mishandling. In a digitalized system, redundancy and data recovery mechanisms would mitigate such risks, ensuring the integrity of land records and preserving crucial information.
- **Land Grabbing and Encroachments:** Unauthorized land occupation and encroachments, both on public and private lands, persist as pervasive

challenges in Pakistan (Ata et al., 2023). These activities, often involving influential individuals or groups, can create formidable legal quagmires and disrupt property rights. For example, consider a case where an influential entity encroaches upon a parcel of public land, using its clout to circumvent legal consequences. Addressing such issues within the existing legal framework can be arduous, requiring substantial time and resources.

- **Urbanization Pressures:** The rapid urbanization sweeping across Pakistan places considerable strain on land administration systems in urban areas (Abdul & Yu, 2020). The challenges associated with urban growth, including issues related to land use planning, zoning regulations, and infrastructure development, often lag behind the pace of urbanization. For instance, envision an urban center experiencing rapid population growth without adequate zoning regulations in place. This mismatch can lead to urban sprawl, inadequate infrastructure, and an inefficient use of available land, ultimately hampering the city's sustainable development.
- **Corruption and Bribery:** Corruption within land administration agencies remains an enduring concern, with the influence of bribes and illicit practices extending into land transactions, property disputes, and land allocation (Hasan et al., 2022). This corruption erodes the principles of transparency and the rule of law, fostering an environment in which illicit gains take precedence over equitable land management.
- **Limited Access to Justice:** High costs and the complexity of the legal process pose significant barriers to justice for many citizens grappling with land disputes (Mughal, 2012). This results in a lack of recourse for individuals whose land rights have been violated, perpetuating a climate of uncertainty and potential injustice. For example, the prohibitive costs of legal proceedings may dissuade, an individual from a marginalized community engaged in a land dispute with a more powerful entity, from pursuing a just resolution, exacerbating land tenure inequities.
- **Fragmented Land Ownership:** The fragmentation of land into small, economically unviable plots is a prevalent issue in rural areas, directly impacting agricultural productivity (A. Ali & Ahmad, 2016; Niroula & Thapa, 2005). Addressing this challenge necessitates comprehensive efforts such as land consolidation and improved land use planning.
- **Policy and Institutional Reforms:** The endeavor to implement comprehensive reforms in land administration may face resistance stemming from bureaucratic hurdles, political considerations, and the need for effective interagency coordination (Ahmad & Khiyal, 2023). This complex landscape can impede the swift adoption of reforms critical for modernizing land management practices.

- **Limited Stakeholder Engagement:** The interests of diverse stakeholders, including local communities, women, and marginalized groups, are often marginalized in land administration processes. Achieving inclusive land governance and equitable land distribution necessitates substantial improvement. This narrow focus can curtail comprehensive land management efforts (Z. Ali & Nasir, 2010).

Mitigating these challenges necessitates a comprehensive approach that includes legal reforms, digitalization of land records, enhanced governance, and heightened transparency. Establishing a land administration system that safeguards property rights, minimizes land disputes, and fuels economic development must also account for the varied needs of the population.

Blockchain for Land Administration: World Perspective

Since the advent of blockchain technology, numerous countries have embarked on the journey of implementing blockchain-driven land administration systems. Instances of such initiatives have been documented in various regions, including Georgia, Sweden, UAE, Honduras, Ukraine, Ghana, India, Bangladesh, and many more (Alam et al., 2022; Ameyaw & de Vries, 2021; Eder, 2019; Graglia & Mellon, 2018; Müller & Seifert, 2019; Thakur et al., 2020).

Ameyaw & de Vries, (2020) undertook a comprehensive examination of the relationship between blockchain technology and the transparency of land administration, with a specific focus on Ghana. The study aimed to identify key elements and connections between the two, ultimately assessing blockchain's potential to enhance transparency in land administration processes. The research findings underscored the importance of achieving comprehensive transparency across all land administration processes and involving all stakeholders simultaneously. A single permissionless public blockchain emerged as a promising means to achieve this goal. However, it was emphasized that standardization within different land divisions must precede the widespread application of blockchain technology to prevent inconsistencies and irregularities in processes. This study holds relevance for a wide spectrum of land stakeholders, offering valuable insights into the social and political dynamics of land administration in Ghana. The paper also outlined policy implications for blockchain adoption, including a thorough review of paper-based land transactions, digitization of land administration processes, and the encouragement of public-private partnerships. Furthermore, it stressed the necessity of intensive public education, particularly for land stakeholders, to ensure a comprehensive understanding of blockchain technology.

Blockchain technology presents a compelling remedy for the issues afflicting land records management in India, tackling concerns such as transparency, accountability, and data consistency across various government departments as noted by Thakur et al., (2020). The study underscored that, within the framework of the National Land Record Modernization Programme (NLRMP), efforts are underway to create a contemporary and transparent land records system, and blockchain has emerged as a pivotal element in this endeavor. This innovative technology has the potential to offer immutable land titles, instilling trust in property ownership while streamlining the entire land records process. In regions susceptible to disasters, such as Kerala, blockchain stands out as a resilient alternative for preserving property rights and ensuring the integrity of land records, the study asserted.

According to Shang & Price, (2019), the government of Georgia has demonstrated a strong inclination toward the adoption of blockchain technology as a pivotal component of its endeavors to rebuild public confidence in government institutions. A notable milestone in this pursuit was the introduction of the Georgia pilot project, which marked the inaugural instance of a national government utilizing the Bitcoin Blockchain for the registration of land titles (Shin, 2017). Benbunan-Fich & Castellanos, (2018); Lazuashvili et al., (2019); Shang & Price, (2019) endorsed that this initiative has yielded substantial improvements in government efficiency and played a pivotal role in reestablishing public trust in national agencies. As of the year 2018, a remarkable total of 1.5 million land titles within the Republic of Georgia had been securely recorded on the blockchain, thereby ensuring the inviolability and permanence of this critical data. The accomplishments of the Georgia project can be attributed to two fundamental factors—education and data quality. In the realm of blockchain-based projects, the education of all stakeholders is of paramount importance. A collective understanding of blockchain technology and the specific challenges it can address is essential. Both the citizens and government authorities must comprehend the rationale behind adopting this technology and the problems it is capable of resolving. Throughout the course of the project, the National Agency of Public Registry (NAPR) undertook the task of enlightening the people of Georgia about how blockchain technology can guarantee the immutability of land title data without compromising privacy concerns.

According to Benbunan-Fich & Castellanos, (2018), in 2015, Factom, a technology company from Austin, Texas, and Epigraph, a Texas-based software title company, engaged with the Honduran government to explore the development of a new land registry system due to concerns about the vulnerability of physical land title records dating back to the 1880s. This effort was closely tied to the creation of Zones for Employment and Economic Development (ZEDEs) in Honduras, with Factom contributing to technology initiatives related to land registry within these zones. Their blockchain-based solution aimed to establish immutable records on the Bitcoin

Blockchain, focusing on proof of existence, process, and audit for land transfers. Despite efforts, the project faced challenges, including political considerations and bureaucratic hurdles, and was eventually halted in 2017, preventing Honduras from becoming an early adopter of a blockchain-based land registry.

Yapicioglu & Leshinsky, (2020) highlighted Cyprus as a prime candidate for harnessing blockchain technology in the recording of contested property rights, presenting innovative possibilities for conflict resolution. It underscored the importance of further research, particularly in exploring how sidechains can streamline the documentation of conflicting land interests and disputed claims. This novel application of blockchain in the realm of property rights presented exciting prospects for future investigation and implementation.

In Brazil, Ubitquity, a blockchain-based real estate startup, has joined forces with Brazil's land records bureau to introduce a pilot program geared towards enhancing property record management in South America. Now blockchain technology is playing a pivotal role in the modernization and simplification of real estate registration processes, particularly within the Municipality of Pelotas, Rio Grande do Sul. This innovative initiative is a response to the country's intricate and fragmented land management system, involving a convoluted 13-step process for property registration, along with the use of various identifiers for the same property, which has led to potential issues related to uncertainty and corruption. The project's primary objectives are to enhance efficiency, transparency, and security in property registration procedures. Blockchain technology is leveraged to guarantee the authenticity of property information and ownership. While a successful pilot program has been conducted, further adjustments and alignment with legal archiving practices are necessary for the broader implementation of this transformative approach (Ian, 2017; Joe, 2018).

The Ukrainian government geared up to launch a blockchain-based land registry trial in October 2017, introducing this technology into the State Land Cadastre and also digitizing state land lease auctions. This forward-looking initiative is designed to enhance transparency, efficiency, and competition in land management, with a particular focus on the agricultural sector, which occupies a substantial portion of Ukraine's territory. Prime Minister Volodymyr Groysman's commitment to auctioning all state land leases underscores the government's determination to stimulate the local economy and curb illicit activities. Furthermore, the trial aims to address prevailing challenges, including low levels of public land registration, inadequate lease payments, a sluggish land market, and limited land taxpayers (Chuan, 2022; Volodymyr, 2017).

Sweden's land registry authority, Lantmäteriet, is progressing with its blockchain technology trial for property transactions, now entering its second phase. Spearheaded by ChromaWay and Kairos Future in partnership with SBAB and Landshypotek banks, this endeavor seeks to establish a transparent system for property dealings through blockchain, potentially reshaping the way real estate transactions are carried out. Despite the current legal requirement for physical signatures, the project is actively exploring digital alternatives and has attracted attention from authorities in other countries, underscoring the global potential of blockchain technology in property transactions, especially in developing nations (Jonathan, 2021).

UK-based HM Land Registry is set to embark on a blockchain technology trial as part of its broader digitization initiative called 'Digital Street.' The primary aim is to boost the efficiency of property title transfers and facilitate nearly instantaneous property ownership changes. This aligns with the government's commitment to digital transformation and providing customer-centric services, reflecting a global trend where public agencies explore blockchain for land registry and property ownership purposes. Nevertheless, potential regulatory challenges could impact the full-scale commercial deployment of these blockchain-based initiatives (Stan, 2021).

Alam et al., (2022) endorsed that Bangladesh's land title management system faces significant challenges, including fraud and lengthy processes. The proposed solution introduces Blockchain technology to enhance data synchronization, transparency, access, and record management while reducing costs and processing time. The phased approach to Blockchain adoption starts with a public Blockchain ledger and gradually transitions to a Full Hybrid Blockchain. This technology is well-suited for land titling as it ensures an immutable chain of ownership records and prevents document falsification. The existing system's problems include fraud, illegal land grabbing, lengthy disputes, and a lack of centralized land information. The proposed system aims to address these issues, improve transparency, and streamline land titling processes in Bangladesh.

UAE-based Dubai Land Department is embarking on a blockchain initiative to digitally record all local real estate contracts, with the aim of enhancing investor confidence and providing electronic conveniences to tenants. This project forms part of the government's broader plan to migrate all documents to a blockchain platform by 2020. The department believes that blockchain technology will bolster global trust among real estate investors and enable tenants to manage leases and payments electronically. Key partners involved in this initiative include Asset Management Group, Emirates NBD, IKEA, and the Emirates Identity Authority. Dubai has been actively exploring blockchain technology for various applications, spanning airport security, trade finance, and immigration controls, positioning itself as a blockchain innovation hub (Marc, 2021).

Overstock.com's blockchain subsidiary, Medici Land Governance (MLG), is partnering with the Zambian government to establish a blockchain-based land title registry, aiming to improve property rights management and stimulate economic development in Zambia (Madeline, 2018).

The Netherlands Land Registry organization, known as the Kadaster, has initiated a land registry project that leverages both Blockchain and AI technologies. This project focuses on recording land title information, including geographical coordinates, with high precision. The use of blockchain and timestamping techniques ensures the accurate storage of this data. While the project is currently in the development stage, it aligns with the government's "Blockchain Pilots" program, which aims to implement blockchain technology across various e-governance applications (Wouda & Opdenakker, 2019).

USA, Cook County, Illinois, planned to pioneer the use of the Bitcoin blockchain for property conveyance, becoming the first government agency to do so. This innovative move, supported by blockchain technology provider Velox, aims to enhance information accuracy related to vacant Chicago buildings, curb fraudulent property transfers, and simplify land records. The Cook County Recorder of Deeds office sees blockchain as the future of land records, emphasizing its potential for security and transparency. The pilot program will assess the compatibility between distributed ledgers and the client-server database model. If successful, it could lead to changes in state laws, ushering in a blockchain-based public record system (Lester, 2021).

Canadian-based British Columbia Land Titles and Survey Authority (LTSA) collaborates with DIACC and IDN to explore blockchain's application in land transaction recording through a virtual design challenge, aiming to innovate LTSA's business processes and understand its social, legal, and business implications. Blockchain@UBC assists in this endeavor, generating insights for future designs and land title registration in British Columbia (Blockchain@UBC, 2023).

The Russian government had plans to initiate a blockchain-based land registration pilot project in 2018, forging partnerships with various agencies such as the Ministry of Economic Development, Rosreetr, the Federal Tax Service, and the Government of Moscow. The primary objectives of this initiative were to enhance transparency in property registry information, safeguard property rights, and bolster citizens' trust in real estate transactions. Prime Minister Dmitry Medvedev's directive to explore blockchain's applications in governance and the economy served as a catalyst for this endeavor, with the high operational costs of Rosreetr acting as a significant driving force (Nikhilesh, 2021).

The Japanese government is embarking on a plan to unify all property and land registries across urban, farmland, and forested areas into a single blockchain-powered ledger. This initiative seeks to enhance the efficiency of real estate transactions and property management. Currently, fragmented data is scattered among various government entities and real estate companies, with the traditional paper-based registry system proving outdated and infrequently updated. The proposed blockchain ledger will encompass property ownership details, sale prices, and collateral information, thereby facilitating improved data cross-referencing and the identification of responsible parties for vacant properties. This endeavor is geared towards streamlining property management, optimizing real estate transactions, and expediting the redevelopment of vacant properties in Japan (Samburaj, 2021).

BLOCKCHAIN FOR LAND ADMINISTRATION IN PAKISTAN

Blockchain has the potential to document and monitor land ownership transactions, granting individuals, particularly farmers, greater control over land utilization (Daniel & Ifejika Speranza, 2020). This technology can significantly enhance the transparency of land administration by maintaining an immutable and verifiable record of all transactions and ownership transfers (Ameyaw & de Vries, 2020). Research findings indicate that blockchain technology is a viable solution for land management. It offers transparency, security, and efficiency in the handling of land-related records and transactions (Müller & Seifert, 2019). Blockchain can simplify the management of transaction records, ensuring consistency and immutability among the various stakeholders involved in land administration (Ameyaw & de Vries, 2023).

In an era where digitization and secure data management are paramount, blockchain technology emerges as a powerful tool to revolutionize land administration systems. This innovation promises a plethora of benefits that not only streamline the processes but also enhance the overall trustworthiness of land records. In the context of mitigating the challenges faced by land administration in Pakistan, blockchain technology stands out as a promising solution with several potential benefits that are described below and summarized in Figure 2.

Figure 2. Blockchain for land administration in Pakistan

- **Transparency and Trust: Blockchain:** Often lauded as a cornerstone of trust, can provide a tamper-resistant and transparent ledger for land records. It achieves this by encrypting and decentralizing data across a network of nodes. Each transaction is cryptographically linked to the previous one, making it nearly impossible to alter historical records without consensus from the network. This not only reduces the scope for fraud but also instills trust in the system among stakeholders. Smart contracts on the blockchain can automate processes, reducing the need for intermediaries and minimizing the risk of corruption. For instance, in Sweden, the Lantmäteriet (Swedish Land Registry) has embarked on a blockchain-based project that can enable the transparent transfer of property ownership (Jonathan, 2021).
- **Mitigate Land Title Fraud:** Blockchain technology can establish an immutable record of land ownership, rendering it exceedingly difficult for fraudsters to manipulate records. Blockchain technology can support to prevention of unauthorized changes to land titles, thereby reducing the risk of land title fraud. For instance, in Ghana, a pilot project has been initiated to register land titles on the blockchain, providing an extra layer of security and trust in land transactions (Ameyaw & de Vries, 2021).
- **Efficient Record-keeping:** Traditional paper-based land record systems are notoriously prone to errors and inefficiencies. In stark contrast, blockchain can streamline record-keeping processes, substantially reducing paperwork. Records stored on a blockchain are easily accessible and can be updated in real time. This can enhance efficiency and accuracy in land administration. The Republic of Georgia, for instance, is in the process of employing blockchain technology to manage land titles, resulting in a significant reduction in administrative burdens and processing times (Lazuashvili et al., 2019).
- **Land Ownership Dispute Resolution:** Blockchain can act as a digital, indisputable repository of land transactions, providing crucial evidence in the resolution of land ownership disputes. Smart contracts can automatically enforce ownership rules, reducing ambiguity and legal disputes. A prime example of this is Sweden, where blockchain-powered smart contracts have been experimented with to automate property transactions, simplifying the resolution of disputes (Jonathan, 2021).
- **Improved Accessibility:** Blockchain can make land records accessible to a broader range of stakeholders, including citizens, government agencies, and financial institutions. Mobile applications and online platforms can provide real-time access to land information, promoting transparency and inclusivity. This is evident in Sweden, where the public can easily access land registry information through a user-friendly interface.

- **Mitigate Corruption:** By reducing the need for intermediaries and automating processes, blockchain technology can diminish opportunities for corruption in land administration. Transparency in transactions can act as a deterrent to corrupt practices.
- **Data Security:** Blockchain can employ robust encryption and decentralized storage, enhancing the security of sensitive land records. Data breaches and unauthorized access are less likely to occur on a blockchain-based land administration system. The state of Andhra Pradesh in India has made significant strides in securing land records using blockchain technology (Singh, 2020).
- **Efficient Land Transactions:** Blockchain can streamline the process of buying, selling, and transferring land, reducing the time and costs associated with these transactions. It can also simplify obtaining mortgages and loans based on land assets. For example, in the United States, companies like Propy are using blockchain to facilitate real estate transactions, making the process more efficient and cost-effective (Propy, 2023).
- **Land Tax Collection:** Blockchain can automate land tax collection, ensuring that landowners pay their taxes promptly and accurately. Governments can receive tax payments in a transparent and efficient manner. This has been successfully demonstrated by the state of Vermont, which introduced blockchain technology to improve the accuracy and efficiency of property tax collection (VADS, 2019).
- **Land Use Planning:** Blockchain provides valuable data for urban planning and land use management, assisting authorities in making informed decisions. Land records stored on the blockchain can be harnessed for urban development and infrastructure planning, as witnessed in Dubai's ambitious project to digitize land records and employ blockchain for urban planning (Marc, 2021).

However, it's important to note that implementing blockchain in land administration is not without challenges. These challenges may include the need for robust legal and regulatory frameworks, capacity building to use blockchain effectively, addressing issues related to data privacy, and ensuring inclusivity to prevent marginalized groups from being left out of the system. Blockchain-driven initiatives aimed at land administration may encounter hurdles, with institutional elements serving as pivotal determinants of their triumph. It is imperative to comprehend and proactively tackle these institutional aspects to foster the adoption and triumph of blockchain technology in the realm of land administration (Ansah et al., 2023).

While blockchain shows great potential, its successful integration into land administration in Pakistan will require careful planning, investment, and collaboration among various stakeholders, including government agencies, technology providers, and legal experts. Additionally, the technology must be adapted to the specific needs and challenges of Pakistan's land administration system to maximize its benefits.

IMPLICATIONS

The adoption of blockchain technology in land administration in Pakistan carries several important policy implications. These implications encompass legal, regulatory, and administrative aspects that must be addressed to ensure a successful and effective implementation of blockchain in this context. Here are some key policy implications to consider:

Legal Framework Development

Pakistan would need to establish a clear legal framework that recognizes blockchain-based land records as legally valid and enforceable. This includes defining the legal status of blockchain records, ensuring their admissibility in courts, and addressing issues related to digital signatures and contracts.

Data Privacy and Security

Policies must be enacted to protect the privacy and security of sensitive land data stored on the blockchain. This may involve complying with data protection regulations, defining access controls, and implementing robust encryption measures.

Interoperability Standards

To ensure that different blockchain systems used in land administration can communicate and share data effectively, interoperability standards need to be established. This is crucial for maintaining a unified and consistent land registry.

Smart Contracts and Legal Validity

Policy considerations must be made regarding the use of smart contracts in land transactions. These self-executing contracts should adhere to existing legal frameworks and be recognized as legally binding.

User Access and Training

Policies should focus on ensuring that all stakeholders, including government officials, citizens, and land professionals, have access to the blockchain-based land registry system. Training and education programs may be necessary to ensure that users can navigate and utilize the technology effectively.

Dispute Resolution Mechanisms

Mechanisms for resolving disputes related to blockchain-based land records should be established. This might involve creating specialized legal procedures or alternative dispute resolution mechanisms that can address issues arising from the technology.

Regulatory Oversight

Regulatory bodies may need to be established or empowered to oversee the implementation of blockchain in land administration. These bodies can ensure compliance with established standards and regulations.

Public Awareness and Engagement

Policies should promote public awareness and engagement in the transition to blockchain-based land administration. Citizens should be informed about the benefits of the technology and how to access and verify land records.

Pilot Programs and Evaluation

It may be prudent to implement pilot programs to test the technology on a smaller scale before nationwide adoption. These programs can help identify challenges and refine policies before full-scale deployment.

CONCLUSION

Blockchain technology has emerged as a revolutionary tool with the potential to address the myriad challenges plaguing land administration in Pakistan. With its inherent attributes of transparency, trust, immutability, security, and decentralization, blockchain offers a promising avenue for modernizing a system that has long relied on cumbersome paper-based processes and struggled with inefficiencies, corruption, land disputes, and inadequate digitization. By embracing blockchain technology,

Pakistan can usher in an era of enhanced transparency, reduced fraud, streamlined record-keeping, efficient dispute resolution, broader accessibility, and improved governance in land administration. While the path forward is promising, it is not without its hurdles, including the need for robust legal frameworks, capacity building, data privacy safeguards, and equitable inclusion. The successful integration of blockchain into Pakistan's land administration system will require a concerted effort and collaboration among stakeholders, including government agencies, technology experts, legal professionals, and the broader public.

As for future work, it is imperative to continue exploring and refining the application of blockchain technology in land administration, tailoring it to the specific needs and intricacies of Pakistan's land management landscape. This includes the development of comprehensive legal and regulatory frameworks that accommodate blockchain, investing in capacity building to ensure the effective use of this technology, and addressing potential privacy and security concerns. Additionally, efforts should focus on ensuring that marginalized groups and communities are not left behind in the adoption of blockchain-based land administration, promoting inclusivity and equitable land governance. Continuous research and pilot projects can help refine the technology's implementation and assess its impact on property rights, land management, and economic development. By addressing these challenges and opportunities, Pakistan can unlock the full potential of blockchain in revolutionizing its land administration system and reaping the associated benefits for its citizens and future prosperity.

REFERENCES

Abdul, L., & Yu, T. F. (2020). Resilient Urbanization: A Systematic Review on Urban Discourse in Pakistan. In Urban Science, 4(4). doi:10.3390/urbansci4040076

Adere, E. M. (2022). Blockchain in healthcare and IoT: A systematic literature review. In Array, 14. doi:10.1016/j.array.2022.100139

Ahmad, M. (2023). Leveraging Blockchain for Spatial Data Infrastructure: Challenges and Opportunities. *Supporting Technologies and the Impact of Blockchain on Organizations and Society*, 177–194.

Ahmad, M., & Khiyal, M. S. H. (2023). Assessment of land administration in Pakistan and the potential role of volunteered geographic information. In Handbook of Research on Driving Socioeconomic Development With Big Data. IGI Global. doi:10.4018/978-1-6684-5959-1.ch014

Alam, K. M., Ashfiqur Rahman, J. M., Tasnim, A., & Akther, A. (2022). A Blockchain-based Land Title Management System for Bangladesh. *Journal of King Saud University. Computer and Information Sciences, 34*(6), 3096–3110. doi:10.1016/j.jksuci.2020.10.011

Alammary, A., Alhazmi, S., Almasri, M., & Gillani, S. (2019). Blockchain-based applications in education: A systematic review. In Applied Sciences (Switzerland), 9(12). doi:10.3390/app9122400

Ali, A., & Ahmad, M. (2016). Analysis of the Barriers to Land Administration in Pakistan. *GSDI 15 World Conference*.

Ali, A., & Imran, M. (2021). National Spatial Data Infrastructure vs. Cadastre System for Economic Development: Evidence from Pakistan. *Land (Basel), 10*(2), 188. doi:10.3390/land10020188

Ali, Z., & Nasir, A. (2010). Land Administration System in Pakistan - Current Situation and Stakeholders' Perception. *FIG Congress 2010: Facing the Challenges - Building the Capacity*. IEEE.

Ameyaw, P. D., & de Vries, W. T. (2020). Transparency of land administration and the role of blockchain technology, a four-dimensional framework analysis from the ghanaian land perspective. In Land, 9(12). doi:10.3390/land9120491

Ameyaw, P. D., & de Vries, W. T. (2021). Toward smart land management: Land acquisition and the associated challenges in Ghana. a look into a blockchain digital land registry for prospects. In Land, 10(3). doi:10.3390/land10030239

Ameyaw, P. D., & de Vries, W. T. (2023). Blockchain technology adaptation for land administration services: The importance of socio-cultural elements. *Land Use Policy, 125*, 106485. Advance online publication. doi:10.1016/j.landusepol.2022.106485

Anderson, M. (2019). Exploring decentralization: blockchain technology and complex coordination. *Journal of Design and Science*.

Ansah, B. O., Voss, W., Asiama, K. O., & Wuni, I. Y. (2023). A systematic review of the institutional success factors for blockchain-based land administration. *Land Use Policy, 125*, 106473. doi:10.1016/j.landusepol.2022.106473

Anusuya, D. (2022). *Building the World's First Blockchain Geospatial Network Backed with Cryptography*. GeoSpatial World. https://www.geospatialworld.net/prime/interviews/building-the-worlds-first-blockchain-geospatial-network-backed-with-cryptography/

Ata, S., Shahbaz, B., Arif Watto, M., & Hussain, N. (2023). Transnational Seasonal Land Grabbing in Pakistan: Power Positions and Resistance. *Journal of Asian and African Studies*, *58*(3), 372–388. doi:10.1177/00219096211063816

Bandeira, P., Sumpsi, J. M., & Falconi, C. (2010). Evaluating land administration systems: A comparative method with an application to Peru and Honduras. *Land Use Policy*, *27*(2), 351–363. doi:10.1016/j.landusepol.2009.04.005

Beck, R., Müller-Bloch, C., & King, J. L. (2018). Governance in the blockchain economy: A framework and research agenda. *Journal of the Association for Information Systems*, *19*(10), 1020–1034. Advance online publication. doi:10.17705/1jais.00518

Benbunan-Fich, R., & Castellanos, A. (2018). Digitalization of land records: From paper to blockchain. *International Conference on Information Systems 2018, ICIS 2018*. Blockchain@UBC.

Chuan, T. (2022). *Ukrainian Government to Start Blockchain Land Registry Trial in October*. CoinDesk. https://www.coindesk.com/markets/2017/06/23/ukrainian-government-to-start-blockchain-land-registry-trial-in-october/

Dale, P., & McLaughlin, J. (1999). Land Administration. In Oxford Press. Oxford University Press. doi:10.1093/oso/9780198233909.001.0001

Daniel, D., & Ifejika Speranza, C. (2020). The Role of Blockchain in Documenting Land Users' Rights: The Canonical Case of Farmers in the Vernacular Land Market. *Frontiers in Blockchain*, *3*, 19. doi:10.3389/fbloc.2020.00019

Demir, M., Turetken, O., & Ferworn, A. (2020). Blockchain-based transparent disaster relief delivery assurance. *SYSCON 2020 - 14th Annual IEEE International Systems Conference, Proceedings*. IEEE. 10.1109/SysCon47679.2020.9275915

Eder, G. (2019). Digital Transformation: Blockchain and Land Titles. *2019 OECD Global Anti-Corruption & Integrity Forum*. OECD.

FAO. (2019). *Measuring Individuals' Rights to Land: An Integrated Approach to Data Collection for SDG Indicators 1.4.2 and 5.a.1*. FAO, The World Bank, & UN-Habitat. https://www.fao.org/publications/card/en/c/CA4885EN/

Gong, J., & Zhao, L. (2020). Blockchain application in healthcare service mode based on Health Data Bank. *Frontiers of Engineering Management*, *7*(4), 605–614. doi:10.100742524-020-0138-9

Graglia, J. M., & Mellon, C. (2018). Blockchain and Property in 2018: At the End of the Beginning. *Innovations: Technology, Governance, Globalization*, *12*(1–2), 90–116. doi:10.1162/inov_a_00270

Haleem, A., Javaid, M., Singh, R. P., Suman, R., & Rab, S. (2021). Blockchain technology applications in healthcare: An overview. In International Journal of Intelligent Networks, 2. doi:10.1016/j.ijin.2021.09.005

Hasan, L., Chaudhry, A., & Jalil, H. (2022). Regulation, Corruption, and Land Grab: A Tale of Illegal Private Housing Societies in Islamabad. SSRN *Electronic Journal*. doi:10.2139/ssrn.4019448

Ian, A. (2017). Blockchain-based Ubitquity pilots with Brazil's land records bureau. *IB Times*. https://www.ibtimes.co.uk/blockchain-based-ubitquity-pilots-brazils-land-records-bureau-1615518

IIPS. (2023). *Land Registration System of Pakistan: History and Challenges*. IIPS. https://iips.com.pk/land-registration-system-of-pakistan-history-and-challenges/

Joe, M. (2018). *Case Study: Blockchain Takes a Spin Around the Real-Estate Block*. RT Insights. https://www.rtinsights.com/case-study-blockchain-takes-a-spin-around-the-real-estate-block/

Jonathan, K. (2021). *Sweden Moves to Next Stage With Blockchain Land Registry*. https://www.coindesk.com/markets/2017/03/30/sweden-moves-to-next-stage-with-blockchain-land-registry/

Kamruzzaman, M. M., Yan, B., Sarker, M. N. I., Alruwaili, O., Wu, M., & Alrashdi, I. (2022). Blockchain and Fog Computing in IoT-Driven Healthcare Services for Smart Cities. *Journal of Healthcare Engineering*, *2022*, 1–13. doi:10.1155/2022/9957888 PMID:35126961

Kshetri, N. (2018). 1 Blockchain's roles in meeting key supply chain management objectives. *International Journal of Information Management*, *39*, 80–89. doi:10.1016/j.ijinfomgt.2017.12.005

Lazuashvili, N., Norta, A., & Draheim, D. (2019). Integration of Blockchain Technology into a Land Registration System for Immutable Traceability: A Casestudy of Georgia. *Lecture Notes in Business Information Processing*, *361*, 219–233. doi:10.1007/978-3-030-30429-4_15

Lester, C. (2021). *Cook County to Use the Bitcoin Blockchain for Property Conveyance*. CCN. https://www.ccn.com/cook-county-to-use-the-bitcoin-blockchain-for-property-conveyance/

Liu, Y., He, D., Obaidat, M. S., Kumar, N., Khan, M. K., & Raymond Choo, K. K. (2020). Blockchain-based identity management systems: A review. In Journal of Network and Computer Applications, 166. doi:10.1016/j.jnca.2020.102731

Madeline, M. S. (2018). *Zambia, Overstock's Medici Ink Deal on Blockchain Land Registry Pilot*. Coin Desk. https://www.coindesk.com/markets/2018/08/01/zambia-overstocks-medici-ink-deal-on-blockchain-land-registry-pilot/

Marc, H. (2021). *Dubai Land Department Launches Blockchain Real Estate Initiative*. Coin Desk. https://www.coindesk.com/markets/2017/10/10/dubai-land-department-launches-blockchain-real-estate-initiative/

Masser, I. (1999). All shapes and sizes: The first generation of national spatial data infrastructures. *International Journal of Geographical Information Science*, *13*(1), 67–84. doi:10.1080/136588199241463

McLaren, R. (2013). Engaging the land sector gatekeepers in crowdsourced land administration. *FIG Working Week 2013*.

Mughal, M. A. (2012). Concept of Access to Justice in Pakistan. SSRN *Electronic Journal*. doi:10.2139/ssrn.2136599

Müller, H., & Seifert, M. (2019). Blockchain, a Feasible Technology for Land Administration? *Geospatial Information for a Smarter Life and Environmental Resilience*.

Nakamoto, S. (2008). Bitcoin: A Peer-to-Peer Electronic Cash System | Satoshi Nakamoto Institute. *Bitcoin.Org*.

Nikhilesh, D. (2021). *Russia's Government to Test Blockchain Land Registry System*. Coin Desk. https://www.coindesk.com/markets/2017/10/20/russias-government-to-test-blockchain-land-registry-system/

Niroula, G. S., & Thapa, G. B. (2005). Impacts and causes of land fragmentation, and lessons learned from land consolidation in South Asia. *Land Use Policy*, *22*(4), 358–372. doi:10.1016/j.landusepol.2004.10.001

O'Sullivan, A., & Sheffrin, S. M. (2007). *Economics: Principles in Action*. Pearson/Prentice Hall. https://books.google.com.pk/books?id=vfxAHAAACAAJ

Park, J. (2021). Promises and challenges of Blockchain in education. *Smart Learning Environments*, *8*(1), 33. doi:10.118640561-021-00179-2

Propy. (2023). *Blockchain for Real Estate*. Propy. https://propy.com/browse/blockchain/

Qurat ul Ain. (2019). The Need for Efficient Record Management System in Pakistan. *South Asian Review of Business and Administrative Studies, 1*(1).

Rajabifard, A., Feeney, M. E. F., & Williamson, I. (2003). *Spatial data infrastructures: concept, nature and SDI hierarchy*. Taylor & Francis London.

Samburaj, D. (2021). *Japan Could Place Its Entire Property Registry on a Blockchain*. CCN. https://www.ccn.com/japan-place-entire-property-registry-blockchain/

Shang, Q., & Price, A. (2019). A Blockchain-Based Land Titling Project in the Republic of Georgia: Rebuilding Public Trust and Lessons for Future Pilot Projects. *Innovations: Technology, Governance, Globalization*, *12*(3–4), 72–78. doi:10.1162/inov_a_00276

Shin, L. (2017). The First Government To Secure Land Titles On The Bitcoin Blockchain Expands Project. *Forbes*.

Singh, P. (2020). Role of Blockchain Technology in Digitization of Land Records in Indian Scenario. *IOP Conference Series. Earth and Environmental Science*, *614*(1), 012055. doi:10.1088/1755-1315/614/1/012055

Stan, H. (2021). *UK Land Registry Plans to Test Blockchain in Digital Push*. Coin Desk. https://www.coindesk.com/markets/2017/05/12/uk-land-registry-plans-to-test-blockchain-in-digital-push/

Thakur, V., Doja, M. N., Dwivedi, Y. K., Ahmad, T., & Khadanga, G. (2020). Land records on Blockchain for implementation of Land Titling in India. *International Journal of Information Management*, *52*, 101940. doi:10.1016/j.ijinfomgt.2019.04.013

Tiwari, U. (2020). Application of Blockchain in Agri-Food Supply Chain. *Britain International of Exact Sciences (BIoEx). Journal*, *2*(2), 574–589. doi:10.33258/bioex.v2i2.233

UN-Habitat. (2012). *A GUIDE ON LAND AND PROPERTY RIGHTS IN PAKISTAN*. UN. https://cms.ndma.gov.pk/storage/app/public/publications/December2020/oeBNJ57eoaK7VbjALelV.pdf

UNECE. (1996). Land Administration Guidelines With Special Reference to Countries in Transition. UNECE.

VADS. (2019). *Blockchains for Public Recordkeeping and for Recording Land Records*. SOS. https://sos.vermont.gov/media/r3jh24ig/vsara_blockchains_for_public_recordkeeping_white_paper_v1.pdf

Volodymyr, V. (2017). *Ukraine Turns to Blockchain to Boost Land Ownership Transparency*. Bloomberg.

Williamson, I. P. (2001). Re-engineering land administration systems for sustainable development - From rhetoric to reality. *International Journal of Applied Earth Observation and Geoinformation*, *3*(3), 278–289. Advance online publication. doi:10.1016/S0303-2434(01)85034-0

Williamson, I. P., & Feeney, M.-E. (2001). Land administration and spatial data infrastructures: trends and developments. *FIG XXII International Congress*.

Worrall, L. (1991). *Spatial Analysis and Spatial Policy Using Geographic Information System*. Belhaven Press.

Wouda, H. P., & Opdenakker, R. (2019). Blockchain technology in commercial real estate transactions. *Journal of Property Investment & Finance*, *37*(6), 570–579. Advance online publication. doi:10.1108/JPIF-06-2019-0085

Yapicioglu, B., & Leshinsky, R. (2020). Blockchain as a tool for land rights: Ownership of land in Cyprus. *Journal of Property. Planning and Environmental Law*, *12*(2), 171–182. Advance online publication. doi:10.1108/JPPEL-02-2020-0010

KEY TERMS AND DEFINITIONS

Land Administration: It is a systematic and organized process of managing and recording land-related information, transactions, and ownership rights. It involves the registration, mapping, and maintenance of land records to ensure secure and transparent land tenure systems.

Blockchain: It is a revolutionary technology that employs a decentralized and immutable ledger to record and verify transactions. It offers high security and transparency by distributing data across a network of computers, making it resistant to alteration and fraud.

Geospatial Blockchain: It is an innovative fusion of geospatial data and blockchain technology. It leverages the capabilities of blockchain to securely and transparently manage geospatial information, allowing for more reliable and efficient management of location-based data and services.

Land Use Planning: It is a strategic process that involves the organized allocation and regulation of land for various purposes, such as residential, commercial, agricultural, or environmental conservation. It aims to balance the needs of communities with sustainable development while considering social, economic, and environmental factors.

Chapter 8
Mechanism for the Systematic Generation of Functional Tests of Smart Contracts in Digital Publication Management Systems

Nicolas Sanchez-Gomez
https://orcid.org/0000-0001-9102-6836
University of Seville, Spain

Javier Jesús Gutierrez
University of Seville, Spain

Enrique Parrilla
Lantia Publishing S.L., Spain

Julian Alberto García García
University of Seville, Spain

Maria Dolores de-Acuña
University of Seville, Spain

Maria Jose Escalona
https://orcid.org/0000-0002-6435-1497
University of Seville, Spain

ABSTRACT

The application of state-of-the-art technologies in functional fields is complex and offers a significant challenge to user and expert teams as well as to technical teams. This chapter presents a mechanism that has been used in a project in the context of digital publications. Ensuring the traceability of digital publications (e-books and e-journals) is a critical aspect of the utmost importance for authors, publishers, and buyers. The SmartISBN project has used blockchain technology to define a protocol for the identification, tracking, and traceability of digital publications. As this was an innovative project that required communication between functional experts (authors, publishers, booksellers, etc.) and technical experts, it was necessary to identify protocols to facilitate communication. This chapter presents the protocol by which the functional tests have been defined and how this has favoured the validation of the project.

DOI: 10.4018/979-8-3693-0405-1.ch008

1. INTRODUCTION

Blockchain is a disruptive software technology that is advancing rapidly (Olea, 2019), being one of the fundamental technologies driving Digital Transformation today and, given its transversal nature applicable to a wide range of industrial and economic sectors, it is enabling disruption in the economy and in business beyond cryptocurrencies. This potential is largely based on its ability to offer individuals or organizations a communication channel that allows the transfer of rights, values, or real assets (tokenization), through the Internet, in a secure and reliable manner.

The publishing industry is one of the economic sectors in which blockchain technology has great applications because the publishing industry is a data and metadata intensive sector. This means that the quality of operations and their automation are linked to the quantity and quality of this data. From a global perspective, the distribution process and supply chain of digital publications (e-books and e-journals, among other formats) in Spain is a complex process (Martínez Alés, 2001). A wide variety of actors are engaged in this process, each with diverse needs and actions. The following is a summary of these actors to help understand the magnitude of the process.

A digital publication, once written, must enter a digital copy distribution process. This process can take several months or even years and requires a significant financial investment. While on demand publishing mechanisms exist with delivery times of days, they do not offer assimilable quality and are pushed to specific niches. Then, distributors take the publications from the publishers to the points of sale. These outlets may be physical bookshops, online platforms, or both (Magadán-Díaz et al., 2020).

The emergence of innovative technologies for data and metadata storage and management, such as the possibility of massively and automatically extracting information from web pages, as well as the development of new technologies, such as blockchain technology for information recording (Gramoli, 2022) (Alharby et al., 2018), open up the possibility of offering novel alternatives within the publishing industry.

Blockchain technology and, above all, smart contracts can make valuable contributions as discussed throughout this article. In short, this recent technology offers more transparency, security, and efficiency in the tracking of publications (books, journals, etc.) at each stage of the process. For example, in this project, it has been possible to track and trace digital publications from their production to their final sale, which has made it possible to know the status of the publication at all times.

However, before deploying a smart contract in a business environment, it is necessary that any smart contract is verified using rigorous mechanisms that allow validating its correct operation, since an error or defect in the code that forms it could cause an unrepairable effect (Legerén-Molina, 2018). From an engineering perspective, the serious and competitive progress in the implementation of recent technologies such as blockchain and smart contracts requires new processes, methods, tools, and techniques to manage quality in software development and, above all, to ensure the quality of the final product.

Currently, there are several blockchain platforms that support the implementation, deployment, and execution of smart contracts without many restrictions. For example, Ethereum, Hyperledger or EOS platforms, among others (Zheng Z., 2020), allow deploying smart contracts without going through any verification and validation process. In this sense, verification of smart contracts remains an unexplored line of research to date. Any blockchain network may be running smart contracts with unexpected behavior, with serious deficiencies, errors and even security vulnerabilities (Luu, 2016). Unlike classical applications, which can be patched when errors are detected, smart contracts are irreversible and immutable, given the characteristics of the underlying technology.

In this context, the objective of this article is to present a proposal to generate functional test plans based on smart contract specifications. For this purpose, the proposal will be based on early testing principles, which will allow validating the functional quality of smart contracts independently of the blockchain technology used and from the requirements specification stage. In addition, this article describes the validation of our proposal in the SmartISBN project, which was carried out between 2019 and 2022.

The SmartISBN project aimed to develop mechanisms to semi-automatically extract a set of data and metadata to facilitate the management of publications, together with the development of a practical case of application of blockchain technology for the registration of transactions throughout the life cycle of a digital publication until it reaches its final purchaser.

This article aims to present the results achieved with this project, focusing the main part of the article on the practical case developed with blockchain, since it is not only a novel technology but there are few references to practical cases of application outside its original scope.

This technology also imposes new challenges. In particular, the main challenge in this project was the testing of blockchain technology and the use of smart contracts. As the distribution and supply chain is a complex process, it was necessary to cover many tests. As part of the SmartISBN project, the generation of a complete set of tests was systematized to verify that the system worked properly in all steps of the process and satisfied all its participants.

The organization of this work is described below. Section 2 presents the objectives of the SmartISBN project and the fundamentals of blockchain technology. Then,

Section 3 presents a comprehensive literature review to identify gaps in the existing models. Next, Section 4 presents the proposed solution for systematic functional test generation in blockchain environments and how it has been validated in the SmartISBN project. Finally, Section 5 presents conclusions and future work.

2. BACKGROUND

This section describes the background to the proposal presented in this article. To do so, on the one hand, it describes the context of the SmartISBN project, delving into its objectives, the problems it aims to solve and the technical and business challenges it faces. On the other hand, the fundamentals of blockchain technology are presented in general terms.

2.1. SmartISBN Project: Context and Approach

When the SmartISBN project started, there was no uniformity in the metadata (data describing other data, e.g., data describing the information to be managed for each specific digital publication) managed in the publishing sector. This is because of the different approaches and because different systems offer different data sets. This results in publishing management systems having to work with the minimum set of common data, which decreases the power of the management that can be applied.

The mission of the SmartISBN project was to address the problem indicated by researching and developing a metadata model applicable to the publishing sector that would enable the processing of data associated with a digital publication in a unified manner. The project also included the development of tools that allow the appropriate management of the information in the publications and the operations that could be carried out with them. To fulfil this mission, the SmartISBN project had to meet the three objectives briefly described below.

The first objective was to store a publisher's complete catalogue information in an automated way. This automation consisted of incorporating the data using tools that detect this data on web pages and then storing it in a system based on the ONIX Standard (Needleman, 2001). ONIX is an open, international standard for the encoding and electronic exchange of bibliographic and commercial information in the publishing industry, with the participation of representatives of the commercial publishing chain from more than twenty countries (including Spain).

The second objective was the processing of the publications data considering the needs of different actors in the sector such as publishers, distributors, etc. In addition, this catalog will be self-verified in the sense that it will report incidences in the information stored in the catalog itself.

The third and final objective was to provide a record of the different operations carried out with the publications in a blockchain registry. This objective allows all transactions to be recorded without the possibility of changes or modifications, which ensures the veracity of the information and makes it possible, for example, to detect fraud or illicit transactions more easily. This third objective is the one most closely related to blockchain technology, whose fundamentals and application to this project are explored in more detail in the following section.

2.2. Blockchain Fundamentals

The origin of digital assets in 2008 with the appearance of Bitcoin also implied the appearance of recent technologies necessary to support these digital currencies and the operations that can be carried out with them. One of these technologies is well known by its English name: blockchain (Gramoli, 2022).

In a simplified way, blockchain technology consists of information that is completed with metainformation designed to guarantee the integrity of the information, so that it cannot be modified, and designed to maintain the time reference so that the temporal order of information generation can be precisely known. Figure 1 shows

Figure 1. How the blockchain works

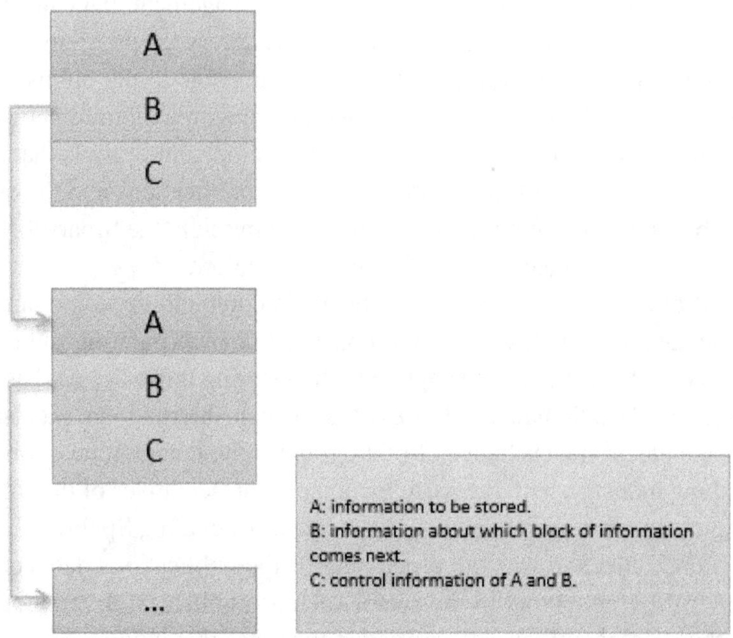

an example of how blockchain technology works. The A blocks are containers of information (e.g., transactions made with publications), and the B blocks link the information so that it is all located and ordered temporally. The C blocks are calculated from the A and B blocks, so a change in the information (an A block), or in the sequence (a B block), would make the C block incorrect and the change would be immediately discovered.

In its first implementation, blockchain technology was used to store all Bitcoin transactions, i.e., who owns which coins. However, this technology quickly became independent of digital currencies and was applied to any area where it is necessary to store an immutable record of transactions, for example, biological samples, domain name registrations, public tenders, etc. Another key aspect of blockchain is server management. The blockchain chain, as seen in the example in Figure 1, must be stored on a computer with external communication.

On the other hand, blockchain technology works through smart contracts. This is a piece of software whose mission is to fulfill and enforce agreements usually registered between two or more parties, for example, to validate the change of ownership of a digital asset. Typically, smart contracts (Figure 2) are used to automate a blockchain system, i.e., the storage of information in a blockchain system is controlled by compliance with the rules and decisions indicated in a smart contract. In the same way, a blockchain system serves as a record of all deployed smart contracts.

Figure 2. Smart contract in blockchain

Although the blockchain itself guarantees that the information is reliable (as we have seen), if the server is not well managed, or suffers physical problems, it can compromise the stored information. To avoid this problem, the non-profit association Alastria exists in Spain to set up blockchain servers.

3. LITERATURE REVIEW

This section presents the state-of-the-art survey of research papers in the context of the development lifecycle of smart contracts in the blockchain. This review focused on the analysis of primary studies addressing some of the phases of the development lifecycle and/or model-driven engineering or other best practices for designing, developing, and testing smart contracts. For this purpose, the SLR (Systematic Literature Review) method proposed by Kitchenham (Kitchenham, 2013), which is one of the most widely applied methods in the field of software engineering, was used. This method proposes three main phases to execute a systematic review: planning the systematic review (planning), which defines aspects such as the need for the research, review protocol and research questions; execution of the review protocol (conducting), where the established protocol is carried out; and presentation of the results obtained (reporting), which presents the final analysis to answer each research question. These phases are described in detail below.

3.1. Planning Review

During this stage of the process, the need to conduct this literature review, the identification of research questions and the definition of the review protocol are established. On the one hand, regarding the need to conduct the review, in recent years, many studies have been published to evaluate and identify current challenges in the application of blockchain technology and smart contracts. Some of these research activities aimed to evaluate the use of blockchain in multiple sectors such as, supply chain (Pranto, 2019), (Hidayanto et al, 2019), education sector (Steiu, 2020), agriculture sector (Yadav, 2019) or healthcare sector (Yaqoob, 2021). Other authors have even published studies partially related to our SLR proposal. For example, Alharby et al. (Alharby, 2018) presented a systematic mapping of smart contract technology, selecting and classifying 188 relevant articles. In this classification, the lack of validation mechanisms for smart contracts is evident. Macrinici et al. (Macrinici, 2018) also conducted a systematic mapping, but, in this case, to identify the application of smart contracts and offer a perspective on current issues. Specifically, the authors presented research trends within this context and gathered sixty-four articles. The work of these authors concluded by indicating that, since 2016, there has been an increasing trend towards the publication of articles related to smart contracts and that the most discussed problems and solutions in the literature were related to security, privacy, and scalability of the blockchain and quality of smart contracts. Dhaiouir et al. (Dhaiouir, 2020) also presented a systematic review of smart contracts, focusing on platforms, languages or applications and selection criteria. Specifically, this study indicates that smart contracts are being adopted in several types of projects, but that they still face many challenges and technical problems, but these authors do not study validation and verification aspects.

In this context, the need to study current methods and techniques that allow quality assurance in the development of smart contracts is identified. Specifically, to analyze techniques for formal modeling of smart contracts, automatic generation of functional tests and/or code from such modeling, in order to characterize and present the state of the art in this field and to identify possible gaps and opportunities for further research. For this purpose, the following research questions (RQ) were proposed:

RQ1: Are there approaches in the literature that promote the application of a Software Development Life Cycle (SDLC)? What phases of the life cycle do the different studies promote? The motivation of this RQ is to find proposals that have been published and to identify their general contexts and the objectives they achieved using SDLC, all in the context of blockchain smart contracts.

RQ2: Do they promote model-based software engineering, early starting of the testing phase or automatic source code generation? The purpose of this RQ is to identify the techniques and guidelines applied in the different proposals, all in the context of blockchain smart contract.

On the other hand, once our research questions were established, inclusion/exclusion criteria were established to filter the primary studies found in some of the main digital libraries, as recommended by authors such as Ngai (Ngai, 2011). In this sense, the libraries selected were ACM Digital Library, IEEE Xplore Digital Library, ScienceDirect, Elsevier's Scopus and Springer Link. In our case, this strategy focused on locating articles published in peer-reviewed journals, presented at relevant conferences, and was done in two steps: (1) the keywords to be used in the search protocol were defined; and (2) preliminary searches were performed to refine the set of keywords and select the most appropriate ones in order to improve the quality of the results. Finally, the keywords systematically applied in each digital library were the following: (Engineering OR Semantic OR Model-based) AND (Requirement OR Analysis OR Validation OR Verification OR Check OR Testing) AND (Blockchain OR Smart Contract).

Regarding the exclusion/inclusion criteria, these were rigorously applied considering five phases as shown in Table 1. Moreover, only articles written in English and published in journals indexed in Journal Citation Reports (JCR) or prestigious conferences (i.e., conference level A*, A, B and C categorized in CORE Conference Rank) were considered. In addition, it was decided to exclude surveys, discussions, reviews, or opinion studies related to the subject matter sought. Finally, following the recommendations given in Kitchenham's method, the SLR protocol was reviewed by an external researcher to obtain a comprehensive review process.

Table 1. Exclusion/inclusion criteria by phase

Phase	Relevance analysis phase description
Ph1	Automatic search was conducted in each scientific database.
Ph2	English only; year of publication greater than or equal to 2016, because after analyzing numerous papers from other years, only from 2016 onwards did we start to identify articles that enhanced the predefined search criteria; full text obtained. Papers not related to the subject were excluded. This exclusion phase included the elimination of duplicate papers and the reading of the title and abstract of the work. In case of any doubt about any document, that document would be preliminarily included. The final decision would be considered and evaluated in the next phase.
Ph3	No new exclusion / inclusion criteria were applied (first meeting), but relevant papers were included. In this phase the researchers also analyzed all "doubtful" papers in detail, considering all their content.
Ph4	In this phase the «snowball» technique was applied, and it was therefore necessary to re-apply the P2 criteria.
Ph5	In this phase (second meeting) no new exclusion / inclusion criteria were applied, but the researchers analyzed all the "doubtful" papers in detail, considering all their content.

In this sense, a Professor of Software Engineering from the University of Seville (Spain) participated as an external expert to validate our review protocol.

3.2. Conducting and Report Review

The aim of this phase is to present the primary papers obtained after applying the search described in the previous section. Table 2 shows the primary papers obtained after applying the inclusion/exclusion criteria set out in the previous section.

Table 2. Primary studies

Data base	Ph1	Ph2	Ph3	Ph4	Ph5
ACM Digital Library	27	6	2	-	-
IEEE Xplore	39	7	3	-	-
ScienceDirect	372	31	7	-	-
Elsevier's Scopus	352	42	6	-	-
SpringerLink	243	24	4	-	-
Snowball technique	-	-	-	10	3
Subtotals	1.033	110	22	10	3
Total	25				

After applying the search protocol and review phases (Table 1), twenty-five primary studies have been identified as the sum of the results of the third and fifth phase of the review protocol. Finally, Table 3 summarizes all the primary papers identified and analyzed, following all the criteria set out in the previous two sections.

Table 3. Summary of studies that have been analyzed

PS	Authors	Title	Year
PS01	Marchesi et al.	An Agile Software Engineering Method to Design Blockchain Applications (Marchesi et al., 2018)	2018
PS02	Liu, et al.	Applying Design Patterns in Smart Contracts (Liu et al., 2018)	2018
PS03	Choudhuret al.	Auto-Generation of Smart Contracts from Domain-Specific Ontologies and Semantic Rules (Choudhuret al., 2018)	2018
PS04	Tateishi, et al.	Automatic smart contract generation using controlled natural language and template (Tateishi et al., 2019)	2019
PS05	Tsai et al.	Beagle: A New Framework for Smart Contracts Taking Account of Law (Tsai et al. 2019)	2019
PS06	Koul, R.	Blockchain Oriented Software Testing - Challenges and Approaches (Koul, R., 2018	2018
PS07	Dolgui et al.	Blockchain-oriented dynamic modelling of smart contract design and execution in the supply chain (Dolgui et al., 2019)	2019
PS08	Porru et al.	Blockchain-Oriented Software Engineering: Challenges and New Directions (Porru et al., 2017)	2017
PS09	Shishkin, E.	Debugging Smart Contract's Business Logic Using Symbolic Model-Checking (Shishkin, 2018)	2018
PS10	Mavridou, A. et al.	Designing Secure Ethereum Smart Contracts: A Finite State Machine Based Approach (Mavridou et al. 2018)	2018
PS11	Parizi, et al.	Empirical vulnerability analysis of automated smart contracts security testing on blockchains (Parizi et al., 2018)	2018
PS12	Lee et al.	Formal Specification Technique in Smart Contract Verification (Lee et al., 2019)	2019
PS13	Mavridou, et al.	FSolidM for Designing Secure Ethereum Smart Contracts: Tool Demonstration (Mavridou, et al., 2018)	2018
PS14	Sillaber et al.	Life Cycle of Smart Contracts in Blockchain Ecosystems (Sillaber et al., 2017)	2017
PS15	Grigg, I.	On the intersection of Ricardian and Smart Contracts (Grigg 2015)	2015
PS16	Kruijff et al.	Ontologies for Commitment-Based Smart Contracts (Kruijff et al., 2017)	2017
PS17	Clack	Smart Contract Templates: Legal semantics and code validation (Clack, 2018)	2018
PS18	Clack et al.	Smart Contract Templates: Foundations, design landscape and research directions (Clack et al., 2016)	2016
PS19	Syahputra et al.	The Development of Smart Contracts for Heterogeneous Blockchains (Syahputra et al., 2019)	2019
PS20	Liao et al.	Toward A Service Platform for Developing Smart Contracts on Blockchain in BDD and TDD Styles (Liao et al., 2017)	2017
PS21	Al Khalil, et al.	Trust in Smart Contracts is a Process, As Well (Al Khalil, et al., 2017)	2017
PS22	Mavridou et al	VeriSolid: Correct-by-Design Smart Contracts for Ethereum (Mavridou et al, 2019)	2019
PS23	Permenev et al.	VerX: Safety Verification of Smart Contracts (Permenev et al., 2019)	2019
PS24	Mao et al.	Visual and User-Defined Smart Contract Designing System Based on Automatic Coding (Mao et al., 2019)	2019
PS25	Clack et al	Smart Contract Templates: essential requirements and design options (Clack et al, 2016)	2016

RQ1: Are there approaches in the literature that promote the application of a Software Development Life Cycle (SDLC)? What phases of the life cycle do the different studies promote?

After analyzing the primary studies, the phases of the software development life cycle that have been most addressed by the authors were: (A1) Requirements, analysis, or design phase (68%), (A2) Coding phase (40%), (A3) Testing phase (28%) and (A4) Other phases (12%).

The work of Marchesi et at (PS01) and Tsai et at (PS05) stands out. Study PS01 proposes a software development process to elicit requirements, analyze, design, develop, test and implement blockchain applications and study PS05 proposes a framework with five stages: development of smart contract templates, from domain analysis, formal model of smart contracts, code development from templates, verification and validation.

It seems, therefore, that some efforts of the scientific community are currently directed towards implementing some kind of development lifecycle. However, in the context of the blockchain, the analyzed processes consist only of a certain number of unlinked phases, as they are not arranged in a clear order of precedence and the inputs/outputs of each stage are also not clearly defined.

It is important to highlight, due to the relevance it has in the blockchain methodology, the fact that the phase with the least impact in the identified literature is the software testing phase. From our point of view, blockchain applications differ quite a bit from other traditional applications, since once a smart contract is implemented, its execution cannot be reversed. Therefore, robust testing is essential, with an emphasis on requirements elicitation, verification and validation, and code debugging. Moreover, testing should involve the simulation of all possible expected and unexpected variables for each smart contract and for the triggers that execute the transactions.

RQ2: Do they promote model-based software engineering, early starting of the testing phase or automatic source code generation?

In recent years, the use of modeling tools or CASE tools, as well as the use of the UML standard have helped to document the functionality of business processes and to use transformations between models. This has made it possible to automate code generation in many cases. For example, among the selected studies, Marchesi et at. (PS01) and Syahputra et at. (PS19) propose the use of UML diagrams to describe application requirements, which makes it possible to start testing at an early stage of system development (early testing). In this sense, performing model-based software engineering is important, as it provides the following advantages (Pohl, 2012): it is possible to implement best practices and generate well-tested code, which reduces the occurrence of vulnerable code; software code is more difficult to understand than models, which makes it easier to test the correctness of a model; and it is possible to apply model-based engineering on multiple platforms.

In this context, the proposals addressed in the primary studies are made by applying different approaches: (B1) Application of model-based software engineering; (B2) Promotion of early testing; and (B3) Proposal of automatic code generation. However, it is possible to observe that although early testing helps to reduce the number of defects, it seems that the efforts of the scientific community are not directed towards this approach. Nevertheless, some authors such as Koul et al. (PS06) highlight the need to ensure software quality from early stages, indicating the challenges currently faced by the testing of this type of applications. These authors also recognize the need to design specific tools and techniques for testing this type of software, in order to ensure high quality standards in the development of smart contracts, achieving greater reliability and lower development costs.

Regarding the automatic generation of smart contracts, an important aspect to consider is the technique that the primary studies have used. The automatic generation of the smart contract code using a model-based software engineering process would eliminate the manual effort required in coding from design and, therefore, speed up the process, while decreasing the possibility of errors compared to the manual coding of the requirements or models. In this sense, the techniques most commonly used or proposed by the authors are: (C1) Generation using ontologies and/or domain-specific semantic rules; (C2) Generation using model-based engineering; and (C3) Generation through templates or other utilities. Interestingly, the study by Syahputra et at. (PS19) proposes the use of a smart contract platform to generate smart contracts for heterogeneous blockchain technologies using UML and OCL (Object Constraint Language).

In summary, after analyzing the primary studies found, it is possible to observe that the phases of requirements specification and software testing are among the aspects least addressed by the research community. However, Marchesi et al. (PS01) proposes a software development process considering the typical phases of the software development life cycle, but they focus on the application of Agile methodologies. In their study they propose the use of UML diagrams to describe the design of the applications and even provide a modeling of the interactions between the traditional software and the blockchain environment. Other authors such as Syahputra et al. (PS05) discuss the development process from a smart contract platform. This platform aims to create a smart contract for heterogeneous blockchain technologies, and they propose the use of UML, in addition to OCL, for the design.

All primary studies, in one way or another, indicate the need to obtain well-functioning software. However, more emphasis needs to be placed on functional, security and performance testing in the case of smart contracts due to its critical factor in ensuring the reliability of blockchain networks. In this sense, some authors such as Koul et al. (PS06) highlight the need to ensure software quality from early stages. Therefore, this study partially coincides with our approach of obtaining test cases in early stages of the smart contract development lifecycle. Furthermore, these authors recognize the need to design specific tools and techniques for testing this type of software, to ensure high quality standards.

Finally, several papers stand out especially due to their proposed verification and testing of smart contracts and blockchain applications:

- Marchesi et at. (PS01) proposes a software development process that allows gathering requirements, analyzing, designing, developing, testing, and implementing blockchain applications. The process is based on Agile practices, using user stories and iterative and incremental development based on them.
- Choudhury et at. (PS03) provides a framework for the automatic generation of smart contracts. This framework uses ontologies and semantic rules to encode domain-specific knowledge and then leverages the structure of abstract syntax trees to incorporate the required constraints.
- Tateishi et at. (PS04) proposes a technique to automatically generate a smart contract from a human-understandable contract document. Specifically, this is created using a template and a controlled natural language. The automation is based on a mapping of the template and that natural language to a formal model that can define the terms and conditions of a contract, including temporal constraints and procedures.
- Mavridou et at. (PS13) argue that, in practice, smart contracts are plagued with vulnerabilities. To facilitate the development of secure smart contracts, these researchers have created a framework that allows contracts to be defined as Finite State Machines (FSM) with rigorous and clear semantics.
- Syahputra et at. (PS19) address a discussion on how the development process of a smart contract platform that aims to generate smart contracts for heterogeneous blockchain technologies should look like.
- Mavrodou et at. (PS22) present a framework for the formal verification of smart contracts using a model based on a transition system with operational semantics and allows the generation of Solidity code from the verified models, which would enable the development from the design of smart contracts.

4. PROPOSED SOLUTION

The objective of this section is to present a model-driven approach to generate functional test plans from smart contract specifications (Section 4.1). After describing our proposal, Section 4.2 describes a validation case on a real business project, the SmartISBN project to solve the challenges described in Section 2.1. To this end, Section 4.2.1 describes the proposed life cycle for managing the production and distribution chain process of a publication. Once this life cycle has been defined, Section 4.2.2 describes, in general terms, the architecture of the SmartISBN platform that supports the proposed life cycle. Finally, Section 4.2.3 explains how the functional tests necessary to validate the smart contracts associated with the proposed publication distribution process were systematically generated.

4.1. Proposal For Systematic Functional Test Generation in Blockchain Environments

The proposal presented in this article for the systematic generation of functional tests of smart contracts in blockchain is based on the principles of early testing, in such a way that it is possible to generate functional test plans based on the specifications of the smart contracts, independently of the blockchain platform used.

To achieve this purpose, our proposal is based on the model-driven engineering paradigm (Bézivin, 2004). Specifically, it is based on: (1) the design of a metamodel containing the definition of all the concepts needed to model smart contracts from functional specifications; and (2) the design of systematic mechanisms to generate functional test plans from the smart contract models designed according to the aforementioned metamodel. Both aspects of the proposal are described below.

On the one hand, Figure 3 shows our proposed smart contract metamodel. This metamodel is based on the following pillars (see Figure 4): (a) a set of legal relations (Legal relation) between stakeholders; (b) Stakeholders (interested parties) that could be considered as a person, an organization or any other entity capable of entering into a legal agreement; (c) a set of internal and external data sources, from which the smart contract is nourished; (d) a set of actions (or behaviors), which are composed of activities and operations on the input data and which are applied on the different business rules of the smart contract; and (e) a set of constraints, which allow controlling the consistency of the smart contract automatically and autonomously during its execution. It is also important to mention that the constraints model the terms and conditions of the smart contract, imposing restrictions as to when an action can be performed, whether the circumstances allow the action to be performed, and so on. Thus, in a smart contract model, a constraint links the execution of an action to the

Figure 3. Smart contract metamodel proposal

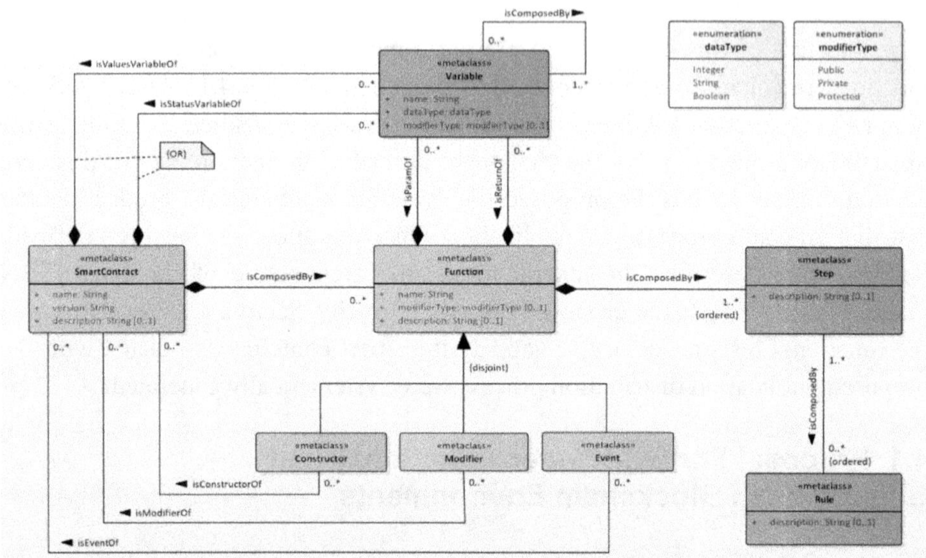

Figure 4. Pillars of the smart contract metamodel

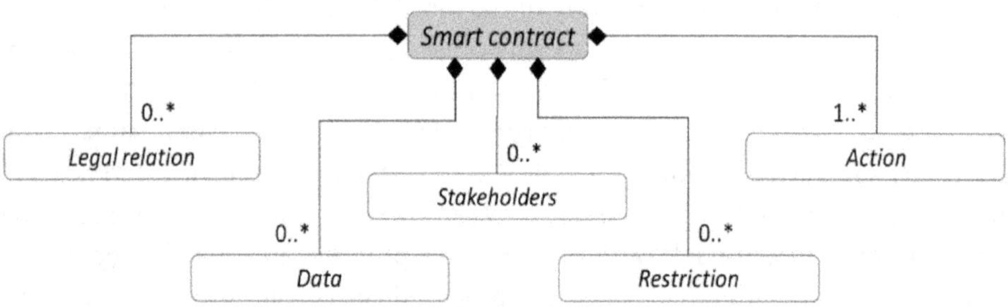

fulfillment of additional conditions and rules. A constraint can affect one or more actions and, in addition, they can read from possible data sources.

On the other hand, once the smart contract metamodel and all its entities have been instantiated, systematic mechanisms are proposed to generate scenarios and functional test cases.

In this sense, the systematic generation of functional tests is done in two stages. First, the skeleton of all test scenarios is generated from each Smart Contract in the model and, then the test case casuistry is generated by combining the test scenario data. Specifically: (1) for each Function of a smart contract, in conjunction with the input data, a test case is created; (2) for each Function Step of a smart contract, a test case step is created; and (3) for each Function Step Restriction of a smart contract, test restrictions are created.

4.2. Validation Case: SmartISBN Project

This section describes the validation context provided by the SmartISBN project. To do so, it first introduces the life cycle associated with the process of the production and distribution chain of a digital publication proposed in the framework of the project. Next, the technological and functional architecture of the SmartISBN platform, which supports the proposed distribution process, is described. Finally, the section presents how the theoretical proposal described in Section 4.1 has been applied to systematically generate the functional tests from the specification of the smart contract that governs SmartISBN.

4.2.1. Proposed Life Cycle of the Production and Distribution Chain of a Digital Publication

As a preliminary step to the design of the SmartISBN technological solution, within the framework of the project, the general process of the life cycle of a publication from the point of view of the production and distribution chain was conceptually proposed. In this sense, Figure 5 represents the distinct stages of this life cycle, as well as the different actors involved in each stage. For this purpose, the UML (Unified Modelling Language) sequence diagram notation (Fontela, 2012) is used to represent the communication flow between the stages described above.

Initially, the distribution process could be considered to begin with the first stage of "E1. Conception and drafting of the publication", in which the Author gives shape, consistency, and meaning to its content until the final manuscript is obtained. Then, the Author would initiate the second stage of the life cycle: "E2. Editorial processing of the publication". In this stage, the Editor receives the manuscript and carries out its review process, cataloging the publication within its editorial line and identifying metadata. Once this processing is completed, the Publisher would initiate the stage "E3. Printing and distribution", establishing different contracts or orders with the Distribution company so that the latter can begin the physical printing and/or digital dissemination of the different editions of the publication. Finally, the life cycle would end with the "E4. Acquisition of copies of the publication" stage, in which Bookshops (or other points of sale) would establish contracts and orders for the publications under distribution.

Considering the above process, it is worth noting that during the transitions between the distinct stages, payments, purchase orders, sales orders, etc., take place between

Figure 5. Life cycle of a publication's overall production and distribution process

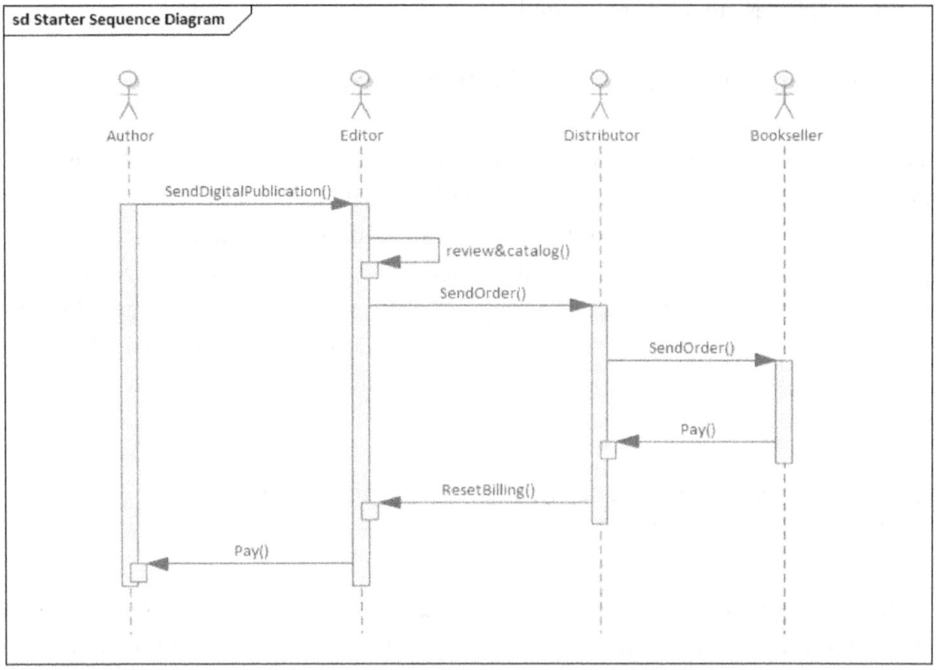

the different actors involved in the process. In this sense, it is crucial to maintain the traceability of all these transactions throughout the entire supply chain process.

4.2.2. SmartISBN Platform Architecture

To meet the objectives of the SmartISBN project and to support the life cycle of the publication's distribution process, a technological architecture is proposed with the subsystems shown in Figure 6.

On one hand, the platform incorporates an administration subsystem so that users with this role can manage users, roles, and access permissions to the platform, as well as control the status of the platform through dashboard utilities.

One of the main objectives of the SmartISBN project was to allow publishers to catalog works correctly within the platform so that users could carry out advanced searches and even receive recommendations based on their previous purchases. The cataloging subsystem is responsible for automating this cataloging process by analyzing the metadata of the digital application, based on the international standard ONIX (XML). However, as a prior step to this automatic cataloging process, the user with the role of Editor must incorporate in the platform, at least, the ISBN

Figure 6. SmartISBN platform architecture

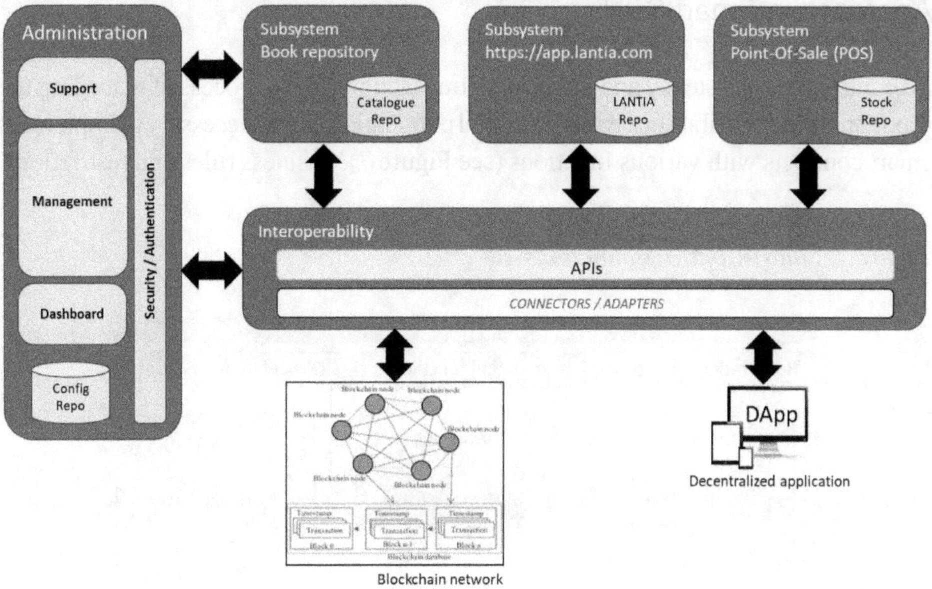

(International Standard Book Number) metadata. Based on this information, the SmartISBN platform includes automatic functionalities to consult the rest of the metadata of the digital publication by consulting public bibliographic sources. SmartISBN is currently integrated with Amazon, Google Book, La Casa del Libro, Todos tus libros and Editorial Lantia, among others.

On the other hand, the SmartISBN platform includes a frontend subsystem and a point-of-sale terminal subsystem, which manages, respectively, the repository of digital publications and their inventory and stock, together with payments and the different order and sales orders. These subsystems will be directly accessible by users with the role of Distributor and Bookshop.

To control the traceability of all order, sales, and distribution orders, the SmartISBN platform includes integration with the Ethereum platform and the use of the Solidity programming language (for the implementation of smart contracts). As part of the SmartISBN project, an Ethereum virtual machine was deployed, and its platform was used to manage the traceability of order and sales transactions in the distribution process of a publication.

Finally, the SmartISBN platform includes an integration subsystem that provides the different communication APIs (Application Programming Interface) to allow the flow of information and data between the different subsystems described above.

4.2.3. Applying the Functional Test Generation Approach in SmartISBN

To control the consistency and integrity of transactions in the process of managing the production and distribution chain of a digital publication, it was necessary to implement smart contracts with various functions (see Figure 7), business rules and restrictions.

Figure 7. Smart Contract Functions

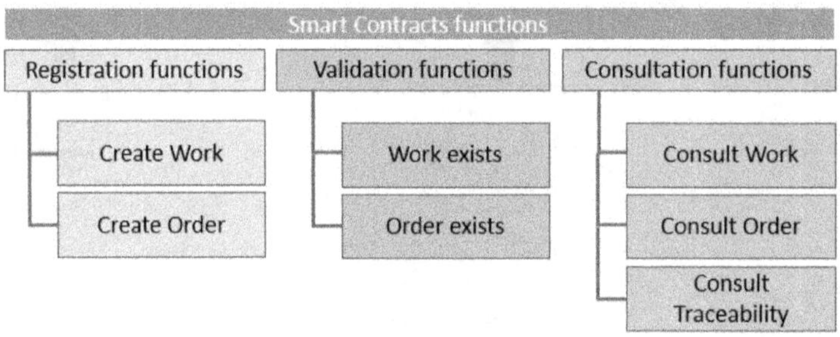

Due to space limitations, it is not possible to describe the complete functional test generation casuistry of this functionality but, as an example of application, we will focus on the following activity diagram. The diagram in Figure 8 shows the expected behavior of the smart contract and specifically the "Create Work" functionality, as well as the rules and constraints to be considered at each step.

Figure 8. Functionality of Smart Contract

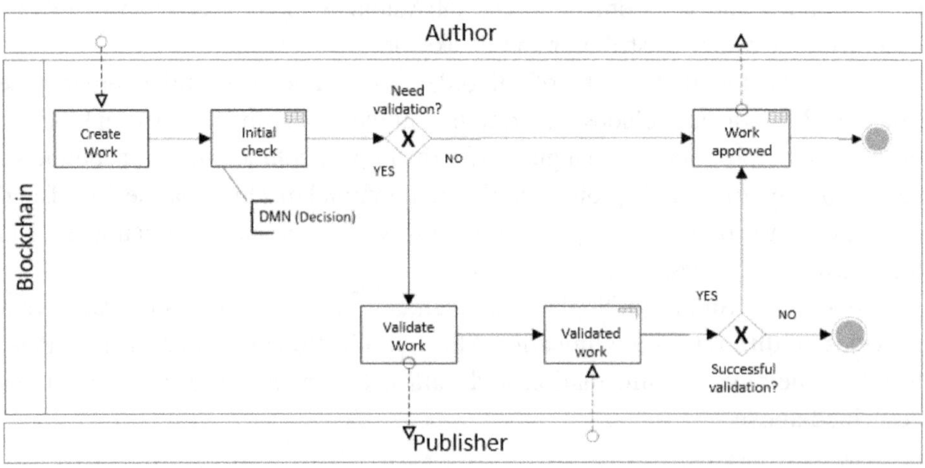

As can be seen, for the rules and constraints it is proposed to use the DMN (Decision Model Note) standard (Janssens et al., 2016). These rules and constraints are supported by a decision table, as shown in Figure 9.

Figure 9. Decision table

Decision table

U	CONDITION 1	CONDITION 2	OUTPUT
	X, Y, Z		*YES / NO*
1	X	< 50	YES
2	Y	[50, 100)	NO
3	Z	[100, 150]	YES
4	Z	> 150	NO

Rules (rows 1–4); Inputs (Condition 1, Condition 2); Output (Output)

Therefore, to systematically generate the test cases of the "Create Work" scenario, it would be necessary to go through all the possible paths and, for each of these paths, the steps are located and added to the test case in the same order. Then as many test cases are obtained as paths have been identified in the functional requirement and each test case will have a different behavior, which will coincide with the path taken.

5. CONCLUSION AND FUTURE WORK

The recent technologies that are emerging offer a major challenge in all functional environments and the world of digital publishing is no exception. Blockchain technology offers a powerful tool for the univocal identification of each digital asset and offers the solution for traceability and tracking of each asset in a secure and appropriate way and at an affordable cost for authors, publishers, and stakeholders. However, the development of solutions in blockchain environments requires fluid communication between users and functional experts throughout the entire lifecycle.

This paper presents the SmartISBN project, an R&D&I project carried out by the company Lantia Publishing and the University of Seville for the application of blockchain in the identification, tracking and traceability management of digital assets. The paper presents how blockchain technology is suitable for this purpose and analyzes the challenges it poses. Specifically, it presents the mechanisms that have been used to generate the functional tests that have facilitated the communication between the experts and the technical team to validate the results of the project. Other mechanisms have been developed in SmartISBN to facilitate this communication in other phases, such as in the requirements identification phase. The results in Section 3 indicate that we have not found any proposal that contemplates formal modelling of contracts and automated generation of artefacts from these models. Marchesi et at. presents a complete process but does not include support for generating artefacts automatically. Choudhury et at., Tateishi et at., Mavridou et at. and Mavrodou et at. describe automations for generating or verifying smart contracts, but none of them include requirements artefact management or test artefact generation.

In future work, we plan to improve our communication protocols to generalize them, as well as to enable mechanisms that allow us to automatically generate smart contract code. In fact, we are currently working on another international project that will allow us to make progress on this. In the context of sotware testing, our idea is to improve test prioritisation mechanisms, not just generation. The idea would be that the technical team could not only generate the functional tests from the requirements, guaranteeing their correspondence with them, but also prioritize them so that, in the event of a lack of resources, the tests could be generated according to the established prioritization.

ACKNOWLEDGMENT

This research article has been elaborated within the following projects: EQUAVEL Project (PID2022-137646OB-C31), which was funded by the Ministry of Economy and Competitiveness of the Government of Spain; and SmartISBN, a technology transfer project, which was funded by the company Lantia Publishing S.L.

REFERENCES

Al Khalil, F., Butler, T., O'Brien, L., & Ceci, M. (2017). Trust in smart contracts is a process, as well. In Financial Cryptography and Data Security: FC 2017 International Workshops, WAHC, BITCOIN, VOTING, WTSC, and TA, (pp. 510-519). Springer International Publishing. doi:10.1007/978-3-319-70278-0_32

Alharby, M., Aldweesh, A., & van Moorsel, A. (2018). blockchain-based smart contracts: A systematic mapping study of academic research (2018). In *2018 International Conference on Cloud Computing, Big Data and blockchain (ICCBB)* (pp. 16). IEEE. 10.1109/ICCBB.2018.8756390

Bézivin, J. (2004). In search of a basic principle for model driven engineering. *Novatica Journal, Special Issue*, *5*(2), 2124.

Choudhury, O., Rudolph, N., Sylla, I., Fairoza, N., & Das, A. (2018). Auto-Generation of Smart Contracts from Domain-Specific Ontologies and Semantic Rules. *Conference: IEEE Conferences on Internet of Things, Green Computing and Communications, Cyber, Physical and Social Computing, Smart Data, Blockchain, Computer and Information Technology*. IEEE. 10.1109/Cybermatics_2018.2018.00183

Clack, C.D. (2018). Smart Contract Templates: Legal semantics and code validation. *Journal of Digital Banking, 2*(4), 338-352.

Clack, C. D., Bakshi, V. A., & Braine, L. (2016). *Smart Contract Templates: foundations, design landscape and research directions.* arXiv. https://arxiv.org/pdf/1608.00771.pdf

Clack, C. D., Bakshi, V. A., & Braine, L. (2016). "Smart Contract Templates: essential requirements and design options". https://arxiv.org/pdf/1612.04496.pdf

Dhaiouir, S., & Assar, S. (2020). A systematic literature review of blockchain-enabled smart contracts: platforms, languages, consensus, applications and choice criteria. In *International Conference on Research Challenges in Information Science* (pp. 249-266). Springer, Cham. 10.1007/978-3-030-50316-1_15

Dolgui, A., Ivanov, D., Potryasaev, S., Sokolov, B., Ivanova, M., & Werner, F. (2020). Blockchain-oriented dynamic modelling of smart contract design and execution in the supply chain. *International Journal of Production Research, 58*(7), 2184–2199. doi:10.1080/00207543.2019.1627439

Fontela, C. (2012). *UML: modelado de software para profesionales*. Alpha Editorial.

Gramoli, V. (2022). Blockchain Fundamentals. In *Blockchain Scalability and its Foundations in Distributed Systems* (p. 1739). Springer International Publishing. doi:10.1007/978-3-031-12578-2_3

Grigg, I. (2015). *On the intersection of Ricardian and Smart Contracts.* IANG. https://iang. org/papers/intersection_ricardian_smart. html.

Hidayanto, A. N., & Prabowo, H. (2019). The latest adoption blockchain technology in supply chain management: A systematic literature review. *ICIC Express Letters, 13*(10), 913–920.

Janssens, L., Bazhenova, E., De Smedt, J., Vanthienen, J., & Denecker, M. (2016, June). Consistent Integration of Decision (DMN) and Process (BPMN) Models. In CAiSE forum (Vol. 1612, pp. 121128).

Kitchenham, B., & Brereton, P. (2013). A systematic review of systematic review process research in software engineering. *Information and Software Technology, 55*(12), 2049–2075. doi:10.1016/j.infsof.2013.07.010

Koul, R. (2018). Blockchain Oriented Software Testing - Challenges and Approaches. *3rd International Conference for Convergence in Technology (I2CT)*, Pune, India. 10.1109/I2CT.2018.8529728

Kruijff, J., & Weigand, H. (2017). *Ontologies for Commitment-Based Smart Contracts*. OTM 2017 Conferences: Confederated International Conferences: CoopIS, C&TC, and ODBASE 2017, Rhodes, Greece.

Lee, S., Park, S., & Park, Y. B. (2019). Formal Specification Technique in Smart Contract Verification. *6th International Conference on Platform Technology and Service (PlatCon)*. IEEE. 10.1109/PlatCon.2019.8669419

Legerén-Molina, A. (2018). Los contratos inteligentes en España (La disciplina de los smart contracts) / Smart contracts in Spain; the regulation of smart contracts. *Revista de Derecho civil, 5*(2), 193-241.

Liao, C., Cheng, C., Chen, K., Lai, C., Chiu, T., & Wu-Lee, C. (2017). Toward A Service Platform for Developing Smart Contracts on Blockchain in BDD and TDD Styles. *2017 IEEE 10th International Conference on Service-Oriented Computing and Applications*. IEEE. 10.1109/SOCA.2017.26

Liu, Y., Lu, Q., Xu, X., Zhu, L., & Yao, H. (2018). *Applying Design Patterns in Smart Contracts*. Springer International.

Luu, L., Chu, D. H., Olickel, H., Saxena, P., & Hobor, A. (2016). Making smart contracts smarter. In *Proceedings of the 2016 ACM SIGSAC conference on computer and communications security* (pp. 254-269). ACM. 10.1145/2976749.2978309

Macrinici, D., Cartofeanu, C., & Gao, S. (2018). Smart contract applications within blockchain technology: A systematic mapping study. *Telematics and Informatics, 35*(8), 2337–2354. doi:10.1016/j.tele.2018.10.004

Magadán-Díaz, M. y Rivas-García, J.I. (2020). *La industria editorial española: dos décadas clave de transformación y cambio (19962016)*. Investigaciones de Historia Económica Economic History Research doi:10.33231/j.ihe.2020.04.003

Mao, D., Wang, F., Wang, Y., & Hao, Z. (2019). *Visual and User-Defined Smart Contract Designing System Based on Automatic Coding*. IEEE Access. Digital Object Identifier., doi:10.1109/ACCESS.2019.2920776

Marchesi, M., Marchesi, L., & Tonelli, R. (2018). An Agile Software Engineering Method to Design Blockchain Applications. *Software Engineering Conference Russia (SECR 2018)*, Moscow, Russia. 10.1145/3290621.3290627

Martínez Alés, R. (2001). *Información Comercial Española, ICE: Revista de Economía*. Dialnet.

Mavridou, A., & Laszka, A. (2018). Designing Secure Ethereum Smart Contracts: A Finite State Machine Based Approach. *International Conference on Financial Cryptography and Data Security*. FC 2018: Financial Cryptography and Data Security. Springer. 10.1007/978-3-662-58387-6_28

Mavridou, A., & Laszka, A. (2018). FSolidM for Designing Secure Ethereum Smart Contracts: Tool Demonstration. *7th International Conference on Principles of Security and Trust (POST) Held as Part of the 21st European Joint Conferences on Theory and Practice of Software (ETAPS)*. Springer. 10.1007/978-3-319-89722-6_11

Mavridou, A., Laszka, A., Stachtiari, E., & Dubey, A. (2019). VeriSolid: Correct-by-Design Smart Contracts for Ethereum. *Cryptography and Security; Software Engineering*. arXiv.org. arXiv:1901.01292

Needleman, M. H. (2001). ONIX (online information exchange). *Serials Review*, *27*(34), 102104.

Ngai, E. W., Hu, Y., Wong, Y. H., Chen, Y., & Sun, X. (2011). The application of data mining techniques in financial fraud detection: A classification framework and an academic review of literature. *Decision Support Systems*, *50*(3), 559–569. doi:10.1016/j.dss.2010.08.006

Parizi, R. M., Dehghantanha, A., Choo, K. K. R., & Singh, A. (2018). Empirical vulnerability analysis of automated smart contracts security testing on blockchains. *CASCON. Proceedings of the 28th Annual International Conference on Computer Science and Software Engineering*. Springer.

Permenev, A., Dimitrov, D., Tsankov, P., Drachsler-Cohen, D., & Vechev, M. (2019). "VerX: Safety Verification of Smart Contracts". Safety verification of Smart Contracts. *Security and Privacy*, 2020.

Pohl, K., Hönninger, H., Achatz, R., & Broy, M. (Eds.). (2012). Model-based engineering of embedded systems: The SPES 2020 methodology. Heidelberg: Springer.

Porru, S., Pinn, A., Marchesi, M., & Tonelli, R. (2017). Blockchain-Oriented Software Engineering: Challenges and New Directions. *2017 IEEE/ACM 39th IEEE International Conference on Software Engineering Companion.* ACM. 10.1109/ICSE-C.2017.142

Pranto, S., Jardim, L., Oliveira, T., & Ruivo, P. (2019, October). Literature review on blockchain with focus on supply chain. In *Atas da Conferencia da Associacao Portuguesa de Sistemas de Informacao 2019*. Associação Portuguesa de Sistemas de Informação.

Shishkin, E. (2018). *Debugging Smart Contract's Business Logic Using Symbolic Model-Checking*. arXiv.org > cs > arXiv:1812.00619v1

Sillaber, C., & Waltl, B. (2017). Life Cycle of Smart Contracts in Blockchain Ecosystems. *Datenschutz und Datensicherheit – DuD, 41*(8), 497–500.

Steiu, M. F. (2020). blockchain in education: Opportunities, applications, and challenges. *First Monday*. doi:10.5210/fm.v25i9.10654

Syahputra, H., & Weigand, H. (2019). The Development of Smart Contracts for Heterogeneous Blockchains. *Enterprise Interoperability, VIII*, 229–238. doi:10.1007/978-3-030-13693-2_19

Tateishi, T., Yoshihama, S., Sato, N., Saito, S. (2019). Automatic smart contract generation using controlled natural language and template. *IBM Journal of Research and Development, 63*.

Tsai, W., Ge, N., Jiang, J., Feng, K., & He, J. (2019). Beagle: A New Framework for Smart Contracts Taking Account of Law. *IEEE International Conference on Service-Oriented System Engineering (SOSE)*. IEEE 10.1109/SOSE.2019.00028

Yadav, V. S., & Singh, A. R. (2019). A systematic literature review of blockchain technology in agriculture. In *Proceedings of the International Conference on Industrial Engineering and Operations Management* (pp. 973-981). Springer.

Yaqoob, I., Salah, K., Jayaraman, R., & Al-Hammadi, Y. (2021). blockchain for healthcare data management: Opportunities, challenges, and future recommendations. *Neural Computing & Applications*, 1–16.

KEY TERMS AND DEFINITIONS

Blockchain: It is a shared, immutable ledger that facilitates the process of recording transactions and tracking assets in a business network. An asset can be tangible (a house, car, cash, land) or intangible (intellectual property, patents, copyrights). Virtually anything of value can be tracked and traded on a blockchain network, reducing risk and cutting costs for all involved.

Digital Publishing Systems: This concept, also called digital publishing platform, allows creators to share, discover, and monetize digital magazines, catalogs and other publications with a global audience.

Digital Publishing: This concept, also called electronic or online publishing, is the distribution of a variety of online content, such as journals, magazines, newspapers, and eBooks. Through this process, any company or publisher can digitize documents and information that people can view online, download, sometimes manipulate, and even print out or share otherwise, if they choose.

Functional Tests: It is a type of software testing that validates the software system against the functional requirements/specifications. The purpose of Functional tests is to test each function of the software application, by providing appropriate input, verifying the output against the Functional requirements.

Smart Contracts: It is programs stored on a blockchain that run when predetermined conditions are met. They typically are used to automate the execution of an agreement so that all participants can be immediately certain of the outcome, without any intermediary's involvement or time loss.

Compilation of References

Abdul, L., & Yu, T. F. (2020). Resilient Urbanization: A Systematic Review on Urban Discourse in Pakistan. In Urban Science, 4(4). doi:10.3390/urbansci4040076

Achhangani. (2023, June 7). *Three challenges in cryptocurrency regulation.* Atlantic Council. https://www.atlanticcouncil.org/blogs/econographics/three-challenges-in-cryptocurrency-regulation/

Adere, E. M. (2022). Blockchain in healthcare and IoT: A systematic literature review. In Array, 14. doi:10.1016/j.array.2022.100139

Agrawal, K., Aggarwal, M., Tanwar, S., Sharma, G., Bokoro, P. N., & Sharma, R. (2022). An Extensive Blockchain Based Applications Survey: Tools, Frameworks, Opportunities, Challenges and Solutions. *IEEE Access : Practical Innovations, Open Solutions*, *10*, 116858–116906. doi:10.1109/ACCESS.2022.3219160

Ahmad, M. (2023). Leveraging Blockchain for Spatial Data Infrastructure: Challenges and Opportunities. *Supporting Technologies and the Impact of Blockchain on Organizations and Society*, 177–194.

Ahmad, M., & Khiyal, M. S. H. (2023). Assessment of land administration in Pakistan and the potential role of volunteered geographic information. In Handbook of Research on Driving Socioeconomic Development With Big Data. IGI Global. doi:10.4018/978-1-6684-5959-1.ch014

Aisyah, E. S. N., Haryani, H., Budiarto, M., Prihastiwi, W. Y., Santoso, N. P. L., & Hayadi, B. H. (2022). Blockchain ilearning platform in education. In *2022 International Conference on Science and Technology (ICOSTECH)* (pp. 01-08). IEEE. 10.1109/ICOSTECH54296.2022.9829160

Al Khalil, F., Butler, T., O'Brien, L., & Ceci, M. (2017). Trust in smart contracts is a process, as well. In Financial Cryptography and Data Security: FC 2017 International Workshops, WAHC, BITCOIN, VOTING, WTSC, and TA, (pp. 510-519). Springer International Publishing. doi:10.1007/978-3-319-70278-0_32

Alam, A. (2022). Platform utilising blockchain technology for eLearning and online Higher Educationfor open sharing of academic proficiency and progress records. In *Smart Data Intelligence: Proceedings of ICSMDI 2022* (pp. 307-320). Singapore: Springer Nature Singapore. 10.1007/978-981-19-3311-0_26

Alam, T., & Benaida, M. (2020). Blockchain and internet of things in higher education. *Universal Journal of Educational Research, 8*, 2164-2174. , doi:10.13189/ujer.2020.080556

Alam, K. M., Ashfiqur Rahman, J. M., Tasnim, A., & Akther, A. (2022). A Blockchain-based Land Title Management System for Bangladesh. *Journal of King Saud University. Computer and Information Sciences, 34*(6), 3096–3110. doi:10.1016/j.jksuci.2020.10.011

Alammary, A., Alhazmi, S., Almasri, M., & Gillani, S. (2019). Blockchain-based applications in education: A systematic review. *Applied Sciences (Basel, Switzerland), 9*(12), 2400. doi:10.3390/app9122400

Alamri, H., Lowell, V., Watson, W., & Watson, S. L. (2020). Using personalized learning as an instructional approach to motivate learners in online higher education: Learner self-determination and intrinsic motivation. *Journal of Research on Technology in Education, 52*(3), 322–352. doi:10.1080/15391523.2020.1728449

Aleskerov, E., Freisleben, B., & Rao, B. (1997). CARDWATCH: A neural network-based database mining system for credit card fraud detection. *Proceeding of the IEEE/IAFE on Computational Intelligence for Financial Engineering*. IEEE. 10.1109/CIFER.1997.618940

Alharby, M., Aldweesh, A., & van Moorsel, A. (2018). blockchain-based smart contracts: A systematic mapping study of academic research (2018). In *2018 International Conference on Cloud Computing, Big Data and blockchain (ICCBB)* (pp. 16). IEEE. 10.1109/ICCBB.2018.8756390

Al-Hashediand, K. & Magalingam, P. (2021). Financial fraud detection applying data mining techniques: A comprehensive review from 2009 to 2019. *Computer Science Review, 40*. doi:10.1016/j.cosrev.2021.100402

Ali, A., & Ahmad, M. (2016). Analysis of the Barriers to Land Administration in Pakistan. *GSDI 15 World Conference.*

Ali, A., & Imran, M. (2021). National Spatial Data Infrastructure vs. Cadastre System for Economic Development: Evidence from Pakistan. *Land (Basel), 10*(2), 188. doi:10.3390/land10020188

Ali, Z., & Nasir, A. (2010). Land Administration System in Pakistan - Current Situation and Stakeholders' Perception. *FIG Congress 2010: Facing the Challenges - Building the Capacity.* IEEE.

Alshahrani, M., Beloff, N., & White, M. (2021). *Towards a blockchain-based smart certification system for higher education: an empirical study*. International Journal Of Computing and Digital System. doi:10.12785/ijcds/110145

Alsobhi, H. A., Alakhtar, R. A., Ubaid, A., Hussain, O. K., & Hussain, F. K. (2023). Blockchain-based micro-credentialing system in higher Higher Educationinstitutions: Systematic literature review. *Knowledge-Based Systems, 110238*, 110238. doi:10.1016/j.knosys.2022.110238

Ameyaw, P. D., & de Vries, W. T. (2021). Toward smart land management: Land acquisition and the associated challenges in Ghana. a look into a blockchain digital land registry for prospects. In Land, 10(3). doi:10.3390/land10030239

Ameyaw, P. D., & de Vries, W. T. (2020). Transparency of land administration and the role of blockchain technology, a four-dimensional framework analysis from the ghanaian land perspective. In Land, 9(12). doi:10.3390/land9120491

Ameyaw, P. D., & de Vries, W. T. (2023). Blockchain technology adaptation for land administration services: The importance of socio-cultural elements. *Land Use Policy*, *125*, 106485. Advance online publication. doi:10.1016/j.landusepol.2022.106485

Anderson, M. (2019). Exploring decentralization: blockchain technology and complex coordination. *Journal of Design and Science*.

Ansah, B. O., Voss, W., Asiama, K. O., & Wuni, I. Y. (2023). A systematic review of the institutional success factors for blockchain-based land administration. *Land Use Policy*, *125*, 106473. doi:10.1016/j.landusepol.2022.106473

Ansari, A. A., Muhideen, S., Das, N., Butt, A. R., & Wei, S. (2018). *North American Academic Research*. Linkedin.

Anusuya, D. (2022). *Building the World's First Blockchain Geospatial Network Backed with Cryptography*. GeoSpatial World. https://www.geospatialworld.net/prime/interviews/building-the-worlds-first-blockchain-geospatial-network-backed-with-cryptography/

Arenas, R., & Fernandez, P. (2018). CredenceLedger: a permissioned blockchain for verifiable academic credentials. Paper presented at the *2018 IEEE International Conference on Engineering, Technology and Innovation (ICE/ITMC)*, (pp. 1-6). IEEE. 10.1109/ICE.2018.8436324

Arndt, T., & Guercio, A. (2020). Blockchain-based transcripts for mobile higher-education. *International Journal of Information and Education Technology (IJIET)*, *10*(2), 84–89. doi:10.18178/ijiet.2020.10.2.1344

Ashford, K. (2022). What is Cryptocurrency? *Forbes*. https://www.forbes.com/advisor/investing/cryptocurrency/what-is-cryptocurrency/

Ata, S., Shahbaz, B., Arif Watto, M., & Hussain, N. (2023). Transnational Seasonal Land Grabbing in Pakistan: Power Positions and Resistance. *Journal of Asian and African Studies*, *58*(3), 372–388. doi:10.1177/00219096211063816

Awaji, B., Solaiman, E., & Albshri, A. (2020, July). Blockchain-based applications in higher education: A systematic mapping study. In *Proceedings of the 5th international conference on information and education innovations* (pp. 96-104). ACM. 10.1145/3411681.3411688

Awerika, C. K., Amerila, Z. M. A., Ameria, S., Ameriya, T., & Atsumi, M. (2023). Exploring Integration in Higher Educationthrough Blockchain Technology. *Blockchain Frontier Technology*, *3*(1), 119–127. doi:10.34306/bfront.v3i1.359

Ayub Khan, A., Laghari, A. A., Shaikh, A. A., Bourouis, S., Mamlouk, A. M., & Alshazly, H. (2021). Educational blockchain: A secure degree attestation and verification traceability architecture for higher Higher Educationcommission. *Applied Sciences (Basel, Switzerland)*, *11*(22), 10917. doi:10.3390/app112210917

Bahmanziari, T., Pearson, J. M., & Crosby, L. (2003). Is trust important in technology adoption? A policy capturing approach. *Journal of Computer Information Systems*, *43*(4), 46–54.

Bal, M., & Pawlicka, K. (2021). Supply chain finance and challenges of modern supply chains. *LogForum, 17*(1), 71–82. https://doiorg.spjain.idm.oclc.org/ 10.17270/ J.LOG.2021. 525.

Bandeira, P., Sumpsi, J. M., & Falconi, C. (2010). Evaluating land administration systems: A comparative method with an application to Peru and Honduras. *Land Use Policy*, *27*(2), 351–363. doi:10.1016/j.landusepol.2009.04.005

Baporikar, N. (2017b). Fundamentals of Higher Education - Fresh Vision (pp. 1- 304). Himalaya Publishing House, Mumbai, India.

Baporikar, N. (2019b). Student Centered Strategies for Quality International Education. In B. Dutta & P. Chaudhuri (Eds.), Internationalization of Higher Education: Opportunities and Challenges (pp. 21-35). MTC Global: India.

Baporikar, N. (2014). *Handbook of Research on Higher Education in the MENA Region: Policy and Practice*. IGI Global. doi:10.4018/978-1-4666-6198-1

Baporikar, N. (2015). Strategies for Promoting Research Culture to Support Knowledge Society. [IJICTHD]. *International Journal of Information Communication Technologies and Human Development*, *7*(4), 58–72. doi:10.4018/IJICTHD.2015100104

Baporikar, N. (2015a). Understanding Professional Development for Educators. [IJSEM]. *International Journal of Sustainable Economies Management*, *4*(4), 18–30. doi:10.4018/IJSEM.2015100102

Baporikar, N. (2016a). Academic Entrepreneurship for Scaling Innovation. [IJEEI]. *International Journal of E-Entrepreneurship and Innovation*, *6*(2), 21–39. doi:10.4018/IJEEI.2016070102

Baporikar, N. (2016b). Stakeholder Approach for Quality Higher Education. In W. Nuninger & J. Châtelet (Eds.), *Handbook of Research on Quality Assurance and Value Management in Higher Education* (pp. 1–26). Information Science Reference. doi:10.4018/978-1-5225-0024-7.ch001

Baporikar, N. (2016c). Technology Integration and Innovation during Reflective Teaching. [IJICTE]. *International Journal of Information and Communication Technology Education*, *12*(2), 14–22. doi:10.4018/IJICTE.2016040102

Baporikar, N. (2017a). Imperatives in Leading Institutions of Higher Learning: Focus B-School. [IJTEM]. *International Journal of Technology and Educational Marketing*, *7*(1), 38–51. doi:10.4018/IJTEM.2017010104

Baporikar, N. (2018). Improving Communication by Linking Student Centred Pedagogy and Management Curriculum Development. In N. P. Ololube (Ed.), *Encyclopaedia of Institutional Leadership, Policy and Management* (pp. 369–386). Pearl Publications.

Baporikar, N. (2019a). Preventing Academic Misconduct: Student-Centered Teaching Strategies. In D. Velliaris (Ed.), *Prevention and Detection of Academic Misconduct in Higher Education* (pp. 98–115). IGI Global. doi:10.4018/978-1-5225-7531-3.ch005

Baporikar, N. (2019c). E-Learning Strategies for Emerging Economies in the Knowledge Era. In J. Pelet (Ed.), *Advanced Web Applications and Progressing E-Learning 2.0 Technologies in Higher Education* (pp. 150–171). IGI Global. doi:10.4018/978-1-5225-7435-4.ch008

Baporikar, N. (2020). Finer Student Engagement via Quality and Lifelong Learning for Sustainable Education. [IJPAE]. *International Journal of Political Activism and Engagement*, *7*(4), 38–55. doi:10.4018/IJPAE.2020100104

Baporikar, N. (2021). Relook at University Planning-Development for Sustainability in Higher Education. [IJESGT]. *International Journal of Environmental Sustainability and Green Technologies*, *12*(2), 13–28. doi:10.4018/IJESGT.2021070102

Baporikar, N. (2022). Entrepreneurial University Challenges and Critical Success Factors to Thrive. [IJAMTR]. *International Journal of Applied Management Theory and Research*, *4*(1), 1–15. doi:10.4018/IJAMTR.300347

Baporikar, N., & Sony, M. (2020). *Quality Management Principles and Policies in Higher Education*. IGI Global. doi:10.4018/978-1-7998-1017-9

Beck, R., Müller-Bloch, C., & King, J. L. (2018). Governance in the blockchain economy: A framework and research agenda. *Journal of the Association for Information Systems, 19*(10), 1020–1034. https://doi-org.spjain.idm.oclc.org/ 10.17705/ 1jais.00518.

Beck, R., Müller-Bloch, C., & King, J. L. (2018). Governance in the blockchain economy: A framework and research agenda. *Journal of the Association for Information Systems*, *19*(10), 1020–1034. Advance online publication. doi:10.17705/1jais.00518

Bedi, P., Gole, P., Dhiman, S., & Gupta, N. (2020). Smart contract based central sector scheme of scholarship for college and university students. *Procedia Computer Science*, *171*, 790–799. doi:10.1016/j.procs.2020.04.086

Benbunan-Fich, R., & Castellanos, A. (2018). Digitalization of land records: From paper to blockchain. *International Conference on Information Systems 2018, ICIS 2018*. Blockchain@UBC.

Bender, J. P., Burchardi, K., & Shepherd, N. (2019). Capturing the value of blockchain. Boston Consulting Group, 9.

Benitez, J., Henseler, J., Castillo, A., & Schuberth, F. (2020). How to perform and report an impactful analysis using partial least squares: Guidelines for confirmatory and explanatory IS research. *Information & Management*, *57*(2), 103168. doi:10.1016/j.im.2019.05.003

Bézivin, J. (2004). In search of a basic principle for model driven engineering. *Novatica Journal, Special Issue*, *5*(2), 2124.

Bhardwaj, A. K., Garg, A., & Gajpal, Y. (2021). Determinants of blockchain technology adoption in supply chains by small and medium enterprises (SMEs) in India. *Mathematical Problems in Engineering*, *2021*, 1–14. doi:10.1155/2021/5537395

Bhasin, T. M. (2018). Analysis of Top 100 Bank Frauds. Central Vigilance Commission India, New Delhi.

Bhowmik, R. (2008). Data Mining Techniques in Fraud Detection. *Journal of Digital Forensics, Security and Law*, *3*(2). doi:10.15394/jdfsl.2008.1040

Bucea-Manea-Ţoniş, R., Martins, O. M., Bucea-Manea-Ţoniş, R., Gheorghiţă, C., Kuleto, V., Ilić, M. P., & Simion, V. (2021). Blockchain technology enhances sustainable higher education. *Sustainability (Basel)*, *13*(22), 12347. doi:10.3390u132212347

Burgess, S. M., & Steenkamp, J. B. E. (2006). Marketing renaissance: How research in emerging markets advances marketing science and practice. *International Journal of Research in Marketing*, *23*(4), 337–356. doi:10.1016/j.ijresmar.2006.08.001

Cahyadi, D., Faturahman, A., Haryani, H., Dolan, E., & Millah, S. (2021). Bcs: Blockchain smart curriculum system for verification student accreditation. *International Journal of Cyber and IT Service Management*, *1*(1), 65–83. doi:10.34306/ijcitsm.v1i1.20

Cai, Y., & Zhu, D. (2016). Fraud detections for online businesses: A perspective from blockchain technology. *Financial Innovation*, *2*(1), 1–10. doi:10.118640854-016-0039-4

Carmichael, J. J., & Eaton, S. E. (2023). Security risks, fake degrees, and other fraud: A topic modelling approach. In *Fake Degrees and Fraudulent Credentials in Higher Higher Education* (pp. 227–250). Springer International Publishing. doi:10.1007/978-3-031-21796-8_11

Ceke, D., & Kunosic, S. (2020) *Smart contracts as a diploma anti-forgery system in higher education—A pilot project.* Proceedings of the 2020 43rd International Convention on Information, Communication and Electronic Technology, Opatija, Croatia.

Chan, C. K. Y. (2023). A comprehensive AI policy Higher Educationframework for university teaching and learning. *International Journal of Educational Technology in Higher Education*, *20*(1), 1–25. doi:10.118641239-023-00408-3

ChatterjeeP.DasD.RawatD. (2023). Securing Financial Transactions: Exploring the Role of Federated Learning and Blockchain in Credit Card Fraud Detection. TechRxiv. doi:10.36227/techrxiv.22683403.v1

Chaudhary, R. (2013, September). Data Mining Tools To Detect Financial Fraud. [IJERT]. *International Journal of Engineering Research & Technology (Ahmedabad)*, *2*(9).

CheHashim, R., & Mahdzan, N. S.Rosmawani CheHashim and Nurul Shahnaz Mahdzan. (2014). Fraud in letter of credit transactions: The experience of Malaysian bankers. *International Journal of Law, Crime and Justice*, *42*(3), 224–236. doi:10.1016/j.ijlcj.2014.01.008

Cheng, H., Lu, J., Xiang, Z., & Song, B. (2020). A Permissioned Blockchain-Based Platform for Higher EducationCertificate Verification. In Z. Zheng, H. N. Dai, X. Fu, & B. Chen (Eds.), *Blockchain and Trustworthy Systems. BlockSys 2020. Communications in Computer and Information Science* (Vol. 1267). Springer. doi:10.1007/978-981-15-9213-3_36

Chen, J., Cai, T., He, W., Chen, L., Zhao, G., Zou, W., & Guo, L. (2020). A blockchain-driven supply chain finance application for auto retail industry. *Entropy (Basel, Switzerland)*, *22*(1), 95. doi:10.3390/e22010095 PMID:33285870

Chivu, R., Popa, I., Orzan, M., Marinescu, C., Florescu, M. S., & Orzan, A. (2022). The role of blockchain technologies in the sustainable development of students' learning process. *Sustainability*, *14*(3), 1406. doi:10.3390u14031406

Chod, J., Trichakis, N., Tsoukalas, G., Aspegren, H., & Weber, M. (2020). On the financing benefits of supply chain transparency and blockchain adoption. *Management Science*, *66*(10), 4378–4396. doi:10.1287/mnsc.2019.3434

Choi, D., Chune, Y. C., Seyha, T., & Young, J. (2020). Factors affecting organizations' resistance to the adoption of blockchain technology in supply networks. *Sustainability (Basel)*, *12*(21), 8882. doi:10.3390u12218882

Choi, T. M. (2020). Supply chain financing using blockchain: Impacts on supply chains selling fashionable products. *Annals of Operations Research*. doi:10.100710479-020-03615-7

Chong, A. Y. L., Lim, E. T., Hua, X., Zheng, S., & Tan, C. W. (2019). Business on chain: A comparative case study of five blockchain-inspired business models. *Journal of the Association for Information Systems*, *20*(9), 9. doi:10.17705/1jais.00568

Choudhury, O., Rudolph, N., Sylla, I., Fairoza, N., & Das, A. (2018). Auto-Generation of Smart Contracts from Domain-Specific Ontologies and Semantic Rules. *Conference: IEEE Conferences on Internet of Things, Green Computing and Communications, Cyber, Physical and Social Computing, Smart Data, Blockchain, Computer and Information Technology*. IEEE. 10.1109/Cybermatics_2018.2018.00183

Chuan, T. (2022). *Ukrainian Government to Start Blockchain Land Registry Trial in October*. CoinDesk. https://www.coindesk.com/markets/2017/06/23/ukrainian-government-to-start-blockchain-land-registry-trial-in-october/

Chukowry, V., Nanuck, G., & Sungkur, R. K. (2021). The future of continuous learning–Digital badge and microcredential system using blockchain. *Global Transitions Proceedings*, *2*(2), 355–361. doi:10.1016/j.gltp.2021.08.026

Clack, C. D., Bakshi, V. A., & Braine, L. (2016). "Smart Contract Templates: essential requirements and design options". https://arxiv.org/pdf/1612.04496.pdf

Clack, C. D., Bakshi, V. A., & Braine, L. (2016). *Smart Contract Templates: foundations, design landscape and research directions*. arXiv. https://arxiv.org/pdf/1608.00771.pdf

Clack, C.D. (2018). Smart Contract Templates: Legal semantics and code validation. *Journal of Digital Banking, 2*(4), 338-352.

Clohessy, T., & Acton, T. (2019). Investigating the influence of organizational factors on blockchain adoption: An innovation theory perspective. *Industrial Management & Data Systems, 119*(7), 1457–1491. doi:10.1108/IMDS-08-2018-0365

Cocco, L., Pinna, A., & Marchesi, M. (2017). Banking on blockchain: Costs savings thanks to the blockchain. [Internet.]. *Future Internet, 25*(9), 25. www.mdpi.com/journal/futureinternetFuture. doi:10.3390/fi9030025

Cummings, T. G. (2008). *Handbook of organization development*. Sage.

Dale, P., & McLaughlin, J. (1999). Land Administration. In Oxford Press. Oxford University Press. doi:10.1093/oso/9780198233909.001.0001

Dan, B. (2015). Blockchainmanoeuvres: applying Bitcoin's technology to banking. *The Banker*. https://www.thebanker.com/Transactions-Technology/Technology/Blockchain-manoeuvres-applying-Bitcoin-s-technology-to-banking?ct=true, 25.06.21

Daniel, D., & Ifejika Speranza, C. (2020). The Role of Blockchain in Documenting Land Users' Rights: The Canonical Case of Farmers in the Vernacular Land Market. *Frontiers in Blockchain, 3*, 19. doi:10.3389/fbloc.2020.00019

Datta, P. K., & Mitra, S. (2022). 7 Application of. *The Data-Driven Blockchain Ecosystem: Fundamentals, Applications, and Emerging Technologies, 103*. doi:10.1201/9781003269281

Dede, C. J., & Richards, J. (2020). *The 60-year curriculum New models for lifelong learning in the digital economy*. Routledge. doi:10.4324/9781003013617

Deepalakshmi, M. U.s, L., S, S., P, S., & K, Y. (2023). Awareness of Cryptocurrency - An Empirical Study. *Innovation in Economy & Policy Research, 4*(1), 46–51. https://matjournals.co.in/index.php/JEPR/article/view/2686

Demir, M., Turetken, O., & Ferworn, A. (2020). Blockchain-based transparent disaster relief delivery assurance. *SYSCON 2020 - 14th Annual IEEE International Systems Conference, Proceedings*. IEEE. 10.1109/SysCon47679.2020.9275915

Demo, G., Neiva, E. R., Nunes, I., & Rozzett, K. (2012). Human resources management policies and practices scale (HRMPPS): Exploratory and confirmatory factor analysis. *BAR - Brazilian Administration Review, 9*(4), 395–420. doi:10.1590/S1807-76922012005000006

Dewangan, S., Verma, S. K., Parganiha, B., & Dewangan, S. (2023). Applications and Implementations of Blockchain Technology Across the Various Sectors. In Building Secure Business Models Through Blockchain Technology: Tactics, Methods, Limitations, and Performance (pp. 1-19). IGI Global. doi:10.4018/978-1-6684-7808-0.ch001

Dhaiouir, S., & Assar, S. (2020). A systematic literature review of blockchain-enabled smart contracts: platforms, languages, consensus, applications and choice criteria. In *International Conference on Research Challenges in Information Science* (pp. 249-266). Springer, Cham. 10.1007/978-3-030-50316-1_15

Di Vaio, A., & Varriale, L. (2020). Blockchain technology in supply chain management for sustainable performance: Evidence from the airport industry. *International Journal of Information Management, 52*, 102014. https://doiorg.spjain.idm.oclc.org/10.1016/j.ijinfomgt.2019.09.010. doi:10.1016/j.ijinfomgt.2019.09.010

Disparte, D. (2017). Blockchain could make the insurance industry much more transparent. *Harvard Business Review*, 2–5.

Dolgui, A., Ivanov, D., Potryasaev, S., Sokolov, B., Ivanova, M., & Werner, F. (2020). Blockchain-oriented dynamic modelling of smart contract design and execution in the supply chain. *International Journal of Production Research, 58*(7), 2184–2199. doi:10.1080/00207543.2019.1627439

Dong, C., Chen, C., Shi, X., & Ng, C. T. (2021). Operations strategy for supply chain finance with asset-backed securitization: Centralization and blockchain adoption. *International Journal of Production Economics, 241*, 108261. doi:10.1016/j.ijpe.2021.108261

Du, M., Chen, Q., Xiao, J., Yang, H., & Ma, X. (2020). Supply chain finance innovation using blockchain. *IEEE Transactions on Engineering Management, 67*(4), 1045–1058. doi:10.1109/TEM.2020.2971858

Eder, G. (2019). Digital Transformation: Blockchain and Land Titles. *2019 OECD Global Anti-Corruption & Integrity Forum*. OECD.

Eliwa, E., & Hameed, H. A. (2023). The Effectiveness of Using Blockchain Technology in Building High-Quality Educational Content Based on A Participatory Learning Environment and Its Impact on Increasing Student Achievement. *International Journal of Intelligent Systems and Applications in Engineering, 11*(1), 50–62. https://www.ijisae.org/index.php/IJISAE/article/view/2443

ElsayedA. N. (2023). The Use of Blockchain Technology in Education: A Comprehensive Review and Future Prospects. SSRN 4523322. doi:10.2139/ssrn.4523322

Emirates News Agency. (2023, 19 July). *University of Dubai successfully publish e-Credentials of graduates on blockchain platform* WAM. https//wam.ae/en/details/1395302866361

Euro Banking Association Working Group on Electronic Alternative Payments. (2016). *Applying cryptotechnologies to trade finance*. Information Paper.

FAO. (2019). *Measuring Individuals' Rights to Land: An Integrated Approach to Data Collection for SDG Indicators 1.4.2 and 5.a.1*. FAO, The World Bank, & UN-Habitat. https://www.fao.org/publications/card/en/c/CA4885EN/

Fauzi, M. A., Paiman, N., & Othman, Z. (2020). Bitcoin and Cryptocurrency: Challenges, Opportunities and Future Works. *The Journal of Asian Finance. Economics and Business*, *7*(8), 695–704. doi:10.13106/jafeb.2020.vol7.no8.695

Fontela, C. (2012). *UML: modelado de software para profesionales*. Alpha Editorial.

Frankenfield, J. (2023, February 4). *Cryptocurrency Explained With Pros and Cons for Investment*. Investopedia. https://www.investopedia.com/terms/c/cryptocurrency.asp

Frizzo-Barker, J., Chow-White, P. A., Adams, P. R., Mentanko, J., Ha, D., & Green, S. (2020). Blockchain as a disruptive technology for business: A systematic review. *International Journal of Information Management*, *51*, 102029. https://doi-org.spjain.idm.oclc.org/10.1016/j.ijinfomgt.2019.10.014. doi:10.1016/j.ijinfomgt.2019.10.014

Furlonger, D., & Uzureau, C. (2019). The 5 kinds of blockchain projects (and which to watch out for). *Harvard Business Review*, 2–6.

Gandhi, H., More, R., & Patil, N. (2019). A blockchain in banking application. *Global Journal for Research Analysis*, *8*(4), 265–276.

Ganeriwalla, A., Casey, M., Shrikrishna, P., Bender, J. P., & Gstettner, S. (2019). Does your supply chain need a blockchain? *The Boston Consulting Group*.

Garg, R. (2021). *Blockchain Ecosystem for Education and Employment Verification*. Paper presented at the 13th International Conference on Network & Communication Security, Toronto Canada.

Gong, J., & Zhao, L. (2020). Blockchain application in healthcare service mode based on Health Data Bank. *Frontiers of Engineering Management*, *7*(4), 605–614. doi:10.100742524-020-0138-9

Götz, O., Liehr-Gobbers, K., & Krafft, M. (2010). Evaluation of structural equation models using the partial least squares (PLS) approach. In V. E. Vinzi, W. W. Chin, J. Henseler, & H. Wang (Eds.), *Handbook of Partial Least Squares* (pp. 691–711). Springer Berlin Heidelberg. doi:10.1007/978-3-540-32827-8_30

Graglia, J. M., & Mellon, C. (2018). Blockchain and Property in 2018: At the End of the Beginning. *Innovations: Technology, Governance, Globalization*, *12*(1–2), 90–116. doi:10.1162/inov_a_00270

Gramoli, V. (2022). Blockchain Fundamentals. In *Blockchain Scalability and its Foundations in Distributed Systems* (p. 1739). Springer International Publishing. doi:10.1007/978-3-031-12578-2_3

Grech, A., Sood, I., & Ariño, L. (2021). Blockchain, self-sovereign identity and digital credentials: Promise versus praxis in education. *Frontiers in Blockchain*, *4*, 616779. https://www.frontiersin.org/articles/10.3389/fbloc.2021.616779/full. doi:10.3389/fbloc.2021.616779

Griffith, & Clancey-Shang, D. (2023). Cryptocurrency regulation and market quality. *Journal of International Financial Markets, Institutions & Money*, *84*, 101744–. doi:10.1016/j.intfin.2023.101744

Grigg, I. (2015). *On the intersection of Ricardian and Smart Contracts*. IANG. https://iang. org/papers/intersection_ricardian_smart. html.

Grima, S., Spiteri, J., & Romānova, I. (2020). A STEEP framework analysis of the key factors impacting the use of blockchain technology in the insurance industry. *The Geneva Papers on Risk and Insurance. Issues and Practice*, *45*(3), 398–425. doi:10.105741288-020-00162-x

Grover, P., Kar, A. K., Janssen, M., & Ilavarasan, P. V. (2019). Perceived usefulness, ease of use and user acceptance of blockchain technology for digital transactions – Insights from user-generated content on Twitter. *Enterprise Information Systems, 13*(6), 771–800. https://doi-org.spjain.idm.oclc.org/10.1080/ 17517575. 2019.1599446.

Guida, P. (2023, September). Council Post: The State Of DAOs And What That Can Mean For Web3. *Forbes*. https://www.forbes.com/sites/forbesfinancecouncil/2022/10/14/the-state-of-daos-and-what-that-can-mean-for-web3/?sh=39711e9e7f37

Guo, Y., & Liang, C. (2016). Blockchain application and outlook in the banking industry. *Financial Innovation*, *2*(1), 24. doi:10.118640854-016-0034-9

Gupta, A., & Gupta, S. (2018). Blockchain technology: Application in the Indian banking sector. *Delhi Business Review*, *19*(2), 89–94. doi:10.51768/dbr.v19i2.192201807

Guustaaf, E., Rahardja, U., Aini, Q., Maharani, H. W., & Santoso, N. A. (2021). Blockchain-based Higher Educationproject. *Aptisi Transactions on Management (ATM), 5*(1), 46-61. https://ijc.ilearning.co/index.php/ATM/article/view/1433

Haber, S., & Stornetta, W. S. (1991). How to time-stamp a digital document. *Journal of Cryptology*, *3*(2), 99–111. doi:10.1007/BF00196791

Hackius, N., & Petersen, M. (2017). Blockchain in logistics and supply chain: Trick or treat? In *Proceedings of the Hamburg International Conference of Logistics* (HICL) (pp. 3–18). Epubli.

Hair, J. F., Tomas, G., Hult, M., & Ringle, C. M. (2021). Partial least squares structural equation modeling (PLS-SEM) using R. OAPEN.

Hair, J. F. J., Hult, M. T. G., Ringle, C. M., & Sarstedt, M. (2014). A primer on partial least squares structural equation modeling (PLS-SEM). *Sage (Atlanta, Ga.)*. doi:10.1108/EBR-10-2013-0128

Hair, J. F. Jr, Hult, G. T. M., Ringle, C. M., Sarstedt, M., Danks, N. P., & Ray, S. (2021). *Partial least squares structural equation modeling (PLS-SEM) using R: A workbook*. Springer Nature. doi:10.1007/978-3-030-80519-7

Hair, J. F., Ringle, C. M., & Sarstedt, M. (2011). PLS-SEM: Indeed a silver bullet. *Journal of Marketing Theory and Practice*, *19*(2), 139–152. doi:10.2753/MTP1069-6679190202

Hair, J. F., Sarstedt, M., Ringle, C. M., & Mena, J. A. (2012). An assessment of the use of partial least squares structural equation modeling in marketing research. *Journal of the Academy of Marketing Science*, *40*(3), 414–433. doi:10.100711747-011-0261-6

Hair, J., Hollingsworth, C. L., Randolph, A. B., & Chong, A. Y. L. (2017). An updated and expanded assessment of PLS-SEM in information systems research. *Industrial Management & Data Systems*, *117*(3), 442–458. doi:10.1108/IMDS-04-2016-0130

Hakizimana, D., Ntizimira, C., Mbituyumuremyi, A., Hakizimana, E., Mahmoud, H., Birindabagabo, P., Musanabaganwa, C., & Gashumba, D. (2022). The impact of Covid-19 on malaria services in three high endemic districts in Rwanda: A mixed-method study. *Malaria Journal*, *21*(1), 48. doi:10.118612936-022-04071-3 PMID:35164781

Haleem, A., Javaid, M., Singh, R. P., Suman, R., & Rab, S. (2021). Blockchain technology applications in healthcare: An overview. In International Journal of Intelligent Networks, 2. doi:10.1016/j.ijin.2021.09.005

Halkiopoulos, C., Antonopoulou, H., & Kostopoulos, N. (2023). *Utilizing Blockchain Technology in Various Applications to Secure Data Flows. A Comprehensive Analysis*. Technium. doi:10.47577/technium.v11i.9132

Han, H., Shiwakoti, R. K., Jarvis, R., Mordi, C., & Botchie, D. (2023). Accounting and auditing with blockchain technology and artificial Intelligence: A literature review. *International Journal of Accounting Information Systems*, *48*, 100598. doi:10.1016/j.accinf.2022.100598

Haque, M. A., Haque, S., Zeba, S., Kumar, K., Ahmad, S., Rahman, M., & Ahmed, L. (2023). Sustainable and efficient E-learning internet of things system through blockchain technology. *E-Learning and Digital Media*, *20427530231156711*. doi:10.1177/20427530231156711

Hasan, L., Chaudhry, A., & Jalil, H. (2022). Regulation, Corruption, and Land Grab: A Tale of Illegal Private Housing Societies in Islamabad. SSRN *Electronic Journal*. doi:10.2139/ssrn.4019448

Hassani, H., Huang, X., & Silva, E. (2019). Big Data and Climate Change. *Big Data and Cognitive Computing*, *3*(1), 12. doi:10.3390/bdcc3010012

Hayati, Y., Mai, F. M., Badrul, M., & Zulnurhaini, Z. (2018). Behavioral intention to adopt blockchain technology: Viewpoint of the banking institutions in Malaysia. *International Journal of Advanced Scientific Research and Management*, *3*(10), 368–377.

Henseler, J. (2017). Bridging design and behavioral research with variance-based structural equation modeling. *Journal of Advertising*, *46*(1), 178–192. doi:10.1080/00913367.2017.1281780

Henseler, J., Ringle, C. M., & Sarstedt, M. (2014). A new criterion for assessing discriminant validity in variance-based structural equation modeling. *Journal of the Academy of Marketing Science*, *43*(1), 115–135. doi:10.100711747-014-0403-8

Henseler, J., Ringle, C. M., & Sinkovics, R. R. (2009). The use of partial least squares path modeling in international marketing. *Advances in International Marketing*, *20*, 277–319. doi:10.1108/S1474-7979(2009)0000020014

Hidayanto, A. N., & Prabowo, H. (2019). The latest adoption blockchain technology in supply chain management: A systematic literature review. *ICIC Express Letters*, *13*(10), 913–920.

Hidrogo, I., Zambrano, D., Hernandez-de-Menendez, M., & Morales-Menendez, R. (2020). Mostla for engineering education: Part 1 initial results. [IJIDeM]. *International Journal on Interactive Design and Manufacturing*, *14*(4), 1429–1441. doi:10.100712008-020-00730-4

Hoy, M. B. (2017). An introduction to the blockchain and its implications for libraries and medicine. *Medical Reference Services Quarterly*, *36*(3), 273–279. doi:10.1080/02763869.2017.1332261 PMID:28714815

Hoyos, C. A., & Kloos, C. D. (2023). Experiences with Micro-Credentials at UC3M: Academic and Technological Aspects. In 2023 IEEE World Engineering Higher EducationConference (EDUNINE) (pp. 1-6). IEEE. doi:10.1109/EDUNINE57531.2023.10102848

Ian, A. (2017). Blockchain-based Ubitquity pilots with Brazil's land records bureau. *IB Times*. https://www.ibtimes.co.uk/blockchain-based-ubitquity-pilots-brazils-land-records-bureau-1615518

Iansiti, M., & Lakhani, K. (2017). The Truth About Blockchain. *Harvard Business Review*, *95*, 118–127.

IBM. (2023). *What is blockchain technology?* IBM. https://www.ibm.com/topics/blockchain

IDRBT. (2017). *Applications of Blockchain Technology to Banking and Financial sectors in India*. Institute for Development and Research in Banking Technology.

IIPS. (2023). *Land Registration System of Pakistan: History and Challenges*. IIPS. https://iips.com.pk/land-registration-system-of-pakistan-history-and-challenges/

Internal Revenue Service. (2023). *Digital Assets*. IRS. https://www.irs.gov/businesses/small-businesses-self-employed/digital-assets

Iyer, S. S., Seetharaman, A., & Maddulety, K. (2020). Higher EducationTransformation Using Block Chain Technology-A Student Centric Model. In *Re-imagining Diffusion and Adoption of Information Technology and Systems: A Continuing Conversation: IFIP WG 8.6 International Conference on Transfer and Diffusion of IT,* (pp. 201-217). Springer International Publishing.

Iyer, S. S., Seetharaman, A., & Ranjan, B. (2021). Researching Blockchain Technology and its Usefulness in Higher Education. *Machine Learning, IOT and Blockchain Technologies & Trends*, 27-48. AIRCC. doi:10.5121/csit.2021.111203

Iyer, S. S. (2022). Adopting a Student Centric Higher EducationBlockchain System. *International Journal of Information and Communication Sciences*, *7*(3), 48–65. Retrieved June 25, 2023, from https://www.researchgate.net/publication/369551569_Adopting_a_Student_Centric_Education_Blockchain_System. doi:10.11648/j.ijics.20220703.11

Jackson, D., Michelson, G., & Munir, R. (2023). Developing accountants for the future: New technology, skills, and the role of stakeholders. *Accounting Education*, *32*(2), 150–177. doi:10.1080/09639284.2022.2057195

Jagtap, V. (2014). To Study Perception of Educated and Working Group of customers towards E - Banking in Thane Region. *Abhinav International Monthly Refereed Journal of Research in Management and Technology.*, *3*(7), 29–35.

Jain, G., Sharma, N., & Shrivastava, A. (2021). Enhancing training effectiveness for organizations through blockchain-enabled training effectiveness measurement (BETEM). *Journal of Organizational Change Management*, *34*(2), 439–461. doi:10.1108/JOCM-10-2020-0303

Jansen, J., Beyer, H-M, & Taschner, A. (2018). Supply chain finance in SMEs: A comparative study in the automotive sector in Germany and The Netherlands. *Logistiek: tijdschrift voor toegepaste logistiek*, (5), 59-81.

Janssens, L., Bazhenova, E., De Smedt, J., Vanthienen, J., & Denecker, M. (2016, June). Consistent Integration of Decision (DMN) and Process (BPMN) Models. In CAiSE forum (Vol. 1612, pp. 121128).

Javaid, M., Haleem, A., Singh, R., Suman, R., & Khan, S. (2022). A review of Blockchain Technology applications for financial services. *Bench Council Transactions on Benchmarks, Standards and Evaluations, 2*(3). . doi:10.1016/j.tbench.2022.100073

JEL classification: G20, G21, G28. (2022, September). *The Financial Stability Implications of Digital Assets.* Federal Reserve Bank Of New York. Www.newyorkfed.org. https://www.newyorkfed.org/research/staff_reports/sr1034

Jensen, T., Hedman, J., & Henningsson, S. (2019). How TradeLens delivers business value with blockchain technology. *MIS Quarterly Executive*, *18*(4), 221–243. https://doi-org.spjain.idm.oclc.org/10.17705/2msqe.00018. doi:10.17705/2msqe.00018

Joe, M. (2018). *Case Study: Blockchain Takes a Spin Around the Real-Estate Block.* RT Insights. https://www.rtinsights.com/case-study-blockchain-takes-a-spin-around-the-real-estate-block/

Jonathan, K. (2021). *Sweden Moves to Next Stage With Blockchain Land Registry.* https://www.coindesk.com/markets/2017/03/30/sweden-moves-to-next-stage-with-blockchain-land-registry/

Jun, M. (2018). Blockchain government-a next form of infrastructure for the twenty-first century. Journal of Open Innovation, 4(1), 7.

Kabashi, F., Neziri, V., Snopce, H., Luma, A., Aliu, A., & Shkurti, L. (2023). The possibility of blockchain application in Higher Education. In *2023 12th Mediterranean Conference on Embedded Computing (MECO)* (pp. 1-5). IEEE. 10.1109/MECO58584.2023.10154919

Kamišalić, A., Turkanović, M., Mrdović, S., & Heričko, M. (2019). *A preliminary review of blockchain-based solutions in higher education*. Paper presented at the Learning Technology for Education Challenges 8th International Workshop, LTEC 2019, Zamora, Spain.

Kamruzzaman, M. M., Yan, B., Sarker, M. N. I., Alruwaili, O., Wu, M., & Alrashdi, I. (2022). Blockchain and Fog Computing in IoT-Driven Healthcare Services for Smart Cities. *Journal of Healthcare Engineering*, *2022*, 1–13. doi:10.1155/2022/9957888 PMID:35126961

Kandaswamy, R., & Furlonger, D. (2018). Gartner report: Pay attention to these 4 types of blockchain business initiatives. *Gartner, Stamford, CT, USA, Tech. Rep., Mar.*

Kaur, M. (2018). A Study on Current Frauds Trends in the Indian Banking Industry and Its Detection Using Data Mining Algorithms. [June.]. *International Journal of Computer Engineering In Research Trends*, *5*(6), 177–186.

Khan, M., & Naz, T. (2021). Smart contracts based on blockchain for decentralized learning management system. *SN Computer Science*, *2*(4), 260. doi:10.100742979-021-00661-1

Kharitonova, A. (2021, March). Capabilities of Blockchain Technology in Tokenization of Economy. In *1st International Scientific Conference" Legal Regulation of the Digital Economy and Digital Relations: Problems and Prospects of Development"(LARDER 2020)* (pp. 28-32). Atlantis Press. 10.2991/aebmr.k.210318.006

Kitchenham, B., & Brereton, P. (2013). A systematic review of systematic review process research in software engineering. *Information and Software Technology*, *55*(12), 2049–2075. doi:10.1016/j.infsof.2013.07.010

Komal & Rani. (2012). Progress of Banking India: Customers' perspectives. *Business Intelligence Journal.*, *5*(1), 28–40.

Korpela, K., Hallikas, J., & Dahlberg, T. (2017, January). Digital supply chain transformation toward blockchain integration. In *Proceedings of the 50th Hawaii International Conference on System Sciences*. Scholar Space. 10.24251/HICSS.2017.506

Kosasi, S., Rahardja, U., Lutfiani, N., Harahap, E. P., & Sari, S. N. (2022). Blockchain technology-emerging research themes opportunities in higher education. In *2022 International Conference on Science and Technology (ICOSTECH)* (pp. 1-8). IEEE. 10.1109/ICOSTECH54296.2022.9829053

Kosba, A., Miller, A., Shi, E., Wen, Z., & Papamanthou, C. (2016). *Hawk: The Blockchain Model of Cryptography and.* IEEE Computer Society.

Koul, R. (2018). Blockchain Oriented Software Testing - Challenges and Approaches. *3rd International Conference for Convergence in Technology (I2CT)*, Pune, India. 10.1109/I2CT.2018.8529728

Kruijff, J., & Weigand, H. (2017). *Ontologies for Commitment-Based Smart Contracts.* OTM 2017 Conferences: Confederated International Conferences: CoopIS, C&TC, and ODBASE 2017, Rhodes, Greece.

Kshetri, N., Miller, K., Banerjee, G., & Upreti, B. R. (2023). International Journal of Emerging and Disruptive Innovation in Education: *Visionarium. 1*(1). https://digitalcommons.lindenwood.edu/ijedie/vol1/iss1/4/

Kshetri, N. (2018). 1 Blockchain's roles in meeting key supply chain management objectives. *International Journal of Information Management*, *39*, 80–89. doi:10.1016/j.ijinfomgt.2017.12.005

Kuleto, V., Bucea-Manea-Ţoniş, R., Bucea-Manea-Ţoniş, R., Ilić, M. P., Martins, O. M., Ranković, M., & Coelho, A. S. (2022). The potential of blockchain technology in higher education as perceived by students in Serbia, Romania, and Portugal. *Sustainability (Basel)*, *14*(2), 749. doi:10.3390u14020749

LalBhasin, M. (2015). An Empirical Study of Frauds in the Banks. *European Journal of Business and Social Sciences*, *4*(7), 1–12.

Lapin, N. (2021, December 23). Explaining Crypto's Volatility. *Forbes*. https://www.forbes.com/sites/nicolelapin/2021/12/23/explaining-cryptos-volatility/?sh=33ab79027b54

Lazuashvili, N., Norta, A., & Draheim, D. (2019). Integration of Blockchain Technology into a Land Registration System for Immutable Traceability: A Casestudy of Georgia. *Lecture Notes in Business Information Processing*, *361*, 219–233. doi:10.1007/978-3-030-30429-4_15

Lee, J. S. (2020, November). *Journal of Korea Trade*, *24*(7), 73–92.

Lee, S., Park, S., & Park, Y. B. (2019). Formal Specification Technique in Smart Contract Verification. *6th International Conference on Platform Technology and Service (PlatCon)*. IEEE. 10.1109/PlatCon.2019.8669419

Legerén-Molina, A. (2018). Los contratos inteligentes en España (La disciplina de los smart contracts) / Smart contracts in Spain; the regulation of smart contracts. *Revista de Derecho civil*, *5*(2), 193-241.

Lerman, R. I., Loprest, P. J., & Kuehn, D. (2020). *Training for jobs of the future Improving access, certifying skills, and expanding apprenticeship.*

Lester, C. (2021). *Cook County to Use the Bitcoin Blockchain for Property Conveyance*. CCN. https://www.ccn.com/cook-county-to-use-the-bitcoin-blockchain-for-property-conveyance/

Li, D., Han, D., Crespi, N., Minerva, R., & Sun, Z. (2021). Fabric-SCF: A blockchain-based secure storage and access control scheme for supply chain finance. *arXiv preprint* arXiv:2111.13538.

Li, W., Bohli, J., & Ghassan, K. (2017). *Securing Proof-of-Stake Blockchain Protocols.* (pp. 297-315). Springer. . doi:10.1007/978-3-319-67816-0_17

Liao, C., Cheng, C., Chen, K., Lai, C., Chiu, T., & Wu-Lee, C. (2017). Toward A Service Platform for Developing Smart Contracts on Blockchain in BDD and TDD Styles. *2017 IEEE 10th International Conference on Service-Oriented Computing and Applications*. IEEE. 10.1109/SOCA.2017.26

Li, J., Zhu, S., Zhang, W., & Yu, L. (2020). Blockchain-driven supply chain finance solution for small and medium enterprises. *Frontiers of Engineering Management*, *7*(4), 500–511. doi:10.100742524-020-0124-2

Lippert, S. K., & Davis, M. (2006). A conceptual model integrating trust into planned change activities to enhance technology adoption behaviour. *Journal of Information Science*, *32*(5), 434–448. doi:10.1177/0165551506066042

Liu, Y., He, D., Obaidat, M. S., Kumar, N., Khan, M. K., & Raymond Choo, K. K. (2020). Blockchain-based identity management systems: A review. In Journal of Network and Computer Applications, 166. doi:10.1016/j.jnca.2020.102731

Liu, Y., Lu, Q., Xu, X., Zhu, L., & Yao, H. (2018). *Applying Design Patterns in Smart Contracts.* Springer International.

Lizcano, DLara, J. AWhite, BAljawarneh, S. (2020). Blockchain-based approach to create a model of trust in open and ubiquitous higher education. Journal of Computing in Higher Education, 32, 109–134.

Lundblad, J. P. (2003). A review and critique of Rogers' diffusion of innovations theory as it applies to organizations. *Organization Development Journal*, *21*(4), 50–64. https://www.proquest.com/scholarly-journals/review-critique-rogers-diffusion-innovation/docview/197971687/se-2

Luu, L., Chu, D. H., Olickel, H., Saxena, P., & Hobor, A. (2016). Making smart contracts smarter. In *Proceedings of the 2016 ACM SIGSAC conference on computer and communications security* (pp. 254-269). ACM. 10.1145/2976749.2978309

Macrinici, D., Cartofeanu, C., & Gao, S. (2018). Smart contract applications within blockchain technology: A systematic mapping study. *Telematics and Informatics*, *35*(8), 2337–2354. doi:10.1016/j.tele.2018.10.004

Madeline, M. S. (2018). *Zambia, Overstock's Medici Ink Deal on Blockchain Land Registry Pilot.* Coin Desk. https://www.coindesk.com/markets/2018/08/01/zambia-overstocks-medici-ink-deal-on-blockchain-land-registry-pilot/

Magadán-Díaz, M. y Rivas-García, J.I. (2020). *La industria editorial española: dos décadas clave de transformación y cambio (19962016).* Investigaciones de Historia Económica Economic History Research doi:10.33231/j.ihe.2020.04.003

Magno, F., Cassia, F., & Ringle, C. M. (2022). A brief review of partial least squares structural equation modeling (PLS-SEM) use in quality management studies. *The TQM Journal*. doi:10.1108/TQM-06-2022-0197

Malik, S., Chadhar, M., Vatanasakdakul, S., & Chetty, M. (2021). Factors affecting the organizational adoption of blockchain technology: Extending the technology–organization–environment (TOE) framework in the Australian context. *Sustainability (Basel)*, *13*(16), 9404. doi:10.3390u13169404

Malik, V., Mittal, R., Mavaluru, D., Narapureddy, B. R., Goyal, S. B., Martin, R. J., & Mittal, A. (2023). *Building a Secure Platform for Digital Governance Interoperability and Data Exchange using Blockchain and Deep Learning-based frameworks.* IEEE. doi:10.1109/ACCESS.2023.3293529

Mallesha, C., & Hari Priya, S. (2019, July – September). A Study on blockchain technology in the banking sector. *International Journal of Advanced Research in Commerce, Management and Social Science*, *2*(03), 123–132.

Maloney, S., Moss, A., Keating, J., Kotsanas, G., & Morgan, P. (2013). Sharing teaching and learning resources perceptions of a university's faculty members. *Medical Education*, *47*(8), 811–819. doi:10.1111/medu.12225 PMID:23837427

Mao, D., Wang, F., Wang, Y., & Hao, Z. (2019). *Visual and User-Defined Smart Contract Designing System Based on Automatic Coding*. IEEE Access. Digital Object Identifier., doi:10.1109/ACCESS.2019.2920776

Marc, H. (2021). *Dubai Land Department Launches Blockchain Real Estate Initiative*. Coin Desk. https://www.coindesk.com/markets/2017/10/10/dubai-land-department-launches-blockchain-real-estate-initiative/

Marchesi, M., Marchesi, L., & Tonelli, R. (2018). An Agile Software Engineering Method to Design Blockchain Applications. *Software Engineering Conference Russia (SECR 2018)*, Moscow, Russia. 10.1145/3290621.3290627

Marlina, E., Hidayanto, A. N., & Purwandari, B. (2022). Towards a model of research data management readiness in Indonesian context: An investigation of factors and indicators through the fuzzy delphi method. *Library & Information Science Research*, *44*(1), 101141. doi:10.1016/j.lisr.2022.101141

Marr, B. (2017). A Short History of Bitcoin and Crypto Currency Everyone Should Read. *Forbes*. https://www.forbes.com/sites/bernardmarr/2017/12/06/a-short-history-of-bitcoin-and-crypto-currency-everyone-should-read/?sh=1b53ac3f3f27

Martínez Alés, R. (2001). *Información Comercial Española, ICE: Revista de Economía*. Dialnet.

Masser, I. (1999). All shapes and sizes: The first generation of national spatial data infrastructures. *International Journal of Geographical Information Science*, *13*(1), 67–84. doi:10.1080/136588199241463

Mavridou, A., & Laszka, A. (2018). Designing Secure Ethereum Smart Contracts: A Finite State Machine Based Approach. *International Conference on Financial Cryptography and Data Security*. FC 2018: Financial Cryptography and Data Security. Springer. 10.1007/978-3-662-58387-6_28

Mavridou, A., & Laszka, A. (2018). FSolidM for Designing Secure Ethereum Smart Contracts: Tool Demonstration. *7th International Conference on Principles of Security and Trust (POST) Held as Part of the 21st European Joint Conferences on Theory and Practice of Software (ETAPS)*. Springer. 10.1007/978-3-319-89722-6_11

Mavridou, A., Laszka, A., Stachtiari, E., & Dubey, A. (2019). VeriSolid: Correct-by-Design Smart Contracts for Ethereum. *Cryptography and Security; Software Engineering*. arXiv.org. arXiv:1901.01292

McLaren, R. (2013). Engaging the land sector gatekeepers in crowdsourced land administration. *FIG Working Week 2013*.

Mecozzi, R., Perrone, G., Anelli, D., Saitto, N., Paggi, E., & Mancini, D. (2022). Blockchain-related identity and access management challenges:(de) centralized digital identities regulation. In *2022 IEEE International Conference on Blockchain (Blockchain)* (pp. 443-448). IEEE. 10.1109/Blockchain55522.2022.00068

Meenakshi, K., & George, A. R. (2018). Green banking through blockchain. *International Journal of Research and Analytical Reviews, 1*(12), 212–220.

Meria, L., Aini, Q., Santoso, N. P. L., Raharja, U., & Millah, S. (2021). Management of Access Control for Decentralized Online Educations using Blockchain Technology. Paper presented at the *2021 Sixth International Conference on Informatics and Computing (ICIC),* (pp. 1-6). IEEE. 10.1109/ICIC54025.2021.9632999

Merlec, M. M., Islam, M. M., Lee, Y. K., & In, H. P. (2022). A consortium blockchain-based secure and trusted electronic portfolio management scheme. *Sensors (Basel), 22*(3), 1271. doi:10.339022031271 PMID:35162016

Mikalef, P., Boura, M., Lekakos, G., & Krogstie, J. (2019). Big data analytics and firm performance: Findings from a mixed-method approach. *Journal of Business Research, 98*, 261–276. doi:10.1016/j.jbusres.2019.01.044

Mikroyannidis, A., Third, A., & Domingue, J. (2020). A case study on the decentralisation of lifelong learning using blockchain technology. *Journal of Interactive Media in Education, 2020*(1), 1–10. doi:10.5334/jime.591

Mishra, S., & Tyagi, A. K. (2022). The role of machine learning techniques in internet of things-based cloud applications. *Artificial intelligence-based internet of things systems*, 105-135. doi:10.1007/978-3-030-87059-1_4

Mohanta, B. K., Jena, D., Panda, S. S., & Sobhanayak, S. (2019). Blockchain technology: A survey on applications and security privacy challenges. *Internet of Things : Engineering Cyber Physical Human Systems, 8*, 100107. doi:10.1016/j.iot.2019.100107

More, D. M. M., & Nalawade, M. P. J. D. K. (2015). Online banking and cyber-attacks: The current scenario. *International Journal of Advanced Research in Computer Science and Software Engineering, 5*(12), 743–749.

Mougayar, W. (2016). *The Business Blockchain: Promise, Practice, and Application of the Next Internet Technology*. Wiley.

Mughal, M. A. (2012). Concept of Access to Justice in Pakistan. SSRN *Electronic Journal.* doi:10.2139/ssrn.2136599

Mulaji, S. S. M., & Roodt, S. S. (2021). The practicality of adopting blockchain-based distributed identity management in organizations: A meta-synthesis. *Security and Communication Networks, 2021*, 1–19. Advance online publication. doi:10.1155/2021/9910078

Müller, H., & Seifert, M. (2019). Blockchain, a Feasible Technology for Land Administration? *Geospatial Information for a Smarter Life and Environmental Resilience.*

Nakamoto, S. (2008). *A peer-to-peer electronic cash system.* Bitcoin. https://bitcoin. org/bitcoin. pdf,

Nakamoto, S. (2008). Bitcoin: A Peer-to-Peer Electronic Cash System I Satoshi Nakamoto Institute. *Bitcoin.Org.*

Nakamoto, S. (2008). *Bitcoin: A Peer-to-Peer Electronic Cash System.* Bitcoin. https://bitcoin.org/bitcoin.pdf

Narayanan, A., Bonneau, J., Felten, E., Miller, A., & Goldfeder, S. (2016). *Bitcoin and Cryptocurrency Technologies: A Comprehensive Introduction.* Princeton University Press.

Needleman, M. H. (2001). ONIX (online information exchange). *Serials Review, 27*(34), 102104.

Nehru, R. S. S., Cuong, T. Q., Prakash, A. R., & Huong, B. T. T. (2023). Higher Education: AI Applications for Blockchain-Based IoT Technology and Networks. In *AI Models for Blockchain-Based Intelligent Networks in IoT Systems: Concepts, Methodologies, Tools, and Applications* (pp. 261–283). Springer International Publishing. doi:10.1007/978-3-031-31952-5_12

Ngai, E. W., Hu, Y., Wong, Y. H., Chen, Y., & Sun, X. (2011). The application of data mining techniques in financial fraud detection: A classification framework and an academic review of literature. *Decision Support Systems, 50*(3), 559–569. doi:10.1016/j.dss.2010.08.006

Ngwakwe, C. (2023). Emerging Regulatory Challenges on The Value and Future Of Cryptocurrency Exchange Business. Acta Universitatis Danubius. *Juridica, 19*(2).

Nikhilesh, D. (2021). *Russia's Government to Test Blockchain Land Registry System.* Coin Desk. https://www.coindesk.com/markets/2017/10/20/russias-government-to-test-blockchain-land-registry-system/

Niroula, G. S., & Thapa, G. B. (2005). Impacts and causes of land fragmentation, and lessons learned from land consolidation in South Asia. *Land Use Policy, 22*(4), 358–372. doi:10.1016/j.landusepol.2004.10.001

O'Sullivan, A., & Sheffrin, S. M. (2007). *Economics: Principles in Action.* Pearson/Prentice Hall. https://books.google.com.pk/books?id=vfxAHAAACAAJ

O'Sullivan, K., Clark, S., Marshall, K., & MacLachlan, M. (2021). A Just Digital framework to ensure equitable achievement of the Sustainable Development Goals. *Nature Communications, 12*(1), 6345. doi:10.103841467-021-26217-8 PMID:34732699

Obal, M. (2013). Why do incumbents sometimes succeed? Investigating the role of interorganizational trust on the adoption of disruptive technology. *Industrial Marketing Management, 42*(6), 900–908. doi:10.1016/j.indmarman.2013.05.017

Oke, A., & Fernandes, F. A. P. (2020). Innovations in teaching and learning: Exploring the perceptions of the Higher Educationsector on the 4th industrial revolution (4IR). *Journal of Open Innovation, 6*(2), 31. doi:10.3390/joitmc6020031

Palihapitiya, T. (2020). *Blockchain in Banking Industry.* University of Moratuwa.

Palma, L. M., Vigil, M. A., Pereira, F. L., & Martina, J. E. (2019). Blockchain and smart contracts for higher education registry in Brazil. *International Journal of Network Management, 29*(3), e2061. doi:10.1002/nem.2061

Pan, G., Seow, P. S., Suwardy, T., & Gay, E. (2011). Fraud: A Review and Research Agenda. *Journal of Accountancy Business and the Public Interest, 10*, 138–178.

Parizi, R. M., Dehghantanha, A., Choo, K. K. R., & Singh, A. (2018). Empirical vulnerability analysis of automated smart contracts security testing on blockchains. *CASCON. Proceedings of the 28th Annual International Conference on Computer Science and Software Engineering*. Springer.

Park, J. (2021). Promises and challenges of Blockchain in education. *Smart Learning Environments, 8*(1), 33. doi:10.118640561-021-00179-2

Pelletier, S. (2018). Blockchain in higher education. *The Chronicle of Higher Education.*

Perisic, A., Perisic, I., Lazic, M., & Perisic, B. (2023). The foundation for future education, teaching, training, learning, and performing infrastructure-The open interoperability conceptual framework approach. *Heliyon, 9*(6), e16836. doi:10.1016/j.heliyon.2023.e16836 PMID:37484382

Permenev, A., Dimitrov, D., Tsankov, P., Drachsler-Cohen, D., & Vechev, M. (2019). "VerX: Safety Verification of Smart Contracts". Safety verification of Smart Contracts. *Security and Privacy*, 2020.

Pirkkalainen, H., Sood, I., Padron Napoles, C., Kukkonen, A., & Camilleri, A. (2023). How might micro-credentials influence institutions and empower learners in higher education? *Educational Research, 65*(1), 40–63. doi:10.1080/00131881.2022.2157302

Pohl, K., Hönninger, H., Achatz, R., & Broy, M. (Eds.). (2012). Model-based engineering of embedded systems: The SPES 2020 methodology. Heidelberg: Springer.

Porru, S., Pinn, A., Marchesi, M., & Tonelli, R. (2017). Blockchain-Oriented Software Engineering: Challenges and New Directions. *2017 IEEE/ACM 39th IEEE International Conference on Software Engineering Companion.* ACM. 10.1109/ICSE-C.2017.142

Pranto, S., Jardim, L., Oliveira, T., & Ruivo, P. (2019, October). Literature review on blockchain with focus on supply chain. In *Atas da Conferencia da Associacao Portuguesa de Sistemas de Informacao 2019*. Associação Portuguesa de Sistemas de Informação.

Prawiyogi, A. G., Aini, Q., Santoso, N. P. L., Lutfiani, N., & Juniar, H. L. J. (2021). Blockchain Higher Educationconcept 4.0: Student-centered ilearning blockchain framework. *JTP-Jurnal Teknologi Pendidikan, 23*(2), 129–145. doi:10.21009/jtp.v23i2.20978

Prewett, K. W., Prescott, G. L., & Phillips, K. (2020). Blockchain adoption is inevitable—Barriers and risks remain. *Journal of Corporate Accounting & Finance, 31*(2), 21–28. doi:10.1002/jcaf.22415

Propy. (2023). *Blockchain for Real Estate*. Propy. https://propy.com/browse/blockchain/

Puthal, D., Malik, N., Mohanty, S. P., Kougianos, E., & Das, G. (2018). Everything you wanted to know about the blockchain Its promise, components, processes, and problems. *IEEE Consumer Electronics Magazine*, *7*(4), 6–14. doi:10.1109/MCE.2018.2816299

Qurat ul Ain. (2019). The Need for Efficient Record Management System in Pakistan. *South Asian Review of Business and Administrative Studies, 1*(1).

Raghavan A.R. & Parthiban, L. (2014). The effect of cybercrime on a Bank's finances. *International Journal of Current Research and Review, 2*(2), 173-178.

Rahardja, U., Aini, Q., Oganda, F. P., & Devana, V. T. (2021). Secure framework based on blockchain for e-learning during covid-19. In *2021 9th International Conference on Cyber and IT Service Management (CITSM)* (pp. 1-7). IEEE. 10.1109/CITSM52892.2021.9588854

Raimundo, R., & Rosário, A. (2021). Blockchain system in the higher education. *European Journal of Investigation in Health, Psychology and Education, 11*(1), 276–293. doi:10.3390/ejihpe11010021 PMID:34542464

Rajabifard, A., Feeney, M. E. F., & Williamson, I. (2003). *Spatial data infrastructures: concept, nature and SDI hierarchy*. Taylor & Francis London.

Rajput, M. (2023, April 28). Top 15 Blockchain Technology Trends to Follow in 2023. *Mind Inventory*. https://www.mindinventory.com/blog/blockchain-development-trends/

Rakshit, A. & Kumar, S. (2022). Fraud Detection: A Review on Blockchain. *International Research Journal of Engineering and Technology (IRJET), 9*(1).

Ramchandra, M. V., Kumar, K., Sarkar, A., & Kr, S. (2022). Assessment of the impact of blockchain technology in the banking industry. *Materials Today: Proceedings, 56*(4), 2221-2226. .(https://www.sciencedirect.com/science/article/pii/S2214785321075763) doi:10.1016/j.matpr.2021.11.554

Ratta, P., Kaur, A., Sharma, S., Shabaz, M., & Dhiman, G. (2021). Application of blockchain and internet of things in healthcare and medical sector: Applications, challenges, and future perspectives. *Journal of Food Quality*, *2021*, 1–20. doi:10.1155/2021/7608296

Rega, F. G., & Riccardi, N. (2018). *Blockchain in the banking industry: an Overview*. (White Paper). Research Gate. https://www.researchgate.net/profile/Federico-Rega/publication/327601993_Blockchain_in_the_banking_industry_an_Overview/links/5bfefaeaa6fdcc1b8d49f252/Blockchain-in-the-banking-industry-an-Overview.pdf

Rieger, A., Lockl, J., Urbach, N., Guggenmos, F., & Fridgen, G. (2019). Building a blockchain application that complies with the EU General Data Protection Regulation. *MIS Quarterly Executive*, *18*(4), 263–279. https://doi-org.spjain.idm.oclc.org/10.17705/2msqe.00020. doi:10.17705/2msqe.00020

Rijanto, A. (2021). Blockchain technology adoption in supply chain finance. *Journal of Theoretical and Applied Electronic Commerce Research*, *16*(7), 3078–3098. doi:10.3390/jtaer16070168

Rijanto, A. (2021). Business financing and blockchain technology adoption in agroindustry. *Journal of Science and Technology Policy Management, 2*(2), 215–235. doi:10.1108/JSTPM-03-2020-0065

Sabry Esmail, F., Kamal Alsheref, F., & Elsayed Aboutabl, A.Fahd Sabry Esmail. (2023). Review of loan fraud detection process in the banking sector using Data Mining Techniques. *International Journal of Electrical and Computer Engineering Systems, 14*(2), 229–239. Advance online publication. doi:10.32985/ijeces.14.2.12

Safiullin, M. R., Elshin, L. A., & Abdukaeva, A. A. (2020). An empirical assessment of the impact of blockchain technologies on the effectiveness of the supply chain development. *International Journal of Supply Chain Management, 9*(4), 887–892.

Samburaj, D. (2021). *Japan Could Place Its Entire Property Registry on a Blockchain.* CCN. https://www.ccn.com/japan-place-entire-property-registry-blockchain/

Sangiuliano Intra, F., Nasti, C., Massaro, R., Perretta, A. J., Di Girolamo, A., Brighi, A., & Biroli, P. (2023). Flexible Learning Environments for a Sustainable Lifelong Learning Process for Teachers in the School Context. *Sustainability (Basel), 15*(14), 11237. doi:10.3390u151411237

Santos, J., & Duffy, K. H. (2019). *A Decentralized Approach to Blockcerts Certificate Revocation.* Github. https://github.com/WebOfTrustInfo/rwot5-boston/tree/master/final-documents

Sarstedt, M., Radomir, L., Moisescu, O. I., & Ringle, C. M. (2022). Latent class analysis in PLS-SEM: A review and recommendations for future applications. *Journal of Business Research, 138*, 398–407. doi:10.1016/j.jbusres.2021.08.051

Satybaldy, A., Subedi, A., & Nowostawski, M. (2022). A Framework for Online Document Verification Using Self-Sovereign Identity Technology. *Sensors (Basel), 22*(21), 8408. doi:10.339022218408 PMID:36366105

Savelyeva, T., & Fang, G. (2022). *Sustainable tertiary education in Asia Policies, practices, and developments.* Springer Nature. doi:10.1007/978-981-19-5104-6

Savelyeva, T., & Park, J. (2022). Blockchain technology for sustainable education. *British Journal of Educational Technology, 53*(6), 1591–1604. doi:10.1111/bjet.13273

Scherer, M. (2017). *Performance and scalability of blockchain networks and smart contracts.*

Schlesinger, W., Cervera-Taulet, A., & Wymer, W. (2023). The influence of university brand image, satisfaction, and university identification on alumni WOM intentions. *Journal of Marketing for Higher Education, 33*(1), 1–19. doi:10.1080/08841241.2021.1874588

Scicchitano, M. (2020, December 12). *How Cryptocurrencies May Impact the Banking Industry.* Wolf & Company, P.C. https://www.wolfandco.com/resources/insights/how-cryptocurrencies-may-impact-the-banking-industry/

Seth, S. (2021, August 25). *Central Bank Digital Currency (CBDC).* Investopedia. https://www.investopedia.com/terms/c/central-bank-digital-currency-cbdc.asp

Shakan, Y., Kumalakov, B., Mutanov, G., Mamykova, Z., & Kistaubayev, Y. (2021). Verification of University student and graduate data using blockchain technology. *International Journal OF Computers Communications & Control, 16*(5). https://univagora.ro/jour/index.php/ijccc/article/view/4266

Shang, Q., & Price, A. (2019). A Blockchain-Based Land Titling Project in the Republic of Georgia: Rebuilding Public Trust and Lessons for Future Pilot Projects. *Innovations: Technology, Governance, Globalization, 12*(3–4), 72–78. doi:10.1162/inov_a_00276

Sharma, S., & Batth, R. S. (2020). *Blockchain technology for higher education system: A mirror review*. Proceedings of the International Conference on Intelligent Engineering and Management, London, UK.

Sharples, M., & Domingue, J. (2016). The blockchain and kudos: A distributed system for educational record, reputation, and reward. *Adaptive and Adaptable Learning*, 490-496.

Sharples, M., & Domingue, J. (2016). The blockchain and kudos: A distributed system for educational record, reputation and reward. In Adaptive and Adaptable Learning: 11th European Conference on Technology Enhanced Learning. Springer.

Shen, H., & Xiao, Y. (2018). *Research on online quiz scheme based on double-layer consortium blockchain*. Proceedings of the 9th International Conference on Information Technology in Medicine and Education, ITME; Hangzhou, China. 10.1109/ITME.2018.00213

Shilpa Parkhi, K. M. (2021). Blockchain enabled technology platform for enhancing supply chain financing for SME's. *Psychology and Education Journal, 57*(9). doi:10.17762/pae.v57i9.2689

Shin, L. (2017). The First Government To Secure Land Titles On The Bitcoin Blockchain Expands Project. *Forbes*.

Shishkin, E. (2018). *Debugging Smart Contract's Business Logic Using Symbolic Model-Checking*. arXiv.org > cs > arXiv:1812.00619v1

Sillaber, C., & Waltl, B. (2017). Life Cycle of Smart Contracts in Blockchain Ecosystems. *Datenschutz und Datensicherheit – DuD, 41*(8), 497–500.

Singh, G., & Kaur, S. (2023). Bank Frauds Reported In India: A Case Study. *Journal of Pharmaceutical Negative Results, 14*(2), 304–309.

Singh, N. P. (2007). Online Frauds in Banks with Phishing. *Journal of Internet Banking and Commerce, 12*(2).

Singh, P. (2020). Role of Blockchain Technology in Digitization of Land Records in Indian Scenario. *IOP Conference Series. Earth and Environmental Science, 614*(1), 012055. doi:10.1088/1755-1315/614/1/012055

Skiba, D. J. (2017). The potential of blockchain in education and health care. *Nursing Education Perspectives, 38*(4), 220–221. doi:10.1097/01.NEP.0000000000000190 PMID:28622267

Smith, S. (2018). Blockchain augmented audit – Benefits and challenges for accounting professionals. *The Journal of Theoretical Accounting Research, 14*(1), 117–137.

Son-Turan, S. (2022). Fostering equality in education: The blockchain business model for higher Higher Education(BBM-HE). *Sustainability (Basel), 14*(5), 2955. doi:10.3390u14052955

Stan, H. (2021). *UK Land Registry Plans to Test Blockchain in Digital Push.* Coin Desk. https://www.coindesk.com/markets/2017/05/12/uk-land-registry-plans-to-test-blockchain-in-digital-push/

Steiu, M. F. (2020). Blockchain in education: Opportunities, applications, and challenges. *First Monday*. doi:10.5210/fm.v25i9.10654

Suh, B., & Han, I. (2002). Effect of trust on customer acceptance of Internet banking. *Electronic Commerce Research and Applications, 1*, 247-263. . doi:10.1016/S1567-4223(02)00017-0

Sun, R., He, D., & Su, H. (2021). Evolutionary game analysis of blockchain technology preventing supply chain financial risks. *Journal of Theoretical and Applied Electronic Commerce Research, 16*(7), 2824–2842. doi:10.3390/jtaer16070155

Swan, M. (2018). *Smart Network Field Theory: The Technophysics of Blockchain and Deep Learning.* SSRN. doi:10.2139/ssrn.3262945

Syahputra, H., & Weigand, H. (2019). The Development of Smart Contracts for Heterogeneous Blockchains. *Enterprise Interoperability, VIII*, 229–238. doi:10.1007/978-3-030-13693-2_19

Tan, E., Lerouge, E., Du Caju, J., & Du Seuil, D. (2023). Verification of Higher EducationCredentials on European Blockchain Services Infrastructure (EBSI): Action Research in a Cross-Border Use Case between Belgium and Italy. *Big Data and Cognitive Computing, 7*(2), 79. doi:10.3390/bdcc7020079

Tapscott, D., & Tapscott, A. (2016). The impact of the blockchain goes beyond financial services. *Harvard Business Review*, 2–5.

Tapscott, D., & Tapscott, A. (2017). Blockchain could help artists profit more from their creative works. *Harvard Business Review*, 2–5.

Tapscott, D., Iansiti, M., Lakhani, K. R., & Tucker, C. (2019). *Blockchain: The insights you need from Harvard Business Review*. Harvard Business Review Press.

Tapscott, D., & Tapscott, A. (2016). *Blockchain revolution: how the technology behind bitcoin is changing money, business, and the world.* Penguin.

Tateishi, T., Yoshihama, S., Sato, N., Saito, S. (2019). Automatic smart contract generation using controlled natural language and template. *IBM Journal of Research and Development, 63.*

Tett, G. (2021). A contest to control crypto is under way. *Financial Times.*

Thakur, V., Doja, M. N., Dwivedi, Y. K., Ahmad, T., & Khadanga, G. (2020). Land records on Blockchain for implementation of Land Titling in India. *International Journal of Information Management, 52*, 101940. doi:10.1016/j.ijinfomgt.2019.04.013

Themistocleous, M., Christodoulou, K., Iosif, E., Louca, S., & Tseas, D. (2020). Blockchain in Academia Where do we stand and where do we go? Paper presented at the *Hicss,* (pp. 1-10). IEEE. 10.24251/HICSS.2020.656

Thomason, J., & Ivwurie, E. (Eds.). (2023). *Advancements in the New World of Web 3: A Look Toward the Decentralized Future: A Look Toward the Decentralized Future*. IGI Global. doi:10.4018/978-1-6684-6658-2

Tiwari, U. (2020). Application of Blockchain in Agri-Food Supply Chain. *Britain International of Exact Sciences (BIoEx). Journal*, *2*(2), 574–589. doi:10.33258/bioex.v2i2.233

Toorajipour, R., Oghazi, P., Sohrabpour, V., Patel, P. C., & Mostaghel, R. (2022). Block by block: A blockchain-based peer-to-peer business transaction for international trade. *Technological Forecasting and Social Change, 180*, 121714. doi:10.1016/j.techfore.2022.121714

Treasury Technology Analyst Report. (2021). Straticic Treasurer. www.strategictreasurer.com

Tsai, C. T., & Wu, J. L. (2022). A Blockchain-Based Fair and Transparent Homework Grading System for Online Education. In *Principles and Practice of Blockchains* (pp. 303–326). Springer International Publishing. doi:10.1007/978-3-031-10507-4_13

Tsai, W., Ge, N., Jiang, J., Feng, K., & He, J. (2019). Beagle: A New Framework for Smart Contracts Taking Account of Law. *IEEE International Conference on Service-Oriented System Engineering (SOSE)*. IEEE 10.1109/SOSE.2019.00028

Tschorsch, F., & Scheuermann, B. (2016). Bitcoin and beyond: A technical survey on decentralized digital currencies. *IEEE Communications Surveys and Tutorials*, *18*(3), 2084–2123. doi:10.1109/COMST.2016.2535718

Tucker, C., & Catalini, C. (2018). What Blockchain Can't Do. *Harvard Business Review*, 2–4.

Underwood, S. (2016). Blockchain beyond bitcoin. *Communications of the ACM*, *59*(11), 15–17. doi:10.1145/2994581

UNECE. (1996). Land Administration Guidelines With Special Reference to Countries in Transition. UNECE.

UN-Habitat. (2012). *A GUIDE ON LAND AND PROPERTY RIGHTS IN PAKISTAN*. UN. https://cms.ndma.gov.pk/storage/app/public/publications/December2020/oeBNJ57eoaK7VbjALelV.pdf

Upadhyay, N. (2020). Demystifying blockchain: A critical analysis of challenges, applications and opportunities. *International Journal of Information Management*, *54*, 1–26. doi:10.1016/j.ijinfomgt.2020.102120

VADS. (2019). *Blockchains for Public Recordkeeping and for Recording Land Records.* SOS. https://sos.vermont.gov/media/r3jh24ig/vsara_blockchains_for_public_recordkeeping_white_paper_v1.pdf

Vaigandla, K. K., Karne, R., Siluveru, M., & Kesoju, M. (2023). Review on Blockchain Technology: Architecture, Characteristics, Benefits, Algorithms, Challenges and Applications. *Mesopotamian Journal of CyberSecurity*, *2023*, 73–85. doi:10.58496/MJCS/2023/012

Varma, P., Nijjer, S., Sood, K., Grima, S., & Rupeika-Apoga, R. (2022). Thematic Analysis of Financial Technology (Fintech) Influence on the Banking Industry. *Risks*, *10*(10), 186. doi:10.3390/risks10100186

Vhatkar, H. V., Singh, H. G., Sonavane, A. S., Singh, S., & Pulgam, N. (2023). Crowdfunding using Blockchain. In *2023 11th International Conference on Emerging Trends in Engineering & Technology-Signal and Information Processing (ICETET-SIP)* (pp. 1-6). IEEE. 10.1109/ICETET-SIP58143.2023.10151618

Vlk, A. (2023). The role of industry in higher Higher Educationtransformation. Research Handbook on the Transformation of Higher Education: 0, 192.

Volodymyr, V. (2017). *Ukraine Turns to Blockchain to Boost Land Ownership Transparency.* Bloomberg.

Voorhees, C. M., Brady, M. K., Calantone, R., & Ramirez, E. (2016). Discriminant validity testing in marketing: An analysis, causes for concern, and proposed remedies. *Journal of the Academy of Marketing Science*, *44*(1), 119–134. doi:10.100711747-015-0455-4

Vukolić, M. (2016). The quest for scalable blockchain fabric: Proof-of-work vs. BFT replication. In *Open Problems in Network Security: IFIP WG 11.4 International Workshop, iNetSec 2015, Zurich, Switzerland, October 29, 2015, Revised Selected Papers* (pp. 112-125). Springer International Publishing.

Wang, H., Chen, K., & Xu, D. (2016). A maturity model for blockchain adoption. *Financial Innovation*, *2*(1), 1–5. doi:10.118640854-016-0031-z

Wang, Y. (2021). Research on supply chain financial risk assessment based on blockchain and fuzzy neural networks. *Wireless Communications and Mobile Computing*, *2021*, 2021. doi:10.1155/2021/5565980

Weerawarna, R., Miah, S. J., & Shao, X. (2023). *Emerging advances of blockchain technology in fiancé: a content analysis.* PersUbiquitcomput. doi:10.100700779-023-01712-5

Wilkie, A., & Smith, S. S. (2021). Blockchain: speed, efficiency, decreased costs, and technical challenges. In The emerald handbook of blockchain for business (pp. 157-170). Emerald Publishing Limited. doi:10.1108/978-1-83982-198-120211014

Williamson, I. P. (2001). Re-engineering land administration systems for sustainable development - From rhetoric to reality. *International Journal of Applied Earth Observation and Geoinformation*, *3*(3), 278–289. Advance online publication. doi:10.1016/S0303-2434(01)85034-0

Williamson, I. P., & Feeney, M.-E. (2001). Land administration and spatial data infrastructures: trends and developments. *FIG XXII International Congress.*

Worrall, L. (1991). *Spatial Analysis and Spatial Policy Using Geographic Information System.* Belhaven Press.

Wouda, H. P., & Opdenakker, R. (2019). Blockchain technology in commercial real estate transactions. *Journal of Property Investment & Finance*, *37*(6), 570–579. Advance online publication. doi:10.1108/JPIF-06-2019-0085

Wu, Y., Cegielski, C. G., Hazen, B. T., & Hall, D. J. (2013). Cloud computing in support of supply chain information system infrastructure: Understanding when to go to the cloud. *The Journal of Supply Chain Management*, *49*(3), 25–41. https://www.proquest.com/scholarly-journals/cloud-computing-support-supply-chain-information/docview/1467435391/se-2?accountid=162730. doi:10.1111/j.1745-493x.2012.03287.x

Wylde, V., Rawindaran, N., Lawrence, J., Balasubramanian, R., Prakash, E., Jayal, A., & Platts, J. (2022). Cybersecurity, data privacy and blockchain: A review. *SN Computer Science*, *3*(2), 127. doi:10.100742979-022-01020-4 PMID:35036930

Xi, P., Zhang, X., Wang, L., Liu, W., & Peng, S. (2022). A review of Blockchain-based secure sharing of healthcare data. *Applied Sciences (Basel, Switzerland)*, *12*(15), 7912. doi:10.3390/app12157912

Yadav, V. S., & Singh, A. R. (2019). A systematic literature review of blockchain technology in agriculture. In *Proceedings of the International Conference on Industrial Engineering and Operations Management* (pp. 973-981). Springer.

Yapicioglu, B., & Leshinsky, R. (2020). Blockchain as a tool for land rights: Ownership of land in Cyprus. *Journal of Property. Planning and Environmental Law*, *12*(2), 171–182. Advance online publication. doi:10.1108/JPPEL-02-2020-0010

Yaqoob, I., Salah, K., Jayaraman, R., & Al-Hammadi, Y. (2021). blockchain for healthcare data management: Opportunities, challenges, and future recommendations. *Neural Computing & Applications*, 1–16.

Yaqoob, I., Salah, K., Jayaraman, R., & Al-Hammadi, Y. (2021). Blockchain for healthcare data management: Opportunities, challenges, and future recommendations. *Neural Computing & Applications*, 1–16. doi:10.100700521-020-05519-w

Yıldırım, H. (2022). Psychosocial status of older adults aged 65 years and over during lockdown in Turkey and their perspectives on the outbreak. *Health & Social Care in the Community*, *30*(3), 899–907. doi:10.1111/hsc.13542 PMID:34390281

Yin, W., & Ran, W. (2021). Theoretical exploration of supply chain viability utilizing blockchain technology. *Sustainability (Basel)*, *13*(15), 8231. doi:10.3390u13158231

Yli-Huumo, J., Ko, D., Choi, S., Park, S., & Smolander, K. (2016). Where is current research on blockchain technology?—A systematic review. *PLoS One, 11*(10), e0163477. doi:10.1371/journal.pone.0163477 PMID:27695049

Zhang, T., Li, J., & Jiang, X. (2021). Analysis of supply chain finance based on blockchain. *Procedia Computer Science, 187*(2021), 1–6. https://doi.org/ doi:10.1016/j.procs.2021.04.025

Zheng, Z., Xie, S., Dai, H., Chen, X., & Wang, H. (2017). An overview of blockchain technology: Architecture, consensus, and future trends. *Proceedings of 6th IEEE international Congress on Big Data* (pp. 557-564). IEEE.

Zhong, J., Xie, H., Zou, D., & Chui, D. K. (2018). *A blockchain model for word-learning systems.* In Proceedings of the 2018 5th International Conference on Behavioral, Economic, and Socio-Cultural Computing (BESC), Kaohsiung, Taiwan. 10.1109/BESC.2018.8697299

About the Contributors

Yanamandra Ramakrishna, is an Associate Dean of Undergraduate Program and Associate Professor in School of Business of Skyline University College, Sharjah, UAE. He is a PhD in Supply Chain Management from Jawaharlal Nehru Technological University (JNTU), Hyderabad, India. His teaching, research and consultancy areas include Logistics and Supply Chain Management, Operations Management, Lean Management and Quality Management. He has presented in reputed international conferences and published articles in leading journals.

Priyameet Kaur Keer is working as Associate Professor, -Research & Placement Coordinator in Department of Management Studies, New Horizon College of Engineering, Bengaluru. She is Faculty of Management subjects like digital, marketing, HR analytics, She has completed her PhD from RTM Nagpur University. She did her MBA in HR/IT from RTM Nagpur University. She is MBA 5 th topper of RTM Nagpur University. She has published several papers in International Journals. She is the Guest Editor for Human Resources Journal (Stress Management at workplace), Science Publishing Group, USA. She is the regular columnist in Deccan Herald, Bangalore & The Hitavada Newspaper, Nagpur. She is into various PhD panels for different universities. Recently she has won Women Excellence Award for the outstanding performance in education by AMP Ninja Group Hyderabad on 24.07.2020. She is VTU Nominee Board of Studies. She has published papers at various national and international levels, Scopus, web of Science, IEEE. Her research interests include Digital Marketing, HR analytics, Management areas – HR,Marketing.

***

Munir Ahmad is a Ph.D. in Computer Science. over 24 years of extensive experience in spatial data development, management, processing, visualization, and quality control. He is dedicated expertise in open data, crowdsourced data, volunteered geographic information and spatial data infrastructure. A seasoned professional with extensive knowledge in the field, having served as a trainer for the latest spatial technologies. With a passion for research and over 30 publications in the same field. In 2022, he got PhD degree in Computer Science from Preston University Rawalpindi, Pakistan. He is dedicated to advancing the industry and spreading knowledge through my expertise and experience. #SpatialData #GIS #GeoTech

Charu Banga is the Subject Lead of Accounting and Finance at the School of Business and Law, De Montfort University, Dubai. With over 16 years of experience in teaching, research, and industry, her areas of interest are corporate finance, business valuations, and market microstructure. She is a Ph.D. (Finance) from the University of Delhi, India; a Certified Financial Risk Manager from GARP, USA, and a fellow of Higher Education Academy (UK). Having an acumen towards research, she has published many research papers in reputed journals and a book on Retail Banking.

Neeta Baporikar is currently a Professor/Director(Business Management) at Harold Pupkewitz Graduate School of Business, Namibia University of Science and Technology, Namibia. Prior to this, she was Head-Scientific Research, with the Ministry of Higher Education CAS-Salalah, Sultanate of Oman, Professor (Strategy and Entrepreneurship) at IIIT Pune and BITS India. With a decade-plus of experience in the industry, consultancy, and training, she made a lateral switch to research and academics in 2000. Prof Baporikar holds D.Sc. (Management Studies) USA, Ph.D. (Management), SP Pune University, INDIA with MBA (Distinction) and Law (Hons.) degrees. Apart from this, she is an external reviewer, Oman Academic Accreditation Authority (2008-2017), an Accredited Management Teacher, a Qualified Trainer, an FDP from EDII, a Doctoral Guide, and a Board Member of the Academic Advisory Committee in accredited B-Schools. She has to her credit many conferred doctorates, 350+ scientific publications, and authored 30+ books in the area of Strategy, Entrepreneurship, Management, and Higher Education. She is also a member of the international and editorial advisory board, and reviewer for Emerald, IGI, Inderscience, Wiley, etc.

Shalini Chandra is an Associate Professor at S P Jain School of Global Management, Singapore. Prior to joining S P Jain, she worked as Research Fellow at Nanyang Technological University (NTU) Singapore, and she holds a PhD from the same university.

M.D. De Acuña received her PhD degree in Physics from the University of Seville in 1992. As a researcher, she developed her research activity at the National Institute of Nuclear Physics (INFN) in Padua (Italy). Since 1998 she has been working as a consultant and project manager on several business sectors, in areas related to methodologies, process improvements, Quality Assurance and PMO. Since 2007 she is an Associate Lecturer in the Department of Computer Languages and Systems at the University of Seville and is currently a collaborator of the Engineering and Science for Software Systems research group (ES3). Her main areas of interest are process methodology, agile methodologies, ITIL and DevOps.

J.A. García-García was awarded his PhD in Computer Science by the University of Seville, Spain, in 2015. Since 2008, he has participated in R&D projects as main researcher. His current research interests include the areas of Software Engineering, Business Process Management (BPM), Model-Driven Engineering and Quality Assurance. He manages several technological transfer projects with companies, and he participates as member committee in several international conferences and journals.

G. V. Satya Sekhar, M.Com, MBA, M.Phil, Ph.D, Associate Professor and Deputy Director, Centre for Distance Learning, GITAM –Deemed to be University, Visakhapatnam, India., has 20 years of teaching and research experience at Post Graduate level. He has published several books viz. 1) Financial Innovation-Theories, Models and Regulation, Vernon Press, USA, 2)The Indian Mutual Fund Industry, Plagrave Macmilan, London. 3) Mangement of Mutual Funds, Springer Nature, Germany, 4) Currency Risk Management, Vernon Press, USA. He has participated and presented papers in various national and international seminars, and published 50 articles in various national and international reputed journals.

Shankar Subramanian Iyer is an astute and result-oriented engineer, management, and finance expert with nearly two and a half decades of comprehensive techno-commercial experience in sales, marketing, business development, and CRM with profit accountability across various sectors including Engineering, Construction, Mining, Projects, Finance, and Education.Lately, he has been developing program and course curriculum, Quality Assurance for Business, Engineering, and Vocational Courses (KHDA), and assisting in their delivery after receiving approval from the sponsors (Dubai Municipality, Mohammed Bin Rashid Housing Establishment, Dubai Electrical and Water Authority, Dubai Road Transport Authority, Dubai Aluminium, Dubai Petroleum and Gas, and Academicians (EDEXCEL). Dr Shankar has also worked for QAD on TVET Approvals as an Internal Verifier and External Reviewer.His research interests include Blockchain in Education, Data Analysis, Big Data, Artificial Intelligence, Virtual Reality, and Augmented Reality.

Dhrupad Mathur has been an Associate Professor in IT Management Area with S P Jain School of Global Management, Dubai, UAE since 2008. Within this tenure, he has served in various administrative positions, including Director of Industry

Projects from 2008 to 2016 and Assistant Dean of the Executive MBA program in 2016–2017. He is currently the Deputy Director – Faculty Management. With approximately 18 years of professional experience in ICT education, policy, and consulting, Dr. Mathur is a Science graduate with an MBA and a master's degree in Public Administration. His doctoral degree from JNVU India (PhD, 2004) is in the area of e-Business Transformations.

Sakuntala Rao, DBA, FCA, MBA, CIMA has 34 years of experience largely in finance transformation in companies across the globe. She is now retired. She has recently been awarded a doctorate for her thesis "Adoption of Blockchain in Supply Chain Financing". She is also a member of MENSA, the high IQ society.

Arumugam Seetharaman is basically a Chartered Accountant with Doctorate in Cross Disciplinary functions of Management. After a successful career of turning a loss making public sector organization into profit in India, he joined School of Management, University Science Malaysia to teach post graduate and under graduate courses including DBA. After a remarkable career at USM, he took over Deanship of the Faculty of Management, Multimedia University, Malaysia. There he got the accreditation of various under graduate and post graduate programmes (including DBA). The uniqueness of the Accounting Degree and DBA of MMU was well appreciated throughout Malaysia. When Dr. Seetha left MMU, the Faculty of Management of MMU, had got 10 under graduate degrees, MBA degree and DBA degree. Dr. Seetha was adjudged as the Best Faculty of Business and Management by MMU. It was the policy of Dr. Seetha to leave an organization when the performance makes him as the finest hour in his career in that organization. When he was in India, he was awarded by Business India magazine as "Unsung Hero of Co-optex". He left that organization at that time. Similarly when he was at the helm of affairs at USM, Penang Malaysia, he left USM and joined MMU. In line with his policy when he was adjudged as the "Best Faculty of the Year", he left MMU and joined S P Jain School of Global Management. At S P Jain he is the Dean of Academic Affairs, in charge of curriculum development, Accreditation of courses, and ranking of degrees. Currently, SP Jain is among the "Top 20 Best International Business Schools" as ranked by Forbes and "Top 100 Global MBA programs" as ranked by Financial Times. Dr. Seetha has more than 150 publications to his credit, including articles listed in ISI-indexed journals. His ambition is to publish 250 articles, mostly in ISI-indexed journals.

Amritha Subhayan is a dynamic practitioner and researcher in Creative Industries, currently doing novel research under the innovation licence provided by Dubai International Financial Centre (DIFC). This research hub, Smart Story

Labs, explores Blockchain and Smart Contracts in Film production, driving future advancements. A skilled creative, academic, and media/business lecturer, Amritha's expertise spans diverse domains. Her trifecta proficiency enriches her role as a Manchester Metropolitan University researcher, Enterprise Outreach Head at Feature Film Production, and Faculty member at Westford University College's Business and Media Department. With filmmaking experience across the UK, EU, India, Oman, and UAE, she brings a compelling edge to research advancements and cinematic enterprise.

Farhan Ujager possesses over 16 years of extensive experience in teaching, research, and management across renowned universities in Pakistan and the United Arab Emirates. Currently, he holds the position of Program Lead for M.Sc. (Artificial Intelligence) and serves as a Senior Lecturer of Computing in the Faculty of Science, Engineering, and Computing (SEC) at De Montfort University (DMU) in Dubai. His research interests encompass several areas, notably Smart and Sustainable Ambiance, Smart Healthcare, Cyber Security, Data Analytics, Wireless Sensor Networks, and Optical Communication. Currently, his research focuses on Context-Aware Smart Ambience and healthcare applications. He has consistently contributed to the academic community by publishing his research in esteemed journals with high impact factors, authoring book chapters and presenting his findings at international conferences in the field of Computing.

Index

F

G

H

I

L

P

S

T

Publishing Tomorrow's Research Today

IGI Global
Publishing Tomorrow's Research Today
www.igi-global.com

Uncover Current Insights and Future Trends in

Business & Management

with IGI Global's Cutting-Edge Recommended Books

Print Only, E-Book Only, or Print + E-Book.

Order direct through IGI Global's Online Bookstore at **www.igi-global.com** or through your preferred provider.

ISBN: 9798369306444
© 2023; 436 pp.
List Price: US$ **230**

ISBN: 9798369300084
© 2023; 358 pp.
List Price: US$ **250**

ISBN: 9781668458594
© 2023; 366 pp.
List Price: US$ **240**

ISBN: 9781668486344
© 2023; 256 pp.
List Price: US$ **280**

ISBN: 9781668493243
© 2024; 318 pp.
List Price: US$ **250**

ISBN: 9798369304181
© 2023; 415 pp.
List Price: US$ **250**

Do you want to stay current on the latest research trends, product announcements, news, and special offers?
Join IGI Global's mailing list to receive customized recommendations, exclusive discounts, and more.
Sign up at: www.igi-global.com/newsletters.

Scan the QR Code here to
view more related titles in Business & Management.

www.igi-global.com | Sign up at www.igi-global.com/newsletters | facebook.com/igiglobal | twitter.com/igiglobal | linkedin.com/igiglobal

www.ingramcontent.com/pod-product-compliance
Lightning Source LLC
LaVergne TN
LVHW080649011026
849160LV00014B/1369